Surviving Solo

Mary Nicholson

Surviving Solo

Mary Nicholson

Address: The Middle of Nowhere, Remotest
Dartmoor, Devon, England, The UK, The World,
The Galaxy, The Mars Bar, The Universe

Phone: no signal

Email: intermittent

DOB: early Victorian times

CURRICULUM VITAE

- PR, Author and Journalist

- Handwriting Analyst

- Motor-Cycle Courier

- Old Etonian

- Entrepreneur: The Wedding Dress Exchange, The Graphology Business,
  The Polar Travel Company, Mary Nicholson PR, Wydemeet B&B and
  Holiday Rental

- Subject of Bill Cole's "The Well-Tempered Clavier" novel and screenplay

- Ex-wife of polar explorer

- Serial Internet Dater

- Lady who Lunches, Teas, Dinners, Breakfasts, Elevenses' etc

- Winner of TripAdvisor's Certificate of Service Excellence

- Working (sort of) Single Mother of a Brace of Teenagers

To My Mate Suz

without whom none of this would have been possible

Contents

∞

A Toe In The Water

∞

B&B and me – a match?

14/12/2012

The computer on my Range Rover says I have enough fuel to last another 65 miles. It's bloody lying again. My ostentatious, (Harrods) green car, with its 'EKO' number-plate, slows to a halt, just inside the school gates.

Jake, the groundsman, sweetly brings me a gallon of red diesel meant for his tractor, and he is very restrained about the brown ruts in his billiard-table-smooth, emerald-green cricket field, made by all the other Mums trying to get round the marooned vehicle.

It's my first venture into B&B today, and I've got a film crew of five arriving at 4.30pm.

Malcolm, my long-suffering 'boyfriend' (if you can call them that when they've got grey hair and they're nearly 60) is working on fitting the new loo into the third bathroom. The main bedroom, which will be needed, is currently still filled with all the furniture that used to be where the bathroom's now going, including an enormous chest of drawers and an extra bed.

Kathy, who cleans for me, and Sashka, who does my horses as well as my cleaning, are due to arrive at 9am, to get everything ready.

Meanwhile I have planned to go swimming, followed by a calming hot tub. I am now £115 down - after dropping in (clearly a bit too late) on Tesco's petrol station to refill my gas guzzling 4x4.

Ashburton is my next stop. I'm stocking up on 'local quality produce' to provide nothing but the best for my discerning guests. Gasp! I find an artisan loaf of bread costs over £2! Paying for it causes me an actual physical pain in my gut. Who buys this stuff? I had heard that this specialist bakery has usually run out of stock by lunchtime. Who are all these millionaires? I normally live off sliced brown wholemeal at 45p a loaf. No crumbs, and no need to wash up a knife or breadboard.

In the farm shop, I discover that some large organic tomatoes on the vine and a few mushrooms cost over £4. Agh!

How do people shop here regularly? Bugger all this upmarket stuff. Guess I might just have to start getting used to it.

I return home to find my house transformed by my incredible little team of workers. But there is no way that the new bathroom is going to be usable in time.

And after all that hard work and effort, too. Perhaps I'd better dig out my rather beautiful antique china chamber pot.

Sashka needs to leave for her next job, but finds that my car, which is blocking everyone in, has developed an enormous hole in its front tyre.

We retire for a coffee and a fag to think about what to do next.

Quite apart from getting the house ready for this film crew today, I'm also trying to prepare for Christmas.

I've organised mulled wine for the Form 4 Mums at Brown's Hotel this evening, before we pick our children up from their Hogwarts-inspired Christmas feast. The film crew is going to arrive while I'm doing that, and will be greeted by Malcolm, who is heavily armed with notes and instructions for preparing supper.

He's to serve the crew two wild mushroom lasagnes from 'Cook', which look home-made, and will taste much better than anything I could produce. The question is, will they defrost and bake properly in my temperamental Aga? The beef joint for tomorrow is still completely frozen. I haven't prepared a full English breakfast for several years, and I can't fry an egg. And even worse, I hate mornings and I loathe making beds.

The AA is on its way to replace the tyre before Sashka can leave or I can set off for the mulled wine fest.

I can't smoke in my own house because I will make it smell.

Am I really cut out for this B&B lark?

Poached vs Fried

15/12/2012

'Dartmoor Killings' is the working title of the film. My friend Peter, who already has a BAFTA to his name, has won the use of a camera worth a million quid, to film a promo in my house which will be used to help source finance for the actual feature film. The trouble is that the camera is so complicated that it takes three people to use it, and that is why he's got such a large crew coming to my house. I hope nobody drops it.

The crew's two nights' sojourn is my opportunity - a trial run - to practise my potentially non-existent B&B skills.

My ultimate aim is to charge the maximum possible rate for a Dartmoor B&B (about £100 a room for a night) which means I have to really try to run the thing in a classy way. I have spent days and nights on the internet tracking down diddy kettles, diddy thermoses for cold milk, and diddy cafetieres for each room. Then there're the individual tea bags (Earl Grey, Camomile etc) and filter coffees; the titchy toiletries and even the baskets to put everything in – I've got to find them all on eBay or somewhere.

But the Christmas rush has meant that the only thing that has arrived in time for the film crew is the kettles. Which turn out to be fitted with continental plugs, and have had to be relocated to my present drawer.

The crew arrives two hours later than anticipated, and, having requested drinks at 8.30pm followed by dinner at 9.00pm, instead film solidly until 11pm. The lasagne miraculously survives the wait and Malcolm and I fall into bed at 1.30am. Up again at 6.30am to prepare Organic Breakfast. God - what order do you cook everything in? Croissants, muesli, Golden Nuggets, fancy bread.. how many sausages? Bacon in the oven, or fried? Eeek! Two people request poached eggs, and two want fried. My poached eggs usually turn out looking like embryo's covered in afterbirth.

Help! Two massive great frying pans (one rusty); a baking tray in the oven with sausages, bacon, tomatoes and mushrooms in it. Baked beans in the microwave. Toast. Plates heating in the lower oven.

Nowhere to hide - we are all in the kitchen together - my mistakes on full display. How much of each thing for whom? I can't let them know that I am a walking zombie and I have never done anything like this before.

Somehow not an egg broken, and my poached ones look bright yellow and white and fairly symmetrical, and not full of mucus. But how to serve them? Genius! I grab a couple of pieces of thinly sliced brown toast and pop them on that. Then I stick the whole lot onto a large platter so everyone can help themselves, which means that I don't have to wonder how much of what to serve to whom.

Pheeeeew! All done. It's been fun! I am a pale ghost of my former self after 48 hours of this. Peter's first 'Dartmoor Killing' perhaps.

But I have done it.

And what's more, I can do it again.

Owners Direct

31/12/2012

Forget Amazon, eBay and Google. There's another monopolistic internet company out there which is quietly taking over the world. It's called 'Owners Direct'.

Innocently looking for a website through which to market my house, I've recently discovered that I'm not alone in finding myself choosing Owners Direct.

It turns out that, of around 100 families paying the fees for my children's posh, expensive school, five of them are renting out their properties to help make ends meet. And all are signed up with Owners Direct.

I discover that both of my friends who rent out their houses abroad also use the company - whether it's called Owners Direct, or 'HomeAway' it's the same headquarters based in Bressenden Place in London, representing nearly 200,000 properties around the world.

I chose it to market my house because there are no fussy agents involved, no 30% commissions, and no one to force me to empty out my cupboards, clean my fridge, and take down the messages stuck haphazardly to the notice board above the phone in the kitchen.

Well. Fancy that! I've signed up, and now I have just received my first enquiry. From a nice-sounding man called Jim, who is looking for three nights, for three families comprising six adults and five children altogether. Perfect. I immediately confirm I have availability.

I then spend nearly £2,000 in a morning, on 100% Egyptian cotton sheets, duvets, duvet covers, mattress protectors; twenty pillows, twenty pillow protectors, and thirty towels.

Jim gets back to me to say he has found somewhere else, cheaper.

I am relieved. It was all too much, too fast.

But it demonstrates that Owners Direct actually works. It could really happen. I might succeed in renting out my home in its entirety for a substantial sum!

How scary. How exciting!

Finding My Voice

∞

Plenty of Room for Willies

17/01/2013

Ben Hardon has contacted me via Owners Direct about renting my house.

This is my third enquiry, even though my entry on the Owners Direct website has only been up for a month or two. It's going to work. I am going to make my fortune by renting out my house! Mr Hardon has completed the form and says he wants to stay with his five children for two nights, January 31st and Feb 1st, 2013.

"I'm single too! love to stay with my children. FYI i have a big willy!" (sic) he writes. I note with increasing dismay that the email address he gives is bigwillywam@hotmail.co.uk

I'm not sure what to do about this - whether to report the incident to Owners Direct or what. So I forward his message to my great mate Susannah, who already rents out two houses via Owners Direct.

She is horrified, having never been contacted by a weirdo through the site, and advises me to play down the 'single mum' bit in the copy of my website entry.

Driving Will back to his school for the beginning of term, when he asks me how the new rental business is going I hesitantly tell him about this incident.

Oh how he larfs.

"That was me! I was typing it up, in the kitchen, while you were cooking the sausages last night," he chortles.

I give myself another mental reminder to amend the predictive text typo that is still on display for all to enjoy on my website entry: Property Ref E7392: "Plenty of room for willies, macs and outside toys in the cloakroom."

The Work/Life Balance

21/01/2013

Oh dear.

I lost it with the garage man yesterday. He'd omitted to phone to tell me that the compressor for my Range Rover hadn't turned up, so he couldn't mend my car after all, now I had taken the trouble to drive the 35 minutes to his garage for our agreed appointment.

"Don't you realise that I've only got twenty hours a week when I can earn enough to support my family?" I ranted when I turned up to find that I'd wasted half my afternoon. "I've bust a gut to get here an hour earlier than I need have for the school run, and all for nothing."

To fill that hour, I should have gone to Costa's for a Skinny Cappuccino, to consider my poor behaviour. Instead I went searching for half-price offers in the Co-op, even though there'd been a Tesco delivery earlier in the day, so I was still late, as usual, to pick Faye up from school.

But I've thought about it since. The reason why I am permanently stressed and in a hurry, is because I visit the health club twice a week, ride my horses twice a week, muck them out most days, watch a child playing in a sports match once or twice a week, and restrict myself to at least one 'Lady Who Lunches' a week. And by 'support the family' I mean 'earn enough to pay my half of the children's school fees'.

I probably ought to feel ashamed of myself for being so horrid. If the nice man knew the real reasons why my every hour is so precious, I doubt he'd be very sympathetic. Perhaps I need to visit a Life Coach. But of course I don't have the time to listen to whatever they have to say.

eBay Addict

23/01/2013

My darling daughter Faye is jumping up and down squeaking. My underarms are sweating and my heart is pounding. We watch the clock - five, four, three..

"It's ours!" We leap about the kitchen in joy, clasping our hands together and grinning at each other.

I have just bought a 1999 Ford Focus off eBay. For only £831. It's in Southampton, and it's blue. Does it work? Who cares? It's ours!

Post divorce I'm now properly broke and I've got to downsize.

The Range Rover has to go. It's haemorrhaging money. £130 a week on diesel for the twice-daily 26 mile return school run across stunning central Dartmoor.

£750 for four new tyres (not much different from buying the whole of this Focus). £500 for a belt. £500 for an air bag and now another £500 for the compressor which turned up in the end.

And that's since December.

So I am going 'reverse chic' with my new old Ford. I can't wait to show it off in the school carpark. It'll be the only one of its kind, whereas there are five other Range Rovers. My new car is straightforward simple proof to one and all, if any were wanted or needed, of the havoc my Nemesis, She, has played in our lives, and of the all too real effects of Her shenanigans. I am going to park it next to Her BMW and grin at Her.

But hey - what am I doing now? I'm at it again. This is all such fun! I've just pressed the button twice and discovered that I'm about to become the proud new owner of a Land Rover (£1,500) and a Mitsubishi Shogun (£2,450). Help! What if I get both? Do I really want either?

I lose the Land Rover (phew!) but eBay emails me to inform me that I am the lucky owner of an old Shogun (silver) based in Swindon.

Oh dear. Now I've got three cars, they're scattered all over the country, and I'm marooned all by myself, snowed in, in the middle of Dartmoor. I am a bit alarmed at what I might find myself doing next.

Stupid Idea

24/01/2013

I think Ex and I have finally agreed our financial settlement, and hopefully now we can get divorced, at last. Tra la!

It's been 3 1/2 years since he left, and I am proud of us both, because I don't think a single cross word about the 'Agreement' has been exchanged between the two of us over the past twelve months. Not since a memorable morning when Ex rolled down his car window crying, "This is War!" And it never was.

A wise solicitor recently advised me that in divorce you will always lose out financially unless you marry someone richer than you are, whatever the rights and wrongs of the marital breakdown. So you need to cut your losses, bury the resentment, and move on.

I am lucky enough to have a 'charm' (collective noun for goldfinches) of grown-up men (yes there are such a things), who, throughout these years have guided me with great tact, gently, kindly, and wisely through the divorce, allowing me to rant and rage, and by the tenth "and another thing" they've heard a million times before, they patiently suggest how I might learn to communicate more pleasantly.

For instance, rather than yelling "That's a bloody stupid idea!" it might be better to calmly describe how a particular course of action might affect me, or make me feel.

I tried it out the other day, during a phone call with Ex, and damn me, it worked.

Perhaps I should have given this approach a bit more of a go during our marriage - I wonder where we would be now if I had?

Anyhow, so, after everything that's happened, Ex and I might soon be properly free to live our separate lives, and on speaking terms too!

Snowed Under

24/01/2013

My part of Dartmoor has been under snow for a week now.

As it's become icier and icier I have left my daughter to board at her school for a couple of nights, and Malcolm is stranded in Ashburton, his ancient Corsa sitting outside my door with a flat battery.

I am marooned, in the middle of nowhere, in a five bedroom house, all alone, surrounded by snow and ice.

It's wonderful!

It did cross my mind that if I slipped and broke my leg getting the horses in, I would die alone in the dark in a blizzard. So I trod carefully.

But otherwise there is suddenly all the time in the world to get on with things. Such as sorting out a picture for next year's personalised Christmas card. I've got real snow, and still haven't put away our Christmas decorations, so there are some suitable props lying around.

Our 2012 Christmas card was a struggle because the winter had been snowless so I didn't have any suitable seasonal happy snaps pictures for Vista Print.

Instead I used one very kindly set up by the film crew's cameraman, of our house glowing in the dark under stars, looking a bit like a pumpkin.

As for Owner's Direct – I haven't got any recent sunny pictures either. All it did was rain last year. How am I going to make Wydemeet look like somewhere you would like to go to?

Midas

25/01/2013

Well Blow Me Down.

I'm sitting here looking at two cheques made out to me. One is for £2,500 for a rental in the Easter holidays; and the other is a £350 deposit for a week's let this July. They both arrived today - the first time the postman has made it to our house in five days, what with the snow.

So it's worked.

I really am going to rent out my home in its entirety. Twice. For a whole week. And be richly rewarded for doing so.

Now all I've got to do is to buy a high chair and a cot, and two blobs to go on the end of the strings that pull the lights on in the bathrooms.

I'm feeling a bit wobbly and spaced out about all of this. It has been a vision for so long. And now it is a reality.

So much less stressful than doing a proper job like PR.

While these strangers are enjoying my house, I think I might go skiing!

And when the second lot come, I have already accepted an invitation from my sister to go and stay with her, in one of the most luxurious country estates there is, just outside Siena, in Italy.

How hard can life be?

They always said my middle name was Midas.

It's A New Life

05/02/2013

A most exciting day today. I have realised that my new life is truly underway.

As you know, I have already had my first B&B customers in the form of the film crew.

I've received my TWO bookings for holiday rental.

I have succeeded in buying two old bangers, Marv - the Ford Focus runabout, and Bill the Shogun, to pull the horses; meanwhile King III, the Range Rover, is for sale on eBay, looking very shiny after an expensive professional valet.

And today I have been immersed in a ring round to speaking agencies on behalf of 'my' poet, Matt Harvey. Matt is a friend of Malcolm's, and the poet on Radio 4's Saturday morning programme. He is one of the most talented, funny, and charming people I have ever met, and I think he should be really, really rich as a result! But like so many artists, he's not.

So that's where I come in:

If Love
If love
can build a bridge
can affection
put up a shelf?

It was really scary doing the ring round, and I dreaded starting it. In the past, when Ex's corporate speaking comprised our main source of income, we employed a string of PAs for whom 'the ring round' on Ex's behalf was top priority. We never found anyone who had the nerve to do it, though, so they ended up not doing anything at all and we had to fire them one after the other.

And now, five years on, here I am, back to the old grindstone, going through our ancient list, endeavouring to coerce old contacts to sign up Matt during a triple-dip recession.

And it's been great. Unbelievably, nearly all the same people are still at their desks, working for the same agencies in the same offices on the same phone numbers. I thought they would all have disappeared. On top of which, they all seem to remember me, and have been really friendly and enthusiastic. Even someone at Brooks International in the States, an agency that books both Blair's, was really nice and encouraging to me!

I've got down to 'D' on my list so far, and I need to send them all the background info. By the time I've finished with 'Z', I look forward to sitting on my bum while the money just rolls on in.

Bye-bye Website Provider

07/02/2013

This website hoster-thing. Well. I've spent so many hours, not to mention quite a lot of money (for me) - nearly a hundred pounds actually - trying to get to grips with the thing, and I have to give up. It's all been an A1 total disaster and waste of time. I just can't work it.

So now, for £36, I've just signed up to another jolly little website-builder equivalent called 'justhost.com', which is potsie-pie to use. I'm having so much fun with it. I can't wait to create my B&B website. I would almost rather be doing this than watching X-Factor!

In the meantime, I've got to sort getting my B&B some sort of profile asap.

Because I've finally discovered, after what feels like months of unreturned emails, impossible-to-find-phone numbers etc, that TripAdvisor won't list Wydemeet as a B&B as well as a holiday rental. It seems that they run two separate businesses, one for rentals, which you have to pay for, and which goes through some company called "Holiday Lettings" and the other is the B&B/hotel listings service that we're all so much more familiar with. And for this, I will have to have my own proper website. Yikes! How do I make one?

The Ashburton Cookery School, to whom I initially sent a sales-flyer, is hardly swamping me with enquiries - they did warn me not to rely on them to see me through. So I really do have to start marketing my B&B side of things a little harder.

I think I am the only B&B on Dartmoor with a hot tub, and for £45 you can also enjoy a relaxing massage, on-site, from Malcolm. He specialises in something called 'trigger points' and if you suffer from a bad back - well your cure lies at my door.

It's up to me I suppose, to make sure that you hear about me. Here goes!

Bevan Trumpington

10/02/2013

Yes - that's his name - Bevan Trumpington. How funny. He's real. He's probably reading this right now!

I have just heard that he is Her new squeeze, now that She and Ex are already over.

Apparently She introduced him at the local hunt meet yesterday, and he is to be Her partner at the hunt's annual smart dinner, in front of everybody – about 100 people whose average age is 152 - in a couple of weeks' time. What will the Great and the Good of the county think of that?

I am surprised by the impact this news has had on me. When I heard of his existence, I found myself reaching for a Cava and a fag.

For some reason I'm not feeling quite so gung-ho about parking Marv next to Her BMW in the school carpark tomorrow.

I'd better tell you the truth though. His actual name isn't exactly Bevan Trumpington. It's something even odder!

Angry of Dartmoor

11/02/2013

The local magistrates are beginning to recognise me.

It's because I go to court so often that I have been up in front of some of the same ones twice now. People like me are known as 'vexatious litigants'.

Have you ever had a go at the small claims? I bet you haven't. Supposedly the system has been set up so that any old person can use it, but I don't think that's true. To manage a small claim yourself, I think you have to be brave, educated, aggressive, and time-rich. The idea of people like my Mum going through with a claim, all on her own, is risible.

I'm not saying I find it a walk in the park - I always have to pay a visit to the loo before venturing into the magistrate's room.

And at the end, even if I win, which so far I usually have, it doesn't mean you get your money back, because so many of the people I have dealt with are already bankrupt and know how to avoid the hapless helpless, bailiffs. But at least, hopefully, I've made sure that their horrible behaviour hasn't gone unnoticed, and I've given them an inconvenient scare.

Over the years I've spent days, weeks and months following up cases.

It's not a pleasant sight - because to be at my most effective I have to wind myself up into a frenzy before opening the dreaded filing cabinet drawer labelled 'Angry of The Moor'. It's just that I don't like being treated like a cretin, oh OK, I'll say it then, a blonde.

I mean honestly. I did warn my plumber that I had sued the previous one, and won.

The new plumber clearly can't have believed me, and now, after foolishly paying him £2000 up front, as it turns out not to mend my central heating, I've sued him too, and won again.

I sue people who I think are trying to rip me off, who I think might rip off people like my Mum, or Ex-mother-in-law.

I don't always come out on top. Once I refused to pay my burglar alarm company because they tried charging double their original quote. I lost that one in court and ended up with a Court Order. Which has meant, drat and double drat, that Santander 123 won't let me set up a savings account with them.

I've won against BT twice - £3000 in all. I've also won against a holiday company, a removals firm, cutlery company, my two plumbers, and a professional horse-riding eventer. I am currently considering whether to sue my electric gate company.

The gate was bought for over £3000, kindly paid for a decade ago by Ex-mother-in-law. Since then, the longest it has ever worked without problems is about two years. The minute it breaks, Scotties, Belted Galloways and wild ponies rampage across my 'lawn' and into the farmer's fields beyond. They all appear to be on automatic pilot – guided missiles aimed at my garden.

It's a heavy 5-bar wooden thing. Underneath it is mud mixed with fresh poo.

Not ideal for suede high heels. And I look like Esther Rantzen if my hair gets wet.

Whenever the gate breaks down, I have to step out of my car, plough through the horizontal rain and wade through the mud, in order to push open and close the heavy mildewed reluctant centrepiece of all my nightmares, climbing back into my prestige vehicle with slime all over my feet, chest and hands.

Last month I made nearly enough money from my film crew of five staying half-board for two nights to cover the cost of the gate's broken control panel, after I had just paid £150 to the same stupid company to supposedly finally put everything right after they'd fitted no less than five faulty open/close switches, causing an invasion of animals every time. On top of all that, just two weeks later they want £645 + VAT because the motor has now broken. 'Unfit for Purpose' I believe might be the legal jargon.

Neighbour next door doesn't appreciate my problem. She suggests I go back to a latch.

Maybe I should go back to London.

I Wouldn't Credit It

25/02/2013

"That's rather clever," said the pretty young dentist, as she peered into my mercury-filled mouth.

She was talking about the way my previous private dentists have artfully smeared some whitish overlay porcelain filler-stuff onto two of my front teeth, making them look straighter and less sticky-outy. The result is that the cutting edge of them is very thick, but I don't care - anything for enhanced beauty.

My little family has been going to the same private dentist in Ashburton for over ten years. We used to see Lucinda who is very nice and takes a lot of trouble over us. But now we are poor I felt we ought to check out the NHS option down the road.

It was totally empty, and the light, bright waiting room upstairs is about 50' by 25', very comfortable, nicely laid out magazines etc, but we didn't have to wait in it, as we were all immediately ushered in to see the dentist.

"Very nice clean teeth," she said to Faye.

"WHAT?!" I jerked out of my reverie dreaming of the ultimate American capped smile - not David Bowie's.

My new, intensive regime to ensure that a reluctant daughter now cleans her teeth twice daily, while Malcolm counts to 100 in Spanish, French and Russian, seems, astonishingly, to have worked. I have been berating myself for the past six months, as last visit she had to have two fillings - clear proof, if you ask me, that I am a Bad Mother.

So we went down to reception, all with 100% clean bill of health, to pay.

The nice lady said, "If you're on child tax credits it's free - you just need to let me have the number on your white card."

"Blimey - that's good," I replied, "But I'm not sure I've got a white card."

"That's OK," the lady said, "You can ring me when you find it, when you get home."

So off we went for macaroni cheese in the Green Ginger, having paid nothing at all for our dental visit with our lovely charming new dentist, in such a glorious ambience, and having enjoyed ourselves a lot.

Later that day I was talking the experience through with a friend who was also born with a silver spoon in his mouth, private school/university education, comfortable family blah blah blah; who had had a crown fitted the very same day. "God how much was that?" I gasped. "£400?"

No, entirely free, because he is on working tax credits.

And I qualify for child tax credits because my ex-husband lives at a different address. Even if he were a millionaire I would still be eligible for child tax credits apparently! In effect, am I wrong, or does this mean that the taxpayer is subsidising men who choose to stray?

And another mate with whom I was discussing this the other day says she spends her child benefit on Cava, as her children's private school fees are already covered.

It's a very odd system. I know it's necessary for some people, but I don't think it should cover people like us. I shall, however, continue to claim if the money's there. Just as I continue to fly, as the planes are there, and drive a car, as Marv's just outside, despite what the eco-warriors tell me to do.

As I retire to bed I turn the lights off and the heating down. But that is because I am mean and own lots of woolly jumpers, not because I think I can influence the rest of the world.

And I hope that in time all these benefits available to people who can, or should be able to pay for them themselves, are eventually eradicated. And when the Daily Mail reports on the changes screaming "Shock horror squeeze on the middle classes yet again", I shall say "Good".

Meanwhile I have just discovered that my income is too high for me to qualify for the 'white card', and I have had to stump up £17.50 for my examination after all.

Yours Anonymously

03/03/2013

The other day one of the few people I'd told about this site said, "If you name me in your blog I will never speak to you again!"

He happens to be one of my favourite men friends, and it got me thinking. Other people are considerably more protective of their privacy than I am, and my not remaining alert to this fact has got me into trouble in the past!

I have checked the issue with another close friend, who was actually the biggest motivator and inspiration behind my starting this in the first place. Let's call her Miriam. She used to be a policewoman, and she was optimistic about all the confidentiality issues that I might find myself facing. She pointed out how much information on anyone you can get, simply by googling them, and she then sent me a list of over 30 sites which can, apparently, be used to track down all your most private moments. Scary or what?

Then I thought about one of my favourite columnists and authors - Lucy Pinney - who wrote "A Country Wife". Apparently she stopped writing because, as a result of her column, she's got no friends left to write about. I will probably call her to find out if this is true or merely conjecture. Either way sad, as she is a far better writer than I am.

And entirely understandable. My friends mean far more to me than a stupid blog does!

Scam!

03/03/2013

Look what I got back to after Faye's riding lesson this morning! At bloody last! A nice friendly email from an oceanographer called Diane Joy who is such a loving Mum that she wants to buy my Range Rover at its published price and give it to her son! What's more, she's a Christian, so she won't be trying any funnies!

She writes:

"Hi there, Sorry for the late reply, Well can you assure me that it's in good state and that i will not be disappointed with it.I'm ready to pay your asking price and to be honest, i wanted to buy this for my son as (Gift) and i want it to get to him as surprise gift, but the issue is i am an oceanographer and i do have a contract to go for which starting today and am leaving any moment from now just trying to send you this message" blah blah blah, saying that she'll pay for it via Pay Pal and send an agent to collect it, ending "God Bless You".

I've had the wretched car on eBay so long that the ad has run out, despite reducing the price and taking out the copy and pictures referring to its various dents and scratches. So only yesterday I signed up to Auto Trader for £45, and now it looks as though I've got a keen buyer already! Hurray for Diane!

A teeny weeny little voice in me whispered 'hesitate'. So I forwarded the email to my friend Miriam who is the ex-policewoman. She screamed back "Avoid! Avoid! Avoid!" and directed me to all the websites detailing identical scams, right down to the oceanographer bit.

So I emailed back:

'Hi Diane
I am so glad you would like to buy my car. And how lovely to be dealing with another believer. I very much look forward to meeting your agent.

God Bless You too

WPC Plod'

Sadly I haven't heard back from her, and meanwhile all three of 'Mazza's Second-hand Motors' continue to block up the drive.

Three and a half years

07/03/2013

Three and a half years since Ex exited.

The sense of disruption is still here. I wonder how long it will take to go away.

I have just been visited by Olga - I bid at a pledges evening for her to come and help me with my garden. She's a widow. Over a cup of Earl Grey and a fig roll, she mused that of course I still feel unsettled. The sense of not being sure whether you're coming or going remains for a long time, following on from a couple of years of shock, bewilderment and disbelief, she said.

I'm feeling like this because I've been wondering why I find myself living alone with two children, in a five-bedroomed house, twenty minutes from a pint of milk, with so many bedrooms that I have to rent most of them out to make ends meet. Potty.

Especially when my fifteen year old son, Will, would much prefer to live on a main road with buses and a railway station, near friends, cinemas and coffee shops. Maybe even London, but being a Dartmoor hillbilly, he is still slightly apprehensive about crossing roads, asking for things in shops, the underground, and muggers. When the children were little, when we played I Spy, they would regularly say, "I spy something beginning with 'H'. The answer was 'House'.

My sense of disruption is caused by considering whether I should move. But no. I think I belong here now. I've promoted myself, after 17 years, from 'Blow In' to 'Incomer', and know most of the people I drive past. My son Will will just have to learn to enjoy walks, while Faye's riding skills must continue on their rapid upward trajectory.

Meanwhile Olga says I have a very nice woodland garden. She is going to come back and plant some 'drought pots' to give it some colour after its initial 'Spring flourish'. Meanwhile I must ask Patrick to come over and pick up sticks, and rake up leaves. We are 'all systems go' before my first guests arrive at the end of the month!

Someone's Found Us At Last!

13/03/2013

Hurrah! Ex has volunteered to drive all the way to Truro to watch Faye play in the netball B-team in sub-zero temperatures, leaving me free, all alone once again, in my rather large and very cold house, to 'Get On', with the whole day to myself and Twiglet the dog.

Trouble is, 'Getting On' can be SO SLOW!

I had been becoming gloomier and gloomier and slower and slower, looking for better pictures to pinch off the internet to illustrate this site with, when - KERRRRPOW!!!!

A very nice lady has just rung, asking whether I am 'Wydemeet'. My first ever proper bed and breakfast enquiry!

I am raised from my lethargy and here I am, straight onto my blog, to report on my success!

"How did you find me?" I asked her. She didn't know - she had been passed my details by her husband, but really - it's only TWO HOURS since the Wydemeet phone number has been listed by BT!

How fantastic is that? So thank God I now have an energy boost and can reapply myself to ringing up the remaining 52 speaking agents on my list, on my poet Matt's behalf, in the hope of getting him a well-rewarded gig.

Yippee! Actually I think I will go and celebrate with a coffee and a fag, I am so excited!

She can't come, by the way - the lady ringing about Bed and Breakfast, as it's during the school holidays. But who cares?!

Another hopefully constructive thing I've done today is to move the published address of my Range Rover to my sister's house in Fulham, and added £500 back onto the price. It's been a month on eBay, and two weeks now on Auto Trader. I haven't had a single enquiry from Auto Trader that wasn't a scam. Four scams in all so far! Beware!

Dating Sites For Total Losers

16/03/2013

I'm a fan of internet dating.

It can work quite well in surprising ways – I speak from personal experience. Malcolm and I met via 'Guardian Soulmates' two years ago, and though he still struggles with the fact that I pay actual money for the 'Daily Mail', we enjoy each other's company a lot and have a very happy time together.

The first personal ad I ever placed was in 'Private Eye' nearly thirty years ago - decades before the internet had been thought of.

I later wrote an article for 'Harpers and Queen' about the people I subsequently met. To illustrate it, they printed a picture of me, taken by society photographer John Swannell, making me look quite different from normal, leaning against the willy of a naked stone statue which didn't have any arms or legs on it. Why did I have to do that? I still have no idea.

The ad went: "Public School/University 5'9" bubbly blonde (26) believes all unattached entertaining men (28-40) are in hiding. Please prove her wrong. Fulham."

I received lots of replies, but unfortunately none of them proved me wrong.

The experience encouraged me to study graphology - the interpretation of handwriting - so that in future I could weed out the more promising respondents from their handwritten letters, instead of finding myself wasting time yawning, getting fatter and fatter from so many dinners spent in London's most expensive restaurants, chatting to boring lonely hearts. (Most of whom paid for me, thank God).

I subsequently practised graphology professionally, both for head-hunting, and for analysing the hand-writing of celebrities. The famous people I came across varied from Michael Jackson to Nurse Allitt the murderess; whilst the media I wrote for spanned anything from the Daily Star to BBC 2's 'Daily Politics' show.

Personal ads were taboo back then, but I felt that most of my single girlfriends were so much prettier, thinner, funnier, more charming and nicer than I was that I had to steal a march on them somehow.

These days though, every single, single person I know has been involved with 'the net'. It offers all of us just a little scrap of hope, whether we're 53 or 83 – everyone wants to love and be loved, don't you think?

So I was fascinated by an article the other day in the 'Daily Mail', written by someone called Liz Hodgkinson (no pic, bet she's ugly), which tells us all that dating sites are for 'total losers'.

So that would be nine million of us, according to your stats, Liz. Wow!

She uses personal experience to prove her theory, based on a total of her three encounters.

She appears to mind that 'bald, white bearded, broke, fat, dull, over-50s men' are using the media to have a crack at finding themselves someone affluent, beautiful, and young, to become their free housekeeper.

From the way that she writes, I wonder whether she might be described as smug, complacent, intellectually arrogant, opinionated, impatient and judgmental.

There's a good chance that she might also be fat-ist, beard-ist, hair-ist, age-ist, and money-ist'.

And if she's over fifty, she's probably got wobbly arms, a floppy fat tummy, saggy large bum, cellulite thighs; criss-crossed wrinkles across her chest and neck; and the moles on her face are probably starting to sprout hair. I bet she's also suffering hormonal mood swings, and wakes up at night in bed sweating.

In short, I would imagine that she's very like me! If I met her I should think that I would really like her!

The thing is, it's no wonder these hideous old grandpas aren't searching for people like Liz and me. At fifty-something we're getting old!

Homeless

17/03/2013

In two weeks' time I'm going to be homeless.

My first ever week's rental is looming.

Kathy, Sashka and I have a 'working elevenses' of coffee and fags twice a week now, sometimes we even sit inside, in the kitchen, because it is so much more comfortable than squatting outside in the wind and horizontal rain, and nobody's going to know.

We are all armed with lists, and because of this powerhouse of a team, I'm not panicking. Quite.

Sashka's got an additional new job overseeing the rental on another Dartmoor house, and the stories she comes back with make me quake in my willies I mean wellies. She says it takes twenty minutes to make each of the house's beds because they all have six pillows, and cushions as well! What are you supposed to do with all those cushions when you're trying to sleep? I can't think of anything more constructive than throwing them on the floor. Susannah, my friend who rents out her luxury home in Helford for about £2 million a week, has only one set of cushions, which she uses for photoshoots, moving them around for each bedroom-shot.

Sashka says the converted barn she now works in has a sunny seating area with views to the sea twenty miles away, one wall being made entirely of glass, and apparently this one room is longer than my kitchen and dining room put together! She says the kitchen is twice the size of mine, all gleaming stainless steel and granite. She couldn't find the plug sockets in it because they are horizontal, built into the work surface.

Huh! Who would want to come to an immaculate shiny show house like that, in the middle of Dartmoor eh? Dartmoor is for MUD.

I have tried to think of a reason why someone would prefer my place to this nouveau barn - and I've come up with one.

At Wydemeet you can shout your head off and no one will hear you except the sheep. Does that count? We've fixed up a karaoke with a couple of mikes coming through Malcolm's PA system, and you sing to karaoke versions of songs you look up on the huge telly screen which you can get via YouTube, resulting in surround-sound underwritten by my special woofer I got second hand off eBay for £400. Leave the French doors open and you can deafen all those belted Galloway's placidly waiting for my electric gate to break down again.

One beautiful gentle balmy sunny evening last summer, Will used our system to serenade a pack of girl-guides camping 1/2 mile away down by the river.

My list of what to do before I say goodbye to my home for the week appears endless, inexhaustible. Malcolm is being amazing and has arranged for Neighbour to put some of the gravel from the council pile outside my gate onto the drive. Patrick is here, coping with the sticks and leaves. I have arranged for a professional contractor to clean and service the hot tub, called the plumber re the water neutraliser, found a bloke to tidy up the carpets, booked the window cleaner, and my next jobs are to arrange insurance and smoke alarms.

Meanwhile Kathy and Sashka are working double hours together cleaning out every cupboard, piece of crockery and glass. I hear them hooting with mirth while I'm trying to Get On. They call me Mad Mary or Lady Muck behind my back, and think it's really funny that I'm still saving the tin of fois gras that my Mum brought back from France for a special occasion, even though its sell-by date was April 3rd 1997.

I am increasingly unsure that I could be going ahead with this, without my amazing little team. They just pack me off, think it all through, arrange their own agenda, and get on with it.

I'm going to stay with my Mum in Dorset for the first two nights of my week away, then hopefully blag a night with a friend, and then I've booked a night in a B&B down the road for £32.50. That will be interesting. Hopefully they won't see me as competition as I'm charging a minimum of £40 per head, based on two sharing, for a minimum of two nights. In truth, I'm anticipating letting out my best en-suite for £120 a night for a minimum of two nights, otherwise I'm not sure I can really be arsed with all this B&B bollocks. Early mornings, being nice first thing, frying eggs .... hopefully I will come up with a solution to such issues if I ever get a customer. No enquiries yet since that first one...

Poisoned!

19/03/2013

Oh help! I think I might have poisoned Malcolm!

He normally has a stomach of iron because, like me, he was brought up on leftovers in a school, where our mothers were at liberty to raid the larder. We share fond memories of giant catering packs containing dried 'Chicken Chasseur' which was enthusiastically served throughout the holidays - in his case on the family yacht, in ours in the VW camping van.

We both had 'war mothers' who believed in saving everything, no waste. In Malcolm's case this meant Izal, and margarine. In my case it meant Izal and hundreds of little plastic pots of moulding scraps stored in the fridge. No matter that both mothers came from rather grand families.

So we are both proud of our inherent embrace of the leftover, and our resulting tiny compost bins.

Yesterday, I came up with the perfect occasion to use my pot of out of date Fois Gras. Granny (82) had driven the eighty miles from her home in Dorset to listen to Faye play "Oops I did it again" on her flute in the school music competition, followed by supper at Wydemeet and an overnight stay.

The little round tin lay innocently, centre piece on the kitchen table. It was so discoloured you couldn't actually read the exact sell-by date (I was embellishing in my last blog), and it had leaked two orange rings of fatty rust. I prepared my version of Melba toast, and opened the lid with a flourish.

There was some brown stuff inside with white, grey and blue marks on it.

"Just what it's supposed to look like," I announced, and sniffed. It smelt fine.

I cut off the blue bits and as Granny, Malcolm and I demolished it we discussed how old it really was. We worked out that Granny had brought it back from a trip to France around ten years ago.

It left a weird sticky fatty sort of layer in your mouth, but tasted fine.

Lidl's De Luxe Three Fish Bake, raspberry cheesecake and profiteroles came next.

This morning Malcolm complained of a feeling of queasiness all night. I also felt a bit sick and headachy, maybe from mixing Cava with white wine and red wine. Granny was bouncing, as she completed our washing up.

Over the past few hours I've left messages on both Malcolm's mobile and landline - to no avail. Where can he be? I hope he's not in hospital.

Gravy in the Bathroom

27/03/2013

"That'll be gravy," I advised Kathy, when she reported that no matter how hard she tried, she couldn't remove the stains from the bathroom carpet.

"How on earth did gravy get into the bathroom?" she asked, astonished.

"It would date back to when the bathroom was Faye's bedroom, and I took her up meals when she was ill," I explained.

Sashka and Kathy are here every day now. The number of coffee and fag breaks we are enjoying, if that's the right word, are on the increase. I have discovered that smoking in my home is illegal, since it became a public place. I'm not sure the mercury has risen above zero for a week now, and at the moment it's snowing yet again, with a wishy-washy wintry sun peeking through for what feels like the first time in living memory.

Just as in the lead-up to the film company's bed-and-breakfast weekend, I can feel myself, despite Sashka and Kathy's best efforts, sliding back into panic-mode. Kathy felt the waves of it hit her too, this morning.

The carpet man didn't turn up, the hot-tub man didn't turn up, the plumber didn't ring back, the gardener didn't turn up, my Auto Trader ad has been hacked into, or 'fished' so that I have had to change my password on everything, and the electric gate man, who hasn't returned a call or email in two months, has finally called to say he will pop by tomorrow. Meanwhile, whilst it is relatively straightforward to insure your house for renting out in its entirety, or for running a B&B business in, it appears to be impossible to insure it for a combination of the two. I have three bespoke brokers on the case, who haven't quite got all the info they need. One of them is querying my use of the word 'entrepreneur' as my stated profession. "Well put 'single mother trying to make ends meet' or something," I suggested instead.

The piles of logs - well actually to be exact tree trunks - outside our house are now nearly touching the sky, and it feels as though the house and I am drowning beneath them. I have warned my guests about them - I am so worried that they will be disappointed as they approach the house and see nothing but a huge pile of timber wrecking what was once a beautiful valley. The wood comprises the livelihood of Neighbour, for whom hill farming no longer pays the bills, so I can't moan about it too much.

Sashka and Kathy have spent days cleaning every cupboard and corner of every room in order to prepare the house properly for our visitors. They have got as far as the main spare, Faye's and Will's rooms to date. Every bed has to have a mattress and pillow protector, duvet, ironed sheet and duvet cover, and there are three towels for each guest. I am going to have to leave the heating on 24/7 with this unseasonal weather - a fact which physically hurts! I really don't think I am going to make any profit at all from this first letting - but I comfort myself with the thought that what we have done would all have been necessary anyway.

I am worried about my horse who is coughing - it is too cold to suddenly leave the horses out so somebody is going to have to visit them twice a day, and muck out while our guests are here. I am worried about packing for three people ie Will, Faye and me, each of us due to spend the next week in two different countries; and I am worried about my stupid car which still hasn't sold and is deteriorating outside my house, and which now has another flat tyre.

And then in the middle of all of this, an email arrives from my lawyer which means I suddenly have to get properly divorced this week, before she goes on holiday! The forms seem to be endless. I have signed off whatever she's asking for this time, and hope for the best.

PS I didn't poison Malcolm after all. He's still alive. He caught a bug, meanwhile his phone was ringing away in the next door room.

Everyone's So Nice!

29/03/2013

"When you arrive, I think I will probably kiss you," I breathe down the phone.

A couple of hours later, and Dave draws up outside the house. He is around 5'6" with grey hair and a beard, slight paunch, is wearing baggy old black track suit bottoms and trainers, and is probably around 70. I rush over, almost jumping up and down with excitement at his arrival. He is the eighth and final carpet-man I have called. I was warned he is semi-retired. He has driven over direct from our phone conversation, ready to work straight away, and if necessary, on tomorrow's Bank Holiday Friday too!

Stephen arrives to see if he can sort out the electric gate using the rams I have bought from eBay for £16 (plus £72 P&P). He is very tired and is planning to take off the Bank Holiday weekend this year. Normally his only days off are Christmas and Boxing Day. He says what I have bought are no good, and I might as well put them back on eBay. He won't let me pay him for his time.

Sashka and Kathy are here again, working at lightning speed cleaning up seventeen years of accumulated family clutter and filth, laughing together as they go.

That was yesterday, and today I have a lump in my throat. Patrick arrives in his giant army Land Rover to finish tidying the garden and to replace the twisted, knotted old piece of electric fence with 6' posts he is planning to bury into the rock-iron sod; Dave is back - hating his job of tidying up the carpet where numerous plumbers have repeatedly pulled it up, and also putting down carpet in the new bathroom, against the advice of my entire family and all my friends; Sashka and Kathy are becoming stressed at the amount there remains to do; and I start swearing because the only thing my guests, who arrive tomorrow at 3pm, have asked for, is a DVD, and it's stopped working.

Sashka phones her friend Carl, who drops everything, drives directly over, and spends two hours going through the maze of wires behind the tangle of wires that is our AV system, in return for a cup of instant coffee. Meanwhile Ken, the insurance man, calls me for the eighth time in his determination to help make sure I have changed my insurance to 'commercial' before my guests' arrival. He, too, is now working on a Bank Holiday Monday.

I don't think I've really done anything to deserve this kind of support. I think people are just generally kinder than I am. I'm not sure I would be this nice to anyone, ever.

It's 2.30pm and I'm eating the remains of last night's leftovers, comprising a sausage and some spinach, when the panic alarm goes off as a result of Kathy dusting the bedhead. I am proud because I haven't lost the key to stop it. But the key doesn't work. Nor does the switch in the airing cupboard, which already reads 'off', yet on and on the sound drums through all of our ears. It has been deliberately designed to drive you so barmy you couldn't even rape someone.

I know! Brilliant! I'll try plugging the code numbers into the burglar alarm! That might stop it. If it doesn't, then I am stumped. I punch the numbers in. Merciful peace.

Blimey, my house is really showing us its tricks today. I pray it will behave itself for the next week. My list of instructions of how to deal with all its quirks has reached three pages!

Maybe this rental won't cover its costs, but it's made me focus on sorting my house out, and we will be much better prepared for the next one. If I have any friends left to help me out by then...

Isolation, not desolation

29/03/2013

God. If I were in my twenties, when I was a young and thrusting PR executive in West London, and could see where I would be in thirty years' time. Well, I would have had trouble believing any of it!

Living alone with my two young children in the middle of nowhere, tonight I find myself in the pub down the road, listening to Faye's young friends playing the recorder and keyboards, while Alicia, daughter of Neighbour, tap dances to the music, on a square white board on the pub floor. I have to admit, the youthful band is jolly good, and so is Alicia, who has now reached Grade 4 in her tap.

It is the perfect jolly, warm scene of rural idyll, and I have recorded it on my camera to show my guests tomorrow how splendid life is in this remote hamlet.

I wonder what everybody might be thinking, if they notice at all, while I sit alone tucking into a surprisingly good Aubergine and Feta bake, the musicians' proud Mums huddled together on the sofa and their Dads standing at the bar, discussing farm subsidies over their Jail Ale.

I feel I'm not such a part of the local community any more, now that my children have moved from the wonderful village primary to their posh schools. The rest of our hamlet, who are mostly slightly older couples without children at home, have reconvened onto a long table in the other bar. I'm not included there either.

I can't think of many other women who would have done what I've done, and remained rattling around in their too big family home, determined to make it pay its way. Who might then turn up at the local pub's jollities, with just their small daughter for company, to take part in a social so that they don't mess up their own kitchen.

I am very lucky indeed to know that Malcolm will definitely be thinking of me, as he marks, literally, a million words of his students' dissertations, cosy in the cabin of his clapped-out trimaran, so stable on its mud bank, somewhere out in southern Portugal.

These feelings of mild isolation might have something to do with my current situation. It's been like moving house today, waiting for someone else to take over my much loved home of so long. Faye and I have both retreated to my bedroom - she's on the hated air mattress, and the things we're going to need over the next week are piled up in the last spare room, needing to be retrieved and packed tomorrow.

Post pub I sit on the floor to watch telly as I don't dare squash or stain the pristine white sofa and its plumped up cushions. (I caught Twiglet lying on it this morning.) All the other rooms are closed to Faye and me, each waiting in its immaculateness for its new inhabitants. I feel as though I am camping in someone else's hotel.

Next time, when we know what to expect and half the things that we've had to worry about on this first occasion will have been done, life will be much easier. You never know – getting ready could almost become fun! The weather will be warmer, and we will be going directly off on a lovely summer holiday too. It may not be pleasant right now, but only a few hours to go and we'll be away! Then there won't be a lot to do except work out how to make the most of the next few days of transience. I feel some retail therapy coming on...

Revenge!

03/04/2013

Ex's old office block bit back.

I've always hated what he calls 'The Bothy'. It is the sort of shed beloved by men for escaping to, from their wives. It is where Ex and his team used to prepare polar expeditions. The only time I set foot in it was to make tea or to find things of extreme urgency that had been lost or forgotten. It's totally cleared of all things polar now, but still the waves of stress hit me whenever I open its door.

A year or two ago, Will somehow persuaded Granny to sign the form at the hardware store allowing him to buy cans of spray paint in black, blue and red.

The next morning I discovered that he and friend had sprayed the entire building inside and out with graffiti, including sophisticated slogans such as "Cheryl Cole Shagable" (sic). Ex took the defacing very well, and a newly matured Will has since repainted everything white, and the Bothy has now become an attractive teen den, housing some old sofas and a ping pong table.

So - I opened its door to show it off to my rental guests, and as I talk, that door takes on a life, or death, of its own. A panel slowly falls out, landing on the earth below. Then a second one goes 'plonk' too. I look down to see a third panel slowly sliding earthwards, and then a fourth. By now the whole of the bottom half of the door is missing. I casually pile up the planks of wood against a nearby wall, and continue with my tour of the house that Sashka, Kathy, Malcolm and I have worked so hard on, for so many weeks, to make look immaculate.

By the time I have finished the tour, left the house to my guests, and reached Granny's house in Dorset, I find myself very upset by the entire experience of renting my home out to strangers, and am relieved to be spoilt silly by her for two days, during which time I slowly regain my composure.

I Met Him!

03/04/2013

Yesterday was the annual Boscastle Football Match between all the boys in Will's year from his old school.

The most interesting aspect of the midday event was either the choice of clothing worn by formerly glamorous Mums, endeavouring to remain warm in the easterly gale blowing across the cliffs direct from Siberia; or the sloe gin/champagne cocktails served in large, real glass glasses by self-styled 'Barman Bill'.

We endured three hours of it, as I cruised car boots scavenging smoked salmon sandwiches, because my life has been too difficult recently to make up a picnic of my own.

Some of us went on to the Hosts' house to continue the merriment. The remaining revellers comprising, as always, Her, Ex, Me, and a couple of others who, seeing who else was there, made a rapid exit.

None too soon, finally, She disappeared too, so I could relax at last. And then Ex went too, leaving me to enjoy myself with my lovely Host friends.

But then the door opened. And. OMG - She reappeared, with... Bevan!

Blimey - what a shock! I felt quite wobbly! I'm not really sure why. I was sitting at the kitchen table surrounded by 14 year old boys, with a cup of coffee and a glass of Cava in front of me, and fag in hand.

I found myself competing with Host (he, I and Bevan had all been to school at Eton at the same time) yelling, "Do you remember ME?!"

"No do you remember ME?!"

"Oh only my sister? Bugger. Everybody always remembers her.."

Poor chap! What has he entered into?! He started talking Green Wellie Shooting with Host so eventually I thought it time to depart in Marv for my cheap and cheerful B&B.

Just before departure, Host showed me round a cottage which he aims to let out as a holiday rental via 'Ultimate Home Stays'. It seems as though we're all at it. He told me that the amount of work he has left to do is doing his head in.

As I drove home I felt a bit tearful. No home, no Range Rover, no family, no dog. All because of Her, still enjoying herself yacking away to all my friends, introducing the new boyfriend, who I don't think is nearly as attractive as Ex, nor, as it happens, as Her ex-husband, who is now a lord.

But then I thought – well actually. I quite like being anonymous, in my funny old car, playing all my favourite songs on my i-trip, off to some jolly little B&B where someone else will do my washing and cook my breakfast. I can just lie in the bath and read my new book. It's called "An Unusual Love Story" and I have just bought it at the Co-op. Then I'll spend the evening watching telly, while tucking into prawns and enjoying yet more Cava.

My Luxurious B&B

04/04/2013

The bathroom is along a corridor and, if I wasn't the only guest, I would have to share it with several other people. It has lino on the floor and is painted light blue. The towel rail appears warm, but the room is icy. The bath and shower gel, body lotions, shampoo and conditioner are all in pump dispensers.

I wander back to my room, my modesty protected (just) by the B&B's tiny towel. There are no pictures on the walls, and no telly in my room, the curtains are thin, and the 'tea and coffee making facilities' are shared, in an area just outside my room. I am cold, as the snow starts coming down again, and the duvet is rather small. All is explained when the hosts tell me later that there is no central heating, but only a lovely log burner in the rather plain sitting room downstairs, which you can fill up with logs at will, while you use the small telly there. It is all very simple and surprisingly cosy.

I am totally cheered up. I feel a whole different person from yesterday. This is real farmhouse B&B, and the hosts are delightful, friendly, chatty, easy-going, young, and can't do enough to be helpful. A couple of years ago they won a 'Best Farmhouse B&B' award in the Sunday Times. It's obvious that being a nice host counts almost as much as the quality of the service that you offer.

I put the daffodils I have brought with me into a coffee cup of water, and excitedly ponder upon the fact that I am quite justified in hopefully charging nearly double what I am paying here for my B&B.

Helen, the proprietor, on hearing about my plans, whizzes off to get me her 'setting up a B&B' book, and I discover that what I am offering might just about count as 'boutique B&B'; or 'complete home hospitality B&B' along the lines of the very expensive Wolsey Lodges. I have spoken to a couple of friends about these. My friends pulled out of the arrangement when they were told the exact dimensions required for the towels that they had to provide. Hmm. Doesn't sound quite 'me' either!

The book tells me that a 40% occupancy is good. My hosts say they're at 25%+; which they're pleased with, and they spend days a week on their marketing efforts and are always open and available. Um. If I am putting myself forward as the most expensive B&B on the moor, only available during weekdays of school term times, for a minimum two people for two nights; hot tub or no hot tub, we're not looking at a lot of guests. I might have to re-think this.

Perhaps I might need to go cap in hand to Alastair Sawday, for his list of wealthy and exclusive potential clients.

Whatever. Any further action will have to wait until I get back from Malcolm's old trimaran in Portugal. I am typing this up on one of Bristol Airport's computers at £1 for every 10 minutes internet access. Luckily it's a very nice computer and keyboard, but I'm buggered if I'm going to keep paying for the privilege, while Ryanair keeps calling out the Faro flight.

Things seem to be coming together though. I just need to call Sashka and Kathy before I board to let them know that ...... oh what was it now?

Oh Hello! Real People!

16/04/2013

A big black man with a sticker on his chest saying 'Gift' stands in front of me. What a funny name!

I love Speeding Courses - you meet a total cross-section of the world at them.

We are divided into 'the red team' and 'the green team' and Gift goes off with the reds. They look like the youngsters. I bet they've all done something really bad – not just 32 in a 30.

We troop in silence (apart from a large woman wearing biker boots who is observing loudly what a profit the organisers must be making out 20 of us paying over £100 to attend this course) into a characterless, very hot, rectangular, off-white room; and I sit down next to a man with a beard whose sticker says 'Anoy'. Oh. Actually it says 'Andy'.

I imagine what a terrifying experience this must have been for Granny, who had been caught by a camera doing her top speed of 34mph, who must have been sitting in this very same room a couple of months previously, wondering what was in store for her, knowing that she has spent her entire life trying to be responsible, to please people, and to behave herself generally. She's not used to people like this, in their t-shirts, hoodies, surfer shorts, and trainers, crew cuts and tattoos.

Meanwhile I've been here before. I know that we're not going to be punished. I've already clocked the smiley matey greetings of the advanced driving instructors welcoming us onto the course, and their prolific use of Christian names. And I know that I will stick out as the most glamorous, best educated, funniest, cleverest, most perceptive and best dressed of the motley crew attending.

Or will I? A lady from Essex, in biker boots, turns to the big lady and says "You ought to be a comedienne on telly you know." Oi – wot?!

Anoy, or Andy, turns out to be cleverer than I am at answering the simplistic questions, and is the natural leader of our little group. I think he probably does pub quizzes. He already knew that in 2004 there had been 2,600 (or something) deaths on the UK roads. He even disputes some of the facts presented by the nice people taking the course!

There is also a funny lorry driver from Newton Abbot who does 130,000 miles a year. His greatest hate is middle-lane hoggers, as his juggernaut has an inhibitor or whatever they're called that won't let him drive faster than 52mph, being a lorry he's not allowed to overtake them in the third lane. The thing that makes me really cross, which I loudly voice, although I know I have gone a little bit pink with heat and embarrassment at my own loud posh accent, is old people drivers. Like my mum, as it happens. Who make impatient people like me do stupid things and cause accidents.

Oh dear. Now an elderly, shy, foreign lady is standing up and describing how her husband died in a bus station. She has been looking rather alarmed by my vehemence. Well whatever. They should all take tests at 70.

The jolly man running the course announces that we are the chattiest group he has ever taken, but don't we want to be away on time? The three hours fly - even the plain digestive biscuit and cheap coffee are delicious.

And then disaster. I am wearing Jaeger black trousers, high black suede boots, and a top quality black coat from Frank Usher, my wardrobe as ever bought in the half price sales of Clarks Shopping Village. I appear rich - well at least that's what I'm hoping! We wander back to our cars, and there's Marv, waiting patiently for me, in all his ordinariness. The other cars are gleaming Toyota's and Honda's, whose remotes actually work. I fumble with the key in Marvin's lock, dive in and drive off, eyes on the road, the myth of posh bitch shattered, never, probably, to see a single one of those people again.

Lying Again

16/04/2013

Champagne three days in a row! Can I really plead poverty?

At my sister's house to toast Faye's 11th birthday. At Saddlers Hall in the City, beginning a family lunch under chandeliers for 49. And at lunch on Sunday in Wimbledon Village – just because the sun's shining and we're feeling good.

Life continues in its crazy surreal way, not helped by staying up drinking and smoking til four in the morning at my best friend Annabelle's house in Putney. It felt so comfortable, and I was concentrating so hard in order to remember every sage word that fell from her lips, that I just didn't feel tipsy at all. It took a while to recover again after all that though, especially having shared a bed with Faye, who suffers from eczema, and scratches and kicks.

From tonight I will be spending three consecutive nights in one bed for the first time in three weeks. I can't wait to fall back to earth. I have returned from London to two enquiries about the Range Rover and a man and a woman have arranged to come and see it. They're coming after Faye's and my horse ride to Princeton before the first dinner party I've thrown for several years.

I leap off wonder-horse Panda and throw her out into her field in the rain. I rush over to inspect the Range Rover, which I haven't looked at in ages. It has earth all around its bottom rims, and muddy wheels and tyres. I rummage around in the Bothy and find a plastic container full of bottles of car cleaning materials. It's raining though - what good is wax in that? I half-heartedly fill a bucket with tepid water and rub some of the mud off bits of the car with a small flannel. I squirt the tyre-cleaner onto the muddy tyres, where it stays in a white goo, and it's time for the potential buyers, armed with £7000 in cash, to arrive.

"I am sad," I explain to the overweight lady, "because if you buy it, I know it's gone and it's worth more than £7000, but if you don't buy it I will be sad too."

They look around it, noting the dent, the scratches and the chewed bit. Luckily when the man presses the button to make the car go up and down, it seems to do its thing, as I am leaning against it at the time and nearly fall over. They open the back door and all my muddy washing water suddenly gushes out. Then they drive off in it, leaving behind their shiny Jaguar with its personalised number plates.

They're rather a long time. I have been too trusting.

Eventually the doorbell rings. It's the lady.

"I think your car's run out of diesel," she explains.

Not again. That bloody fuel indicator. This time it says there's 100 miles of fuel left. And my hard-won potential buyers have been left stranded outside the garden in the rain. Bloody car. Lying again.

I join them and the wretched car in the hurricane, having happily found a container of diesel to help them get up the last few yards of driveway.

The couple say they will call me in an hour or two, when they've had time for a little think, over a meal at the Plume of Feathers in Princetown, where the horses, Faye and I have just had lunch. The call will interrupt my dinner party.

What a surprise! It never comes.

Decree Nisi

25/04/2013

If it were as difficult and expensive to get married as it is to get divorced, I am sure there would be far fewer marriages, and far fewer divorces as a result. The lawyers would be put out of business!

My lawyer charges £25 for every email sent and received by her, even if it's just one word long! I emailed her at vast expense saying "Sorry I haven't been very polite recently, but I feel I can't email to say 'thanks' if it costs me twenty-five pounds every time."

I have just discovered from some form that a Decree Nisi, if that's how you spell it, was issued to me last November. News to me. Haven't a clue what it means. Or what it looked like.

Anyway, apparently our financial arrangements have been 'sealed' so I am now officially broke, and am about to have to ask my Mum to help me out for the first time since I was 35.

I have also just signed a thing applying for a 'Decree Absolute' which means we should be divorced in a few weeks' time.

Hurray! At bloody last! This has all taken so long - the process started back in October 2009 - that I feel I hardly care anymore.
It must be horrid being a divorce lawyer, or in 'family law' or whatever they call it, because as far as I can tell, there's just absolutely nothing remotely pleasant about anything to do with the whole experience.

The worst bit for me has been listing our belongings, and allocating them. Walking from room to room writing them all down - it brought back memories of eighteen years ago when life was all so exciting, moving into our new home, deciding where all his antiques and glassware, and our wedding presents still arriving from Harrods and John Lewis, would go best - the years ahead beckoning in a sunny sort of way. We've agreed that he's going to keep all his family's 'wealth' - including six Royal Worcester miniature porcelain coffee sets, and I will keep the modern things you can't sell, such as curtains.

Let's hope he doesn't decide to take everything away immediately, or there won't be anywhere to put things down on.

Growing Up

25/04/2013

I'm getting really old now. I've got much fatter and much wrinklier this year - my 54th. Wrinkles AND spots. That really is unfair. I'm trying out some new moisturisers to try to reverse the signs - I've moved from Boot's Protect and Perfect, to Neal's Yard Frankincense Nourishing Cream, to Olay's Regenerist 3 which has apparently got special peptides in it. But nothing's working, and they all seem to curdle with any foundation I may try putting on top. I don't suppose my diet of Cava, fags, riding through the horizontal rain of Dartmoor, and getting divorced, would be terribly helpful for anyone's complexion, nor my penchant for deliberately getting sunburnt.

Nobody's commented on my demise in the looks department yet, except my children, who cheerfully let me know that I'm beginning to look like Granny.

Meanwhile Ex is, annoyingly, looking better every day! He appears to be keeping to some diet and regime prescribed by his personal trainer, and anyway, fifty year old men, with their greying temples, do tend to look better than fifty year old women, it would seem. Bum.

I am so grown up that I included him in the dinner party I threw the other day, once I had confirmed with Malcolm that he was happy with the idea.

I guess this was payback after Ex brought Will home from school to me, with no comment nor demand for exaggerated thanks. Ex is actually just the best company if there are people around, and I was really pleased that he joined us. He helped make the evening go with a real swing, no matter how surprised our friends were to see him there!

I am so intrigued about what his next girlfriend will be like. I think he would be happier with a straightforward outdoorsy-type who camps, than with the manipulative film-star types he has favoured of late.

But it must be quite hard for him (as the actress said to the bishop or whoever) as there is just so much temptation for men in the public eye. During his speaking gigs when he went on about how he 'did it all for his family', women would still pass him napkins with "I want to have your babies" written in lipstick on them.

Honestly. What sisterhood?

Back to (slimming) Black

26/04/2013

The Jilted Wives Club, comprising Loelia, Juliette and me, lost six stone between its members, shortly after we were all dumped by our better/worse/other halves.

Juliette, in her miniscule hot-pants, soon pulled a blind man in Costa's, and then a little later, two men who could see, and therefore could properly appreciate her pert bum.

Loelia was repeatedly hooted at by lorry drivers on the Launceston A30, as we chatted outside Spud-U-Like. Her Elle MacPherson giraffe-legs encased in skin-tight jeans and long boots, and her thick, brunette Kate Middleton hair waving in their slip-stream, could not be ignored. Will at the time awarded Loelia the honour of 'fittest mother in the school'.

Meanwhile, immersed in my diet of misery, fags and Birds Eye Frozen Platters For One, I initially found keeping the weight off quite easy, and for the first time found myself branching out into coloured clothing!

We were proud of ourselves.

But now I am back to black.

As all women know, black reliably coordinates with itself, and makes you look thinner, as well as not showing the dirt, so I wear the same outfit every day until it smells – each one normally lasts a bit over a week before I put it in the washing basket. I alternate each black outfit with my blue riding clothes, which I wear every other day until they really smell.

Occasionally I may venture into navy leisure clothes, and I celebrate summer with a little white, to lift the black. My walk-in wardrobe as a result is terribly dark.

When I came down for breakfast this morning, Malcolm commented, "Black again?"

Being Divorced, Absolutely

03/05/2013

Well. Apparently I got divorced just now. Ex has sent me an email 'truly hoping for only good things' for me.

I say. What an anti-climax! After ALL that! I mean not just the year of planning the wedding and the £10,000+ that it cost, but all the anguish of the split, and the incredible hassle and vast expense of getting all the right bits of paper together from the bottom of old drawers, and making sure we'd got the exact, precise wording onto the divorce forms - and now it's done. Bingo. Without me even noticing!

I really don't know what to feel - if anything much at all. Is it an excuse to share one of the £12 Lidl bottles of champagne I have carefully put by, with Malcolm? That would make a nice change from Cava, and he will be pleased to hear that I am now a genuinely 'Free Woman'. I think it is very touching that he cares about that.

Or should I go and smoke a fag at the bottom of the garden by the manure heap and feel sad about the waste? I simply don't know.

What I do know is that I must hurry off in Marvin to reach the school in time to hear Faye singing 'For All the Saints' in the school Church Choir. Perhaps I should first change into a Little Black Dress in which to mourn the end of my eighteen year marriage properly.

Range Rover Over

06/05/2013

With butterflies in my tummy, I carefully stuck up the sign reading "£8450, MOT until November, 149,000 sedate miles" in the windscreen of my Range Rover, using the piece of selotape I had prepared earlier, slammed the door shut, locked it, and ran round the corner to Malcolm's house, so that he could drive me home, as I sat shaking in his passenger seat.

I had driven my beloved Range Rover, 'King III', named after Jeremy Clarkson described the Range Rover as 'The King' of the road, eight miles down off the moor, and parked it on the grass in front of a bench, just behind a bus stop, by the Ashburton junction of the A38, opposite Ashburton Motors, which sells second hand four wheel drive cars at twice the price of mine.

'Foolhardy' was how Malcolm described my action, through gritted teeth.

'You're mad!' exploded Sashka, when I told her what I'd done.

But ho ho to both of them. Within 24 hours I received a phone call about it from someone calling himself 'Kouros', and was in a muddle because I didn't know whether he had seen it in real life, or come across it advertised for auction on eBay. I have now been trying to sell the thing since February!

Anyway, Kouros called back and said his friend had seen my car parked on the grass, and that he would come and give it a go on Sunday.

'Fat chance' I thought, by now quite used to no one wanting my adored car. And as anticipated, no further phone call was forthcoming. 'Who cares, anyway – F*** it; I'll keep the Range Rover and flog Bill the Shogun."

But I had to give it one more try.

That evening I asked a couple of friends to bid for King III on eBay, to make it look as though somebody was actually interested in buying him. I did get one enquiry and then countdown began... four hours left for someone to bid £7,500 and it was theirs. Three, two, one .... Nothing. Gone. Auction over. Nobody. Another £17 in advertising costs down the Swannee.

Meanwhile, every time the phone rang I thought it might be the police saying they had towed my Range Rover away at vast expense and added several points to my licence, or Malcolm reporting that someone had covered it in scratches, or that the wipers and/or wheels had gone missing, or, indeed, the entire car. After five days I could bear the tension no more, and Malcolm dropped me off by the car, for me to drive it home again. Instead I went into Ashburton Motors and asked the very nice staff there if they would like to sell it for me, for a huge commission.

"No one would ever do that," they assured me (very nicely).

So I went to the Country Wholesalers to buy some horse-food and bumped straight into the arms of riding-boyfriend James, and told him my sad story. James used to own the identical car, same colour, year, mileage and price, only his had since cost him £12,000 in repairs whilst mine, much to James' envy, continued to work most of the time. "My friend John will sell it for you," he said cheerfully. "He sold mine."

And the next thing I know is my Range Rover is on the forecourt of a small country garage in Ugborough, and James is driving me twenty miles home, with a stop for a baguette in the sun as a thank you in the Church House Inn on the way.

Saying goodbye to my car was like walking away from a much-loved dog or horse. I will probably never see King III again. In the meantime, for £300 John will make it look immaculate, and for whatever it costs more, the rattle in its engine will be eradicated (I hope).

And , young John is only going to take a 10% commission! He's going to call me in a couple of months to let me know how things are going, but in the meantime will thoroughly clean King III on a daily basis. That will make a change. And now, finally, I've got some space in my driveway. And in my head.

Fashion Tips for the Maturer Man

08/05/2013

It has come to my attention that some of you chaps out there, back on the dating game, just don't get it that you're missing out on potential love-matches because you've forgotten how to dress. Or how to stay properly clean. Or your hair is now growing in the wrong places. Et cetera.

Do you think you're sliding into Sad Old Gitness? Perhaps you think that love should conquer all - whatever you look, smell or feel like. Wrong. We girls mind. Even if we're desperate and over 50.

It's worth remembering that like you, we're also learning to fancy middle-aged people with crepey necks, thin grey hair, paunches, bad backs - etc. The last time we were all on the market everybody was in their twenties and thirties! We've got to get our eye in!

Proof that we no longer look as we did comes when you pass a building site. The silence is even worse than the wolf whistles used to be!

Anyhow. I think it's still worth bothering so I've put together a little guide for blokes, what I think is important anyway, moving all the way down his body from the top of his head to the tips of his toes:

HAIR (or lack of it) ON YOUR HEAD
Long hair dark - good; long hair grey - bad.
Cut it! Bald with straggly sides? Give me strength.
Comb-overs – like limp handshakes.
Proper regular haircuts are important for old blokes.

FACE
Eyebrows, nose hair, ear hair, toe hair needs to be regularly trimmed or you'll look like an old tramp, or Dennis Healey. Those trimmer gadgets make great stocking fillers!
Contacts or a laser operation – lose years!
Light specs frames if you must, unless your face is so ugly it needs covering up.
A big no to light-reactive lenses – we'll think you're blind rather than cool.
Brown/black stubble - tick. Silver stubble - cross.

Just because you can now grow hair more easily on your chin than on the top of your head doesn't mean that you should!

BODY

Choose your look, not a combination. Country caszh? Town caszh? Nautical, beachy, sporty, dinner party; but not all at once. A fleece, lamb's wool sweater, floppy linen trousers and leather boots all together and you will look like a dog's dinner.

Tuck in all shirts - the 'vertical hang' from even the tiniest paunch does few favours, and, presumably, is also draughty. Beware of floppy old fleeces and jumpers that might further draw attention to this problem.

A 'non' to thick shirts under thin jumpers.

White polo neck jumpers are a deal-breaker (unless you're in the Alps and ypu're thin).

These days creased clothes make you look like an old tramp rather than a young hippy.

Thick woolly jumpers make you look fat.

No anoraks unless they're Musto

LOWER HALF

Tailored and fitted looks better on saggy old bumpy bodies than floppy trousers or combats which are designed for young surfers devoid of excess flesh and skin.

Hurray! None of us is old enough for elasticated waistbands yet!

Are your trousers long enough?

Open toed shoes are a challenge, now our toenails are becoming thick and yellow. Women's advantage is that we can cover them with Shellac.

Flip-flops, provided they come complete with the bit that goes between your toes could be OK.

Sandals with socks – noooooooooooooooooooooooooooo!

Trainers (unless you're going to the gym) noooooooo! They're for people with arthritis. Bright white trainers? Any white shoes at all? AAGGGHH!

Thick crepe soles – avoid!

Long, thin willies, I mean wellies – yummy! Short, wide ones – yuck!

Skinny swimming trunks? OK – but only if you're Daniel Craig or Tom Daley.

SMELL

I've received a couple of reports of men who live singly smelling 'musty'.
Really. Well. No one can kiss someone new who actually smells 'old'.
Wash your rarely worn clothes and air your cloakroom and coats.
Make sure your home doesn't smell of cat.
BO might be OK on Venice Beach, but it's horrid on old bloke.
Clean your teeth twice a day.

I've found that charity shops aren't bad if you're a bit broke after the
divorce. I've just returned from Newton Abbot with two lamb's wool
jumpers and a Saville Row morning suit for smart weddings, all for £25.
I'll sell the morning suit on eBay for a profit if nobody I know wants it.

And now I've just checked the internet for a similar list of do's and don'ts
for dressing the older man. Oh dear. There's a site hosted by some
ghastly white-haired American moron with a beard, wearing a stupid
jacket and tie, who says the exact opposite of what I've said above.

B&B in Central Dartmoor Up and Running!

08/05/2013

Well! Here we are! How exciting that we are up and running at last! It is
lovely that you are reading this, and we hope you will choose to come and
stay at Wydemeet Bed and Breakfast very soon. We much look forward
to meeting you, and hope to provide you with a luxury break of 5 Star
standard!

The house martins have arrived and are swirling around the gardens and
barn; and after this late Spring we have never before seen so many
flowers blooming down the banks towards the garden gate onto the
moor.

Finally the grass is growing and we must deal with it; and watch out that
naughty pony Elwyn is away safe in his 'prison', before he contracts that
horrendous spring grass disease: laminitis.

So above is the bland loveliness that I have made public on the blog page
of my classy, all-new, ringing and dinging B&B's website. I've called it:
www.wydemeet-dartmoor.com. Enjoy!

How Honest A Friend?

08/05/2013

I seem to have gone a bit 'lookist' recently - or perhaps this is a permanent state of mind. You certainly wouldn't believe it to look at me, for all the time it might appear that I devote to the subject.

If you're not interested in appearances I don't care at all if you skip the next few blogs. I am going to write about headaches (the cure for) next anyway, so that'll make a change from moisturisers.

Last Monday, I leaped out of bed, threw on a few clothes, and rushed downstairs to prepare Faye's pony for her, just in time for her to join Neighbour for a short ride.

As we went out of the gate together, me in a vest, no bra, a fleece, some jodhpurs and no knickers; my hair matted, and what was left of yesterday's mascara and eyeliner smeared down the sides of my face reaching down to my chin, Faye casually commented, "You look better without make-up."

A conclusion that I had been slowly moving towards on my own. But why? Make-up is designed to improve your looks, not make you look worse.

I think this is a touchy, sensitive, intensely personal subject area.

Should you, for instance, tell your best friend that her teeth are yellowing and need bleaching, her heavy green eye shadow makes her look like a 70s retro, her eye-liner and mascara are all blotchy, her foundation is much too thick and exaggerating her open pores and wrinkles, her haircut does her face-shape no favours, the colour she's chosen for it makes her look older than if she just left the grey streaks in, and that the clothes she's wearing make her look fatter than she is underneath?

I think that commenting on this kind of thing is helpful, and the mark of brave, real friendship, if they are true, and if they are something that she can do something about. Especially as we all get older and our eyesight worsens, so we can't see ourselves very well in the mirror anymore.

I had been trying to emulate all those young people with apparently flawless matt skin, who embrace the use of these new kinds of foundation that didn't exist in my day. I've also borrowed some black, black eyeliner from my great friend Annabelle who works in the city in central London.

But Faye is correct. It all just looks wrong, wrong, wrong in the back of beyond in Dartmoor, so I am returning to tinted moisturiser, a bit of mascara, and chapstick as a cheap and natural alternative to lipstick. Thank you, Faye! You are my true friend!

Nothing Works Faster than Anadin

12/05/2013

I'm going to make Malcolm Rich and Famous (even though he doesn't want to be).

Just as I did with Ex (who did).

And you heard about it here first!

You see, Malcolm can cure headaches! It's true, because I know! First hand! And it's so, so simple!

That ancient Anadin ad, 'for tense, nervous headaches' has caused SO much misunderstanding. Malcolm explained that your actual brain can't hurt. So my constant, on-going headaches aren't being caused by stress. They are simply caused by my holding my head in the same place for too long - writing this for instance.

He says the little muscles in the back of the neck aren't designed to hold up such a big heavy thing in one place for hours on end. They are meant to dip and dive as you move your head a lot, when you're not doing unnatural things like sitting in front of a PC screen all day. He says everybody knows this already, but I don't think they do. I certainly haven't read about it in the Daily Mail recently. And I've been under the impression for years that Nothing is just as ineffective as Anadin.

I call Malcolm 'Artist of Touch'. He releases these seized muscles by gently putting increased pressure on the 'trigger points' which are causing them to jam resulting in the pain that you feel in the muscles further up around your skull. I sat quietly in a kitchen chair while he exercised his technique on me. It took about 15 minutes, while my sceptical mother, back towards us, carried on washing up the family lunch.

Well blow me down. It worked. I mucked out the horses and came back smiling.

And the next day I consciously moved my head around as I was bashing away on the keyboard (no one was looking, so it didn't matter that I looked like a crazy woman (or 'special', in the rather unattractive words of my revered son, Will). Come 4.30am that night, and no daily dreaded headache appeared. Wow!

AND. Malcolm can do the same thing for backs too. In fact it was problems with his own back that got him into researching trigger points. He is probably the greatest expert on them in the South West, but is currently too modest to blow his own cornetto. He could change the lives of thousands and thousands of pain-racked people.

So I am going to tell the world about him and his special powers! But I am not quite ready to yet. I've got to market my B&B, House Rental, and Poet first. Then I will be Onto It. Watch this space!!

Green Shoots

21/05/2013

I bet we're the only house in the world with daffodils still blooming in the garden in May! What a cold winter's tale.

As they're about the only thing that's blooming. Or so I thought. By yesterday lunchtime (spent with the Jilted Wives Club at the Endsleigh, the poshest hotel in the South West, total bill £12.50 each for the best sandwiches and Spritzer available in the universe) I was becoming despondent.

I have been pouring myself into my five post-breakup-money-making-ventures for over a year now, and all have come to nothing.

Not a single B&B enquiry, despite having spent three solid weeks on creating a fabby-dabby-doo website complete with SEO (Search Engine Optimisation - which means all the things you have to do to get it to the top of Google, which I believe has now become an even more significant skill as part of the marketing mix than advertising or PR).

Breaking about even on my first house rental and no sign of the follow-up cheque, now due, for the second. No further bites for my poet. A blank in my brain about how to make this bloggy thing commercial, and 40,000 words written of a book.

I am now actually overdrawn for the first time in 25 years. And no sign of things improving.

And then yesterday tea-time: Ping! An email from a Swiss couple wanting to stay for a couple of nights in August! And then, Ping! My July rental lady emails to say she would like to drop the cheque round personally! Wowee! There are signs of life after all! Fancy that!

Never mind that I don't want to do August B&Bs because the children will be at home, and that the mower's at the menders, so if my potential rental turns up she'll run a mile if she sees that jungle.

All is not lost. TripAdvisor must have sprung into life. I will forward the Swiss couple to my friends' fantastic hotel, Prince Hall, just up the road, and perhaps they and I might enter into some mutually beneficial arrangement over time, in case this happens again.

Just when you think there is no light in sight, bingo! I now have the energy to get back to my poet's ring rounds, investigate getting advertising onto this site and going public on it to my 2000+ email contacts, and adding to my book. It would seem that I just need a little kick up the arse now and then, and off I spin!

Cutting Down On the Lunches

21/05/2013

I've told everybody that now I need to spend some time making money, I am going to limit myself to just one Lady Who Lunches a week.

So this week I'm doing three.

Yesterday was the Jilted Wives Club, and today I simply couldn't resist joining my brother and his two edible male friends on their yacht , as they sailed back from the Scillies via Newton Ferrers in Devon, and on to Chichester. Their dropping by in Devon seems to be becoming an annual event, and as usual they treated me like Lady Muck and took lots of pictures of me looking just that.

In fact it was on the previous occasion that I had lunched with them when they took the picture that I subsequently used in all my internet dating sites, when I was a couple of stone lighter than I am now.

I like sitting on boats in the sun, but am not too keen if they start moving along, over waves. So as the boys fussed over me with delicious 'Bladder Wine' (wine served from the 'bag-box', the cardboard part having been discarded to save space) and cold meat and salad, I found myself expounding on what had been bothering me during the night.

Once you are no longer part of a nuclear family, you don't fit in. Jack winningly tried to reassure me that other people's wives are just terrified of a glamorous single woman like me getting anywhere near their husbands. "That's just a silly cliché!" I reprimanded him.

I think people generally like to be involved with people in similar situations to themselves – their own 'tribe'. But I don't have anyone in my position living anywhere near me.

Ex has just bought a two-bed flat at the poor end of Parsons Green in London, and I think he is going to have loads of fun. There are millions of single people like him living within a stone's throw of his new home.

No one at all lives within a stone's throw of my house, let alone someone like me. I'm wondering whether I am mad to be so determined to stay in this large, expensive, worrying, demanding, inaccessible place, especially assuming both my children will soon be at boarding school. I am at a crossroads. Ex has started a whole new life. Perhaps I should consider that too.

The boys on the boat, all in happy marriages, didn't really have any views on this line of thought of mine, and wandered off, slightly uninterested, doing the washing up and preparing to make the most of the sunshine and wind by sailing on to Salcombe that afternoon.

This Thursday my favourite Auntie Rhonda is coming down from Edinburgh to stay with my mother, who lives not all that far away in Dorset. I feel the irresistible urge of another lunch coming on. Yes. No. Yes. No. Yes! So that's three in five days! Hurray! I'll work at making some money next week instead.

∞

Bedding In

∞

Decayed and Neglected

29/05/2013

The gate is still broken. The logs are still piled up to the sky on either side of it. It's raining again. I squelch out of the car into the cow-shit and in my cream cashmere top and salmon pink manicured finger nails reach around the orange bailer-twine which is vaguely keeping the gate held to, and pull the wooden five-bar structure open, as usual getting the green lichen into my finger nails and all down my front; my 'top stylist at Toni and Guy hairstyle' matted wet to the top of my head, making me look like Esther Rantzen.

I have been waiting nearly three months now for my new friend to sort out the electric 'ram' which makes the gate work automatically, without my having to get out of the car. I think I might prefer to just pay a stranger to sort it out, today!

The wind's in the wrong direction again, so I have to lean down and pick up a huge, heavy slimy stone to keep the gate open while I get back in the car, drive it through the gate opening, and get out again, and kick away the stone with my damp, stained suede high heeled boots, lean over the mossy stone pillar to get hold of the twine and shut the slippery gate; get back into the car and gaze with dismay up my potholed drive and the mad jungle that now runs along either side of it, while the house stands above, looking grey and forlorn, the paint peeling off all the rotten window frames.

I pray that my second house-rental hasn't been here and seen it all like this, while I have been out collecting Faye from school.

I collect the post from the box outside the door, and a letter with no stamp or address falls away from the pile of letters. I open it, and inside is a cheque for over £2000 from my July rental, no additional comments. God she must have been disappointed, I think to myself.

I email her to thank her for the cheque, and to once again apologise for the sense of neglect and decay that must emanate from my wonderful home.

By return she writes: 'I thought the house looked lovely, huge, and very pleased that it was straightforward to find and quite close to Ashburton for shopping (I like Ashburton). The dog and I had a bit of a wander down to Hexworthy and around which is also very pretty. My American sister-in-law will love it.

'We are quite serious walkers so some recommendations for good walks close by would be great if you have some. And my daughter and her boyfriend would love a recommendation for a good hacking stables, she doesn't get much chance to ride in Paris!'

Well blow me down. I write back that I never go for walks - that is what the horse is for, so I can sit down going uphill. But thinking about it we could not be more perfectly placed for short, middling or long walks, including pubs and/or total wilderness, north, south, east or west. And I am very familiar with all the hacking stables nearby, each offers something slightly different so that there's a choice for people of every riding standard.

This entrepreneurial life is such a roller-coaster. Depressing, elating, frustrating, all-consuming. Perhaps my home is nicer than I thought! And maybe I'm not very rural. Although I was exaggerating about the cashmere and the manicure. All my jumpers are black! And I don't have any fingernails.

Domestic Drudgery

29/06/2013

I've just learned how to turn the hoover on. After nearly ten minutes of trying all the switches I could see on it, I was beginning to panic. It was already noon, and my First Ever Proper Customer was due to arrive at 4pm. Followed an hour later by no less than The King, no, The Emperor, no God of global B&Bs.

That is how my life works. No customers at all for three months, and then God Himself invites Himself to stay without my even having to pray for Him. Sending me reeling with panic and focus.

I immediately bought 21 things off eBay, including a pair of giant ears for Faye, who is playing the Mad March Hare in Alice in Wonderland next week; and a Singer Steam Press, for which I bid £75.

So it was then, at the height of my apprehension and butterflies, that I received an email from the aptly named (in this case) LateRooms (who have, after three weeks of nagging on my part, managed to get Wydemeet onto their map), telling me that they are sending me my first proper, paying customer in 24 hrs time, which will coincide with God's arrival. I don't even know if, or how, to charge the guy! I only have one room ready for B&B, which I have already reserved for my Deity and his wife. The room I must put the customer in has a hole in the carpet, bare walls where pictures belonging to Ex used to be, and domestic bedlinen which has been 'Twigletted' - ie it's covered in muddy paw-prints.

Luckily, a week ago, Faye, aged 11, taught me how to use the mowing machine. She mowed the entire garden - about an acre of meadow grass, in an hour and a half, so I gave her £5. I've lived here for nearly twenty years, but have never used a mower. Just banged my head against the wall when endless gardeners didn't turn up whatever the weather, while the grass went on growing, and I looked helplessly on.

Well now I know what to do. And it's quite fun. A bit like hoovering really. I had always assumed that it's man's work, but if an eleven year old girl can do it, I guess I can too.

And another fun bit about all this domestic drudgery is that I can get it done how and when I choose, instead of waiting for people who don't turn up, or forgetting to tell my wonderful team exactly what I want, and expecting them to work on telepathy.

Anyway, all this work and preparation is why I've been a bit silent of late.

You will have to wait to find out what happened.

Egyptian Cotton

18/07/2013

I'll tell you something. 100% Egyptian cotton with a 200 thread count is a complete bummer. After washing, its creases resemble the complexion of an old woman, and it's impossible to iron them out.

But. This B&B lark. It's brilliant! I am really loving it! I still simply just can't believe that I ever possibly could!

I mean. You actually get paid for doing your own hoovering and mowing, and making your house look like a show home! Well, you would, assuming you had some customers. Which I'm sure I will eventually.

My freaky scary night with my first guests was really great. Malcolm and I had dinner with God and his especially delightful wife, just after I got back from listening to Faye singing 'Swing Low" particularly wonderfully in our local parish church.

I asked God whether it would be OK to serve my guests food from 'Cook', the manufacturers of my film crew's offering of mushroom lasagne. Cook is based in Kent and makes home-made food in bulk, freezes it, and gets it to you within 24 hrs of ordering. Most courses cost £3.95 a serving, and taste exquisite - words can't really do it justice. It's delicious, and completely reliable and consistent, unlike my cooking.

It seems that God is most comfortable with honesty and personality - two things that I rather pride myself on actually. He said it would be fine to serve Cook's food, provided I was open about doing so. He also commented on the hideous piles of timber piled sky high just outside my gate, which have been growing so fast over the past decade that my poor home is now drowning behind it all.

"It's real," he said. "It's what the moor's all about these days. What's really going on now that the hill farmers are forced to diversify." He made me feel completely better about it.

God, his wife, the LateRooms couple, Malcolm and I all sat around the polished dining room table for breakfast the next morning, and it was really like a jolly house party. The freshly baked (from frozen) croissants and pain-au-chocolats that I had found the day before in Sainsbury's went down particularly well. And I was especially pleased that one of my guests had come down in her onesie. I felt that she set exactly the right tone, and I have consequently used the website to encourage guests to have breakfast in their pyjamas.

Later I joined God and his wife for lunch at the Rugglestone Inn in Widecombe – possibly the best pub on Dartmoor - after they had wandered down the River Swincombe, which winds down the valley from just outside our house, to join the East Dart. They were stunned by the beauty of what they had seen. I have recently discovered that people who have lived on Dartmoor for years choose my out-of-the-way very spot to celebrate their most special occasions. It is so important not to take where I live for granted. There is truly nowhere else like it in the world!

I had spent the morning filling in God's B&B form, and rushing around tidying, clearing up dining room, bedrooms and kitchen, washing up, straightening flowers in vases and straightening beds, wiping around bathrooms and hoovering. Stuff that I have never really done in my life before - well at least not for about thirty years, since my mother made me do it during the school holidays.

For the price of an overnight stay - averaging £100 a room for one of my three rooms - I really can't complain about this. All the books say that to run a B&B is such hard work. Well, not compared with a proper job, in my probably not as humble as it should be opinion. It just gives you an excuse to keep your house in good nick and hopefully, in the end, to entertain a steady stream of people staying the night, and to cook breakfast for them, and chat to them. All of my favourite things.

Roll on that steady stream!

And in the meantime I'll gird my loins and get experimenting with my new steam press. I got it for £52 in the end, from a very nice lady just down the road from my unhealth club. All the books agree that a decent B&B must offer Egyptian cotton. So I have to have a proper ironing device. Personally, I really can't see the problem with polyester, but there we are.

The Best B&B

19/07/2013

I have decided that I am going to offer the best B&B experience on the moor.

By this, of course, I mean the most expensive. But I'm still cheaper than a hotel, and I'm not liable for VAT yet, which means 20% off for guests – or, more accurately, 20% more for me. If I have sufficiently few guests so that I can manage to do all the work myself, I should be quids in!

The reason I have been 'off air' recently is because I have been trying to market the thing. After all these months I have felt as though I have been banging my head against a brick wall until it bleeds. I have become increasingly frustrated and irritable as nothing I do seems to work, and all appears out of my control.

I used to style myself modestly as 'Queen of PR'. I could make anyone famous, and get any crappy old product into the national papers for free. Well such talents now appear redundant. These days I have just one simple marketing goal. That if you plug 'Dartmoor B&B' into Google's search engine, up comes Wydemeet. Simples. Not. Over all this time I have got nowhere with it.

Owners Direct - for holiday rentals - no enquiries since January, despite my putting a 20% reduction on my prices.

TripAdvisor - after three months I still don't appear to be on their map, and I'm languishing at No 47 in their 'Top 166 B&Bs in Dartmoor National Park'. They won't include any contact details in your entry unless you pay them, or do it through another agent. So now finally I've succeeded in organising a link on the Wydemeet entry from TripAdvisor direct to LateRooms. What an effort though! It seriously doesn't just happen!

AdWords - they're the ads that come up in the yellow box, or are listed down the side of your screen when you do a Google search. Every time somebody clicks on an AdWord it costs the advertiser anything from around 25p, according to a complicated kind of auction-system. You're supposed to make up several very short ads, and fill in columns and columns of keywords and phrases (I completed over 200 in the end) to make sure the ads come up according to the various searches potential guests might make (including spelling mistakes such as 'acomodation'). I put my budget at a maximum of a £5 total spend a day, and my ads started appearing on the front Google search page occasionally, but still no one has booked through it, so I have cancelled my subscription.

LateRooms - I spent hours sorting out details of what should go on their website, and subsequently changed to a company called Eviivo, which covers LateRooms, TopRooms, LastMinutedotCom, Expedia and about 30 others, all at once. So I needn't have bothered with the LateRooms-only website after all that. It took two weeks to get up and running with Eviivo - quite quick relatively speaking in this business. They were sensible and efficient to work with. Hurray!

Booking.Com – currently operates separately from Eviivo. It insisted on writing its own copy and choosing which pictures to use to advertise Wydemeet, and in what order. The result was that Wydemeet's greatest asset, according to Booking.com, was its 'easy access' to Torquay, and the first picture they used to advertise the B&B was one of a silver horse and some glasses on the dining room table. Eventually I did manage to work with them to make the entry sensible.

Air BnB - operates differently from the above agencies. The others mostly charge me 15% + VAT commission per booking. Air BnB charges both customers and operators. Canny! And they are flying, judging by the number of enquiries I have been getting from them. And it's straightforward to set up.

God of B&Bs has gone away to France so I won't be on his website until after he gets back.

Search Engine Optimisation. Otherwise known as SEO. Hah! Aren't we modern now, to know that? I have been working on it really hard. As in AdWords, you have to list lots of 'key words' in your copy and behind the scenes in special hard-to-find sections of your website builder-thing, add a blog, use captions with capital letters under your photo's, etc etc etc. Apparently it can take six months for all these little touches to start working to make sure you come high up on Google searches, once Google's 'spiders' have crawled all around them. It is an ancient myth that the more clicks your entry gets, the higher up you appear. Whatever - so far I'm nowhere - not even on page 12 of search results!

YouTube: on one of our rare sunny days I grabbed the opportunity to film the garden and a bedroom I've called 'Dartmeet', and put the results up on YouTube, using as many keywords in the accompanying copy as I could think of, including a backing track of a Chopin Nocturne for the bedroom, and a quick blast of Beethoven's Pastoral for the so-called garden. This has resulted in Wydemeet's appearance on page 6 of a Google search, but somebody not very kind has added a 'dislike' little sign to my bedroom film. Perhaps they thought the use of one of the most beautiful tunes ever written, to advertise a B&B, was naff.

So I have been busy. With zero result. No other accommodation in the area is following up so many marketing avenues, as far as I am aware. So what's the problem? That I am up there too late in the season, that I am too expensive, that I am too dictatorial demanding a minimum of two nights, that the place is let out for a week in July, that I am new, so that I am at the bottom of all the marketing arms with no reviews as yet and have no repeat business? Or possibly just because I am horrid. I've got the feeling that Malcolm and Faye think I've been pretty horrid recently anyway.

So any results remain to be seen. At least I now have an on-line presence. Which means that I can calm down, get away from my computer for a few minutes a day, and be a bit nicer generally.

And I remain firmly optimistic that very soon all will begin to gather momentum, and in due course I will be over-inundated with bookings. Watch this space!

Cracked It?

23/07/2013

Well, I was going to write about my perfect moment as follows:

Wow! Wow! Wow! I am reclining here in the dark, on my newly-oiled teak sun-lounger, with a full moon gazing down upon me through the gap in the trees, picking on Lidl's 70% cocoa solids 'dark chocolate with raspberries', enjoying a fag at the same time, and a chilled glass of Naked Wine's Mar del Sur; while Will lies back in the hot tub before me, using the moonlight to read a dodgy-looking novel called 'The Vincent Boys', the blue, orange and blood red disco-strobe lights flashing under the water of the tub; his tea, lap-top and i-pod next to him on the shelf by his head, music (some of which I know and actually quite like) blaring across the moor from the ghetto blaster, the gorgeous heavy evening scent of honeysuckle permeating all around.

The house is clean and tidy, the lawn and patio immaculate, the tubs of flowers and herbs still alive, my pots of cooking oil, beverages, preserves, baked beans, herbs and spices all in neat OCD rows in their kitchen cupboards, everything just as I like it, awaiting the arrival of our guests on Saturday, while we catch EasyJet to Pisa and drive on to Siena, to stay in a luxury converted monastery (the sort of place prime ministers reside in during their holidays) to relax for a week with 14 other members of the immediate family, courtesy my lovely sister.

Tomorrow the window cleaner, telly man, hot tub man, and my 'Mr Fixit Team' arrive to finish everything off, while I live up to my new persona of 'Mad Mower of the Moor'.

I've just received a B&B booking for two rooms for mid-August for a couple of nights from a German family.

We've arrived! We're going to be OK!

And the unforeseen bonus is that this holiday lettings/B&B thing means that I can spend time and money making my home really nice, just as I'd always hoped it might be, guilt-free - and get paid for the privilege. Bingo! All is right in my world!

Or was. I have now spent 45 minutes trying to get my i-pad to log on to this site so I could tell you all about how happy I am and the bloody thing won't work. So I've had to come indoors, up two flights of stairs to my normal computer, and even that took another 20 minutes to sort itself out because we're so far from a proper broadband connection, and it is now well past bedtime at one o'clock in the morning, so I am in a bait.

Well I Never!

28/08/2013

I thought it would never happen. No one came.

And then suddenly - floodgates!

This is the first moment I've had, since before we went on our uber-luxury holiday in Tuscany, that I could properly put fingers to keyboard and draft a blog.

We've had breakfast in the dining room and in the garden, the weather has been out of this world, and we have developed what we call 'The Wydemeet Challenge' - a twenty mile yomp there and back across the most varied terrain of central Dartmoor, to 'The Warren House Inn' - the second highest pub in England.

I always offer to collect anyone who gets too tired on their walks, but have only been asked to once. The second person to complete the challenge was a Swiss twelve year old boy, who set out with the rest of his family at 10.30am, and returned at 6.30pm, ready for a sumptuous dinner at Prince Hall Hotel.

We don't have plans to start making it into a race at this stage.

Today I served my 100th breakfast since everything went mad. Phew! I am exhausted. I haven't been able to do or think about anything apart from Bed and Breakfast now for nearly a month.

Sashka is laughing her head off to see Lady Muck with her head down a loo cleaning up other people's poo. I have gone back to being a (relatively well remunerated) chambermaid - a job I last did when I was 17.

I thought this B&B lark was money for old rope to begin with.

Wrong! Instead, I have found I have never worked so hard, under such pressure, for such a sustained period of time, in my life! Well actually since I was publicising Ex succeeding in his world record attempt on the North Pole back in 2003.

My current guests are a jolly band of six from down the road in Plymouth, who were looking for somewhere remote to stay, so that they could make as much noise as they liked without disturbing anyone, celebrating their 26th wedding anniversary with champagne and several bottles of gold leaf cinnamon flavoured vodka. I wanted to give them an award for receiving my 100th breakfast complete with its 'Very Best Eggs In The World', courtesy Neighbour, but I couldn't think what to give them, so I didn't bother.

Tonight I get my own bedroom back at last. I have been dossing down in whatever bed happened to be available at the time, with all my things packed into a green Tesco crate, as I moved from room to room. Last night it was Will's bed again (he was away at a party in Dorset, and I am dreading finding out what he got up to there), which is two floors away from the nearest available plumbing.

The past few weeks have proved an extraordinary and surreal experience. Ask me for 'sunny side up', 'easy over', 'egg over hard', fried, poached, scrambled, baked or boiled - I can do the lot.

It has been terrifying, but at last I am gathering up the blobs on TripAdvisor and everybody appears to be having a very jolly time here. Hurray! I love my home being used for what it does best. A really good party!

I'm a Mole

30/08/2013

I feel as if I'm a mole. That's been underground for a long time and has suddenly emerged into the light and air, and who, all of a sudden, after days and weeks, has space in which to move around and stretch.

I've got time to write a blog, play the piano, have a bath in my own bathroom, and go out to dinner at the Peter Tavy Inn with Malcolm to celebrate the clear fact that my B&B and house rentals are, without any doubt at all, a resounding success.

I am such a perfectionist in my work that it has been something of a roller-coaster though. Sometimes it has felt that anything that can possibly go wrong will. And because I suffer from early onset dementia - well it feels like it to me anyway - I always seem to forget something. And I simply cannot bear to make mistakes. Or get told off. I have been moving around in a state of exhausted, permanent, apprehension.

All my guests have been extremely nice about this though, and many have just laughed at the inevitable errors of an inexperienced B&B proprietor.

My first four visitors, post God and the girl in the onesie, all arrived at once, and honestly, they were so nice, and so along the same lines as Malcolm and myself, that I really felt, had they lived around here, they would have become close friends.

When the new loo lever went wrong, Robert mended it himself, and when the adapter for the silly continentally plugged kettles blew up because it was meant for 1 amp shavers, he personally drove to Newton Abbot to buy three sensible ones from the pound shop, and refused to accept payment for them.

A more mature couple, with the most delightful little dog called 'Spud', found that despite my changing all the tellies from 'Freeview' to 'Freesat' at late notice and vast expense, they still didn't work, nor did the light switch in their bathroom. Having silently lost my temper inside my head on both counts, I subsequently discovered there was nothing wrong with either - we had simply been using the wrong switches. I wrote down their breakfast requests, but then didn't read my notes and only gave them one poached egg instead of two, and forgot to lay any cups or glasses; yet despite all this I felt they became very fond of, and paternal towards me.

I have repeatedly not quite finished laying the table when my guests appear for breakfast at the time they said they would come down, and on one occasion I forgot to offer them tea or coffee! Sometimes I forget to wear an apron, or even put on shoes!

I have finally learned how not to over-book, with all the calendars I have to complete for every booking; but the worst moment was when I came back to find the kitchen awash. 'Agh, those delightful Swiss children have left the bathwater running with the plug left in," I thought. But no - water was pouring through the ceiling into my £90 per night bedroom, 'Bellever'. Meanwhile a car came up the drive, which was the guest that I had already double-booked, and who I had had to move down to Bellever from the poshest room (my room) which he originally asked for.

We sat at the garden table in the sun, as I had a Cava and a fag and explained the situation to him, while Malcolm hot-footed it over from Ashburton to help solve the problem, as the water continued to pour in.

I will tell you what happened next if I get around to it!

Uncle Tom Cobley and All

09/09/2013

Tomorrow it's Widecombe Fair. This takes place on the second Tuesday of every September. It's a cross between a kind of Henley for the local community, mixed in with tourists coming from all over the place, even from abroad.

It nearly always rains so hard that the pony area, where we hang out with all the horse trailers, becomes a quagmire. Tomorrow's forecast isn't too bad, I don't think.

We will have to leave at 7.45am to drive around the one way system to arrive at 8.30am and be ready for Faye's first class - Best Hunter/Hunter Pony. She's also in the Best Pony and Best Rider competitions. The showground is very uneven and on a steep slope. Showing consists mostly of going round and round in circles with everybody else, then demonstrating a figure of 8 on your own, and finally standing still a lot. Elwyn, Faye's bouncy pony, will hate the ground (like last year) but he's so pretty and posy, and Faye has got to grips with him, so he should do well. She is Number 4; so it doesn't look as though the classes are going to be very full anyway.

Sashka is kindly cooking breakfast for my very nice guests, who will be coming along to join in the fun a little later.

What larks! I love Widecombe Fair, complete even with Uncle Tom Cobley in his ancient white smock astride his old grey mare (which I believe some years is a gelding).

Still Busy!

17/09/2013

Now the holidays are over and everyone's back to school I thought things might calm down a bit. But no! The bookings just keep on coming! I am beginning to wonder whether I might soon move back into my (the best, obviously) room, and then someone else books it! Good! I am very comfy in Will's hideaway in the attic, while the money pours in and he is away at boarding school.

I had wondered how logistically it was going to work, incorporating Faye's school run with preparing breakfast. But so far it's fine. If anyone wants a Full English between 8.05am and 9am Sashka is kindly available to help on Monday's and Friday's; and I'm here on Saturday's and Sunday's. Which leaves Tuesday's, Wednesday's and Thursday's for the odd occasion when this might prove a potential issue. In which case Faye will have fun enjoying a sleepover at a friend's house; or flexi-boarding at the school.

So all appears to be working remarkably well to date, and I'm looking forward to meeting six more guests/potential new friends this weekend!

Only Four Blobs!

25/09/2013

I think 'management of expectations' is critical to enjoying almost anything in life.

I was very upset the other day, because a nice, and, I believe, well intentioned, lady called Tina gave me the most fantastic write-up on TripAdvisor, with full marks for everything they list such as room, value, service, sleep quality etc; but overall she only gave me four blobs. This is worse than no write-up, as it will pull down my ratings. It's already made me slip down from No 34 to No 46 out of 172 B&Bs on Dartmoor. And I am determined to be Numero Uno!

I've been battling with myself since, about what, if anything, to do about it. Should I contact her? Was it a mistake? If it wasn't, I just don't want to know what she didn't like about my perfect home. Perhaps it was too quiet and remote for her?

But I've come up with an answer. I must make sure that these lovely guests of mine don't expect to find the equivalent of a Holiday Inn in my family home nestling in the wilds of Dartmoor.

So I've amended my website and told them! "Expect to come across drawerfuls of stored ski-clothes, family photographs and old lipsticks, the odd muddy paw-print and a shower with a mind of its own," I've written on the Home Page. I am very curious as to whether this is going to increase, or decrease, bookings. I don't really care either way, because it is all going so well that I wouldn't object to a bit of a rest. What I really, utterly, absolutely couldn't stand, is the idea of someone arriving with the wrong expectations, and being disappointed.

The most expensive room on offer, which I've called 'Hexworthy', costs a rather substantial £260 (£130 per night, 'including scrumptious breakfast of local produce', available only for a minimum of two nights), largely because it is my bedroom, and I don't want to go to the trouble of moving out of it for less. The result is that it must be the most pricey B&B bedroom on Dartmoor, so I think some of my guests are a little surprised to find themselves sharing my walk-in cupboard complete with underwear shelf, and the dressing table drawers all stuffed with unused nail varnish and body lotion. And to get rid of every carpet stain made by children and dogs over the past fifteen years would have meant re-carpeting the whole thing. So I haven't.

Instead we have to play on Wydemeet's unique location, and my magnetic personality. Seems to be working most of the time. I nearly cried when by chance just today I came across lovely Tracy's review, complete with the full quota of blobs, headed: "Perfection!!! Great Host, Wonderful Setting and the Best Night's Sleep away from Home in Years!!!!"

And I was most gratified by a recent American guest's reaction when I showed him Hexworthy in all its glory. "Holy Cow!" he exclaimed.

Don't Steal Our Dog

03/10/2013

What has caught me most by surprise since I started this business, is how much our guests love our mutt, Twiglet.

They keep smuggling him into their bedrooms, where he leaves muddy paw prints on my best white Egyptian cotton bedlinen; and nearly all the comments in our visitors' book appear to be more about him than anyone else!

Faye has started a website about him. It is called www.gotwiglet.com; so if you have any nice pictures of him, feel free to send them there!

B&B-itis

10/10/2013

I can't think about anything else! Every spare minute - while Faye practises Ballade on the piano, or gorges herself on Nutella and B&B leftover bread for breakfast - here I am on my i-pad, checking my ranking on TripAdvisor and making myself frustrated and envious as I compare my marks with other establishments' 10 out of 10s on Booking.com. I had no idea I was so competitive. I think it's an addiction.

Further to my last post, I've been tweaking my website daily, so that when guests arrive they are braced to find no hanging space and a total absence of what I have rather cleverly referred to as 'slick, sleek, urban chic'.

As I said before, I want them to realize that I am the most expensive B&B on Dartmoor (I have started losing blobs under the 'value for money section') because of (1) the amazing location, and (2) my brilliant service and personality. Not because I offer the most utterly incredible rooms in the universe.

I've pulled back from the 'you may find muddy paw prints, and the shower's temperamental' allusions, but on the inside pages I have broadly hinted at such things.

Anyway, the results of my obsession are now there for all to see. I am inordinately proud, smug and boring about it. Read on.

I had my monthly meeting with my local girlfriends (The Thunderbirds) plus partners last night, and asked them to play my new game. "Anyone with Safari on their phones, plug in 'Luxury Dartmoor B&B' on Google Search " I ordered them.

Hah hah!!! Up came Wydemeet!! SECOND!!!! Out of 180 B&Bs on Dartmoor!! Page ONE! Along with Bovey Castle and Browns Hotel in Tavistock! How clever am I? So all these hours and days spent giving myself headaches and getting irritable, immersing myself in Search Engine Optimization (SEO to geeks), has been worth it! Maybe I have a new career here!

So all is going according to plan, and my next stage will be to sack all the agents who charge me 15% + VAT commission on every booking made through them, and wait for guests to come flooding in to me direct!

Except that they're not. Demand has fallen off a cliff. Null pointes. Zero. I've got two more couples in October and then that's it.

Meanwhile I think I've booked the house out for a week over Christmas to a lovely sounding extended family with small children and three dogs (eek); as well as receiving my first enquiry for summer 2014. Directly through my newly highly visible website, as is now usual. Preen.

So dear Sashka is back to catering just for Lady Muck, who lies in bed til 10.30am now she's got the chance to do so after all these weeks. The difference is that I am feeling financially secure again, for the first time since the marriage bust-up four years ago. Yes - those children will benefit from an elitist, privileged, divisive education, turning them into people who haven't got a clue about the real world. Why? Why do we kill ourselves to achieve that? God knows.

Website Visibility

10/10/2013

One of the many fascinating things about starting Wydemeet B&B has been learning to use the social media and maximising website visibility.

I have spent just about as much time on this as preparing the house for my guests!

A vast proportion of B&B bookings are made through agents such as Booking.com and Eviivo. The agents are useful because they pay AdWords to be right at the top of any search you may make on Google, so going through them makes sure we get noticed.

But now most of my bookings are coming direct to me via my website, rather than the agents' ones, which means that potential guests should get the right idea of what to expect, and they can easily call to discuss anything which is unclear before they are committed to a deposit.

I am terribly pleased and excited by all this, and boring friends and family stupid about it!

One way of ensuring you stay at the top of Google is by continually changing and adding to the website - hence this blog! It certainly appears to be having some effect anyway, so I will keep on with it!

Thank you for reading this far!

What's the Point?

17/10/2013

So, what's the point of it all?

I've turned into a total B&B bore and am still short of time because I'm trying to write a proper book alongside this blog, but it's got completely held up after 40,000 heartfelt words, and now needs an entire re-write as things I was going to write about in it haven't quite panned out as planned.

With demand for my B&B services having recently fallen off a cliff I must now move on to Stage 3, which is to promote Wydemeet's existence to every contact I have, to get back the demand for my B&B. At the moment I have over 2000 'contacts' on my computer – that's everyone I've ever exchanged an email with over the past ten years.

I am pretty scared of this prospect - my contacts range from national press editors, to people I've sued, to speakers' agents, to past and existing B&B customers, and even include Her and Her ex-husband etc! I am bound to say something that will offend somebody somewhere.

And after that I have to move on to selling the B&B service via Facebook and Twitter. Even worse than the above - I gather I have to 'hashtag' the entire world - not just a handful of contacts - and entice all and sundry to come and stay at my place by saying something short and pithy about it, which will go viral. I wish!

And then finally somehow I have to make this blog commercial, after so much time, effort and thought has gone into it, or there's not really much point in its existence. How? I suppose I've got to draw the attention of my 2000 contacts to it for a start, and hope there's not too much that's too offensive in it anywhere. And then include advertising space on it or something.

I may be a marketing person to my core, but the thought of people I vaguely know being bothered by stupid emailed messages saying "There's been a lot of action on your Facebook account recently" or "Here's the latest news from Twitter" as a direct result of my trying to flog them something, fills me with horror!

I gather this is how things get sold these days, though, and people accept the process.

I guess the only way to find out is to try it.

eBay Addict (reprise)

17/10/2013

Not only am I addicted to looking up Wydemeet B&B on Google and TripAdvisor.

I am also, as you know, a total addict for eBay. With this new B&B business I feel I have an excuse to buy new (or sometimes old) things all the time, and at the moment I am making about 20 bids a week!

Yesterday I bid £2 for a black and white spotted apron for Faye, who has offered to clear up breakfast and tidy our guests' rooms for £3 per hr on Saturday, while I visit Will at his school because it is his 15th birthday.

My latest approach to using eBay is to press the 'time left' column, so up come all the things that no-one really wants, and with no time left for anyone else to make a bid. Try it - you'll find that ebay is selling a car almost every five seconds, lots of them at silly prices.

Anyway, my latest triumph was buying a carpet. A few years ago, at vast expense I stupidly covered our kitchen floor with that sisal grass stuff, where all the old bits of food go down the cracks, it shrinks if you get water anywhere near it, you can't wipe anything off it, and it stains with immediate effect. Well it did look nice on the first day. So to protect it I bought a rug from Trago Mills for about £90, which very quickly also got stained with all the gravy, coffee and red wine which we habitually spill on it.

Sashka has been desperately but hopelessly trying to make our kitchen look clean and hygienic for when I offer 'tea and cake' to my guests on their arrival. An impossible task. It actually looks a bit disgusting.

So what sort of flooring should I replace the sisal with? And how on earth much would that cost to get it all fitted properly? And then bingo. Brainwave. If I could get a big carpet just the right size, I could pop it on top of all the stained ones and no-one would be any the wiser.

So I measured up and put 'carpet 111" x 85" ' into the eBay search. And do you know what? Up it came! An all wool, earth red, unused carpet from Trago with its £299.99 price tag still attached! No bids, a minimum price of £60, and located not too far away in Truro.

So it's mine now. Malcolm kindly picked it up on his way back from Falmouth, and brought it home, collecting Faye on his way, the carpet sticking through the sunroof of his old Vauxhall Corsa (he had checked the weather forecast before setting off). He was gobsmacked to find it fitted my kitchen perfectly, with a 1/2" margin all the way around. He should have predicted my immaculate planning. I'm clever like that.

With all the mank old carpets still underneath, it's so springy it's like a trampoline. I just hope nothing below goes actually mouldy.

Love

21/10/2013

"I'm a bit nervous, because I'm going to ask her to marry me when we come to stay," my B&Ber rang to warn me in advance.

"Oh no, now you've given me butterflies too!" I exclaimed. "But I know just the place to pop the question - down at the stepping stones, where the Swincombe meets the West Dart."

So after he disappeared with his girlfriend for 'a walk' on Saturday afternoon, Faye, her little friend from next door, and I excitedly put champagne in the fridge, opened our best Kettle crisps, lit the fire in the sitting room, arranged red roses in their bedroom, poured ice into the under-used Tiffany's ice bucket - a wedding present from my best mate; displayed under-used champagne flutes - a wedding present from my other best mate - on a tray, all ready for Wydemeet B&B's first betrothal.

As we heard the couple returning, the girls were jumping up and down, poised to rush out bearing our gifts.

"No, no - wait!" I entreated them. "What if she said 'no'?"

"Here they come!" shouted Faye.

"Has she got a ring on?" I asked.

"Yes, no, yes - it's on the wrong hand - oh no - yes, no - it's on the right hand!!!" cried Faye, and we all flew down to congratulate the happy couple.

Missing You

28/11/2013

Dear old blog.

I've been missing you.

I've broken, or cracked, or bruised some ribs. I was walking along in the dark, holding a torch and a bucket, and tripped over a tiny ledge of the ramp up to the horses' barn, my ribs landing on my hand with the torch in it. The world went sssshhwwissshh,, and then I was back to normal, and carried on.

At four in the morning, Faye came through to be sick in my loo. I was about to get up to look after her, and found I couldn't move. At all. Not even raise my head.

So despite having contracted some dreadful virus, she found herself having to call the NHS number, and a couple of hours later, after driving round and round the Dartmoor lanes in the dark, a bloke turned up in his car. If I couldn't get myself to the loo, I was going to have to go to hospital – my eleven year old Faye wouldn't be able to deal with bedpans etc.

He spent a further couple of hours filling in forms, gave me some morphine, and finally called an ambulance to take me away.

One more try to stagger to the loo before being rolled onto a stretcher, and I made it there, on my own. My God did I feel ill afterwards though. Apparently I am 'drug intolerant'. I would imagine that is a very good thing.

So the ambulance went away again, and here is the result. I can hardly get out of bed, and have to come up with clever ways of rolling onto the floor in order to reach the lavatory. Six weeks they say it will take to get better.

Well call that three. Or two. I am a single mother with children to organise, a business to run, and horses to exercise. I can't afford to be out for one day, let alone 42.

So this morning, after ten days in bed, I have hauled myself upstairs and onto my computer, to tell you how I've been spending my time.

Shopping.

I've lost count of how many pairs of jodhpurs and electric blankets I've bought. So far I've got four pairs of jods, and Faye's got three, and four electric blankets have been delivered. Also a cream coloured set of tea, coffee and sugar tins, and a Rock Box.

I have also been learning things. I now know more about showers than anyone in existence, and we've got the wrong one. That's why it works all funny. So I've bought a new second-hand twin-ended pump and thermostatic head to replace it with.

Satellite broadband! It's coming on Saturday! This will add years to my life! It's only £500 to install with a hideous white satellite dish, and £28pm thereafter for speeds of 20mb/s. That's 153 times faster than what I have now!

Android mobiles! Yeah! You can use your mobile without a phone signal via Wi-Fi! I've bought two by mistake. One will have to go to Faye for Christmas.

Renewable Energy Sources! A windmill, heat exchanger, bio-mass boiler, solar panels? Or the whole lot?! A company is calling me tomorrow to discuss it all.

I am truly a woman of the modern world. With a broken rib or two.

Poor Lonely Me

28/11/2013

This Christmas I shall be all by myself in the cheapest B&B on Dartmoor, while my two children wake up to their stockings with their father in his new pad in Parsons Green, and go on to join their cousins in Sussex for a jolly family Christmas Day.

We originally bought Wydemeet as a 'Christmas Home', which it is perfect for, and swore to spend every Christmas in it, for ever. And now I have rented it out for another family to enjoy.

Hurrah! I am free! I have been struggling to prepare a Christmas meal in a 2-ovened Aga for sixteen years now, without a break. I've missed the telly! I've missed the riding! I've been stressing for weeks in advance...

So I've organised this arrangement on purpose, and I just can't wait for the 'me time' to begin. I shall be on that horse, jacuzzi-ing at my health club, coming back from parties (if I get asked to any) to someone else's lovely, warm, friendly, cosy house, and having breakfast prepared for me every day.

And on the day itself, lovely Malcolm is preparing Christmas Dinner for me, his wife, their daughter, my Mum, his wife's sister, and any other waifs and strays who knock on his door, I assume. How modern!

So I think it's going to be really, really fun! (Although a little part of me thinks I'd like my children back next year.)

More eBay Madness

28/11/2013

I have just bought Faye a flute which cost more than my car. It's solid silver, unlike my car which is solid Ford Focus.

I bought it mostly because it was a quarter of the price that I was expecting. Her teacher had told me that a silver one, called a straight, open-holed Yamaha 481 or something, which professionals use, would be around £4000. So when I saw this one advertised for £1100 on Gum Tree I just ordered it then and there.

I'm wondering whether Gum Tree is the next eBay. You can advertise on there for nothing.

But I think, despite its best efforts, it might be a portal for prostitution.

Two people rang up in one morning, directly after I'd posted an ad on it for Malcolm's massage business. Sashka answered the phone, and not being briefed said "No, this is not a massage parlour, it's a bed and breakfast business".

Aaggh! So that's two even fewer customers for Malcolm then. I returned the next call from a chap called 'Dave' asking for 'Mary'. Well honestly - there's a pic of a bloke massaging someone who's fully dressed in the ad; and the copy is all about long term pain relief with particular reference to backs and trigger points. Dave never called back.

My final enquiry came from someone trying to get me to pyramid sell health food products.

I might go back to eBay.

And now, to make things fair, I suppose I'll have to buy Will a new sax. No doubt this will be made from solid gold, and will cost more than my house.

Well Hello Everybody!

06/12/2013

Oooeerrr...

Today I managed to transfer the 50 blogs I've written over the past year privately, while attempting to 'find my voice', onto this public site for all to see and despair at: 'wydemeet-dartmoor.com'.

I'm wondering whether I'm being completely stupid.

These blogs weren't really originally intended for public scrutiny. They were an experiment for me to find my style and work out what I was talking about, to search for my own personal muse, to see if I was actually capable of writing, because so many of my friends told me I had to, and I thought it might somehow result in a few extra pennies one day. Now I'm not so sure.

How many of you am I going to offend, frighten, or generally put off coming to my lovely B&B, once you've had a look at my ramblings?

I'm also still mulling over whether to launch my new B&B business to my 2,000 contacts - telling them all how fantastic my B&B is, and imploring them to come to stay.

Even though I now seem to have enough 'footfall' already.

Is this just my loathing of wasted resources gone mad?

Time will tell.. watch this space if you haven't fallen asleep already!

What I Love about Running a B&B

12/12/2013

I have just said goodbye to my latest guests. They have been a complete larf and generally brilliant, and I am going to miss them. I am smiling warmly to myself now, just thinking about how funny they were!

In fact this weekend is going to be my first weekend without guests since July! Time for a lie-in! Except we get those anyway sometimes. Last weekend I served 'my doctor' breakfast at 5pm! It suited us both very well.

I have been amazed at guests' reactions when I ask them what time they'd like breakfast in the morning. They nearly always say, "When would suit you?" I mean WHAT???!!! I am here to serve! That is my job! Breakfast, anywhere, any place, any time, whatever you can think of, except kedgeree because it makes the whole place smell.

Sometimes I almost have to force guests to say what will suit them, everybody is so astonishingly nice and obliging. Inside my head I am often trying to convey what I really want them to say by telepathy. I concentrate hard, focussing on their brain, saying "Say 10 o'clock, say 10 o'clock!!" and usually they pause before replying with "Would 8.30am be too late?"

Well now I am sad that my latest couple have left, because I have had to go around the house turning off all the radiators and the wall lights (which I only use on special occasions because they are very expensive on bulbs), and I won't have any more fresh flowers now until my next guests arrive. Horrid cheap croissants, nasty spreadable Lurpac, grotty bland orange juice and plastic bread are what we live off when there are no guests around.

Before I started the B&B business my house was becoming a tatty old mess, to such an extent I felt like moving, rather than attempting to get it all together.

The very idea of porcelain tea cups, scatter cushions and throws in each bedroom did my head in. Getting everything immaculate with not a single 'curly' anywhere to be seen (a disgusting word I have learned through my recent addiction to 'Four In a Bed'), no flaking paint, and no dust even on top of a 7' wardrobe, filled me with utter horror and dread.

But nine months later, I wander around my establishment with its cut grass, swept gutters, filled tubs, clean patio's and (almost) everything working, including the mended glass pane in the dining room window that had clearly once had a bullet shot through it at head height. I'm feeling good.

And also cold, until my next guests arrive and I have an excuse to heat the whole house at 20C all over again. Roll on Monday!!

A Thoroughly Modern Christmas

30/12/2013

Granny sat on the squishy white sofa of the main room in Malcolm's wife's house, sipping a cup of tea, while Sonya, his wife, completed the hoovering. Malcolm basted the venison haunch, I positioned the presents under the tree, and Malcolm's 19 yr old daughter emerged from the bathroom, radiant, to join us for dinner at 5pm.

Malcolm, Granny and I had returned from a hobble along the River Dart in the rain - Malcolm with his broken heel; 83 year old Granny with her dodgy ankles; and sulky, childish me, loved and treated as 'tiresome' in equal measure by the sensible adults immersed in conversation pottering along ahead of me, as I fiddled, staring at the ground, with the toggles on my oversized anorak.

I am polar opposite to Malcolm's wife, who is much cleverer and kinder than I am; and she is even more polar opposite to my Mum, being an intellectual liberal, while my mother was quietly at a total loss as to why we hadn't organised the entire day around the queen's speech. But we all had a very jolly time, and finally wandered back for a B without the B, 100 yards away, alongside the A38 dual carriageway, where Mum, Malcolm and I had booked in for the night.

We were the only people in its 20 bedrooms. It was warm and quiet, with masses of hot water, clean, comfortable beds, and a peaceful view of the carpark directly outside the window, and quite a good breakfast the following day from the garage next door.

Perhaps that's really all you need from a B&B?

Christmas Break

05/01/2014

Pandora (13) is giggling on the computer next to me, enjoying her first Facebook flirtation with a boy called Ted (12). Ted says he loves her.

It's my first visit to what's laughingly called my unhealth club for a month. It's neither healthy (we've just shared a chocolate brownie) nor a club (a small glass of wine costs a fiver and members don't get to share out the profits - those all go to that bloke with the woolly jumpers and the beard, who also owns an airline amongst other businesses, and who, unsurprisingly, appears to laugh a lot).

2014 is about to begin. B&B proper.

Since my lovely funny outward-bound guys, I've had a family of rock climbers, and three days later let out the house for Christmas week.

I mind very much that people are happy in my home. I waited for my rental family's arrival with bated breath, having booked myself the previous night into my cheap B&B, to ensure I didn't crease anything or leave any drips on the basins of my immaculate home before they arrived.

My guests turned out to be the perfect 'fit'. Three siblings, their families, and a grandparent. Just like our own family Christmas of 2012. I was quite emotional about it. "The house is made for you," I said. "I am so very happy that it is you."

I will never know how much I should have enjoyed eight nights of me-time. I wasn't well and had lost my voice for almost the entire break, but despite all of that, I spent most of it talking, and the rest of it trying to get my voice back. Nothing is ever quite as much fun as it should be, when you only feel 90%.

Home Sweet Home

12/01/2014

This is only the second weekend I've had without guests since everything went mad back in August. It feels strange to think I am earning a living from B&B, and yet this week I have been almost entirely uninvolved with the business. It is nice to have my home to myself and use whichever loo I feel like, whenever I like!

And lie-ins!

My last visitors were a sort of hybrid between guests and friends. I am very fond of them, but hadn't seen them for nearly a decade!

Here was a murky B&B area. Already some best friends have changed their minds about visiting me because they were not sure about coming to see me and taking up a potentially profitable bedroom, whilst strangers, using the other rooms, wander about the house. The result is I haven't had any friends or family - not even Mum - to stay since it all took off.

I also rather foolhardily gave away a free night at a recent charity pledges evening. I begged my mate Richard, who was attending the dinner, and who had persuaded me to part with the night in the first place, to bid for it.

Thankfully, he kindly did - he bid £90 for a night in Dartmeet, which hopefully is good news for everybody. Why I was so keen for Richard to win it was so that I could get away with providing domestic worn-out un-ironed sheets which I wash at home, no 'hospitality trays', and a relaxed supper and breakfast with cheap orange juice in the kitchen with me. Otherwise my little gesture might have turned into a rather time-consuming, expensive, generous one!

Richard is looking forward to his visit very much I think, and in the meantime, I like to believe my friends-who-paid had a nice time too. I gave them rather a late dinner on the first night (there was just so much to catch up on!), and they took Faye and me out to the local pub on the second. I provided them with my best quality ironed Egyptian bedlinen, designer toiletries, and hospitality trays complete with ground coffee, cafetieres, and fresh milk-in-a-thermos and biscuits as usual, but didn't do the room-straightening thing, as it felt more intrusive with people you know.

Our final evening was spent in our cosy sitting room in front of its log fire, listening to their son playing some of the hardest concertos ever written for the flute, as a YouTube backing track streamed through Faye's buskers box - a rather successful new use for my satellite broadband.

Google Google

18/01/2014

I might buy one of those things to make my expensive butter into curls - it looked good in somebody else's breakfast shot I was recently studying on TripAdvisor. But possibly that level of presentation might be a bit 'Surrey' for the middle of Dartmoor. Tongs for placing breakfast ingredients on the plate aesthetically, however, are my new 'must'.

All a bit academic really, since I won't have had a single guest to stay throughout January!

To me, though, of equal interest to the actual running of the B&B, is the marketing of it, and how Google is changing the world.

In my opinion, Google has transformed the selling process - and also, what can be sold.

Malcolm's massage service, for instance. Despite my best efforts pushing the fact that what he does can be life changing in terms of relieving/stabilising chronic pain possibly for ever, while 'extras' are not an option, people are just refusing to buy into what he offers via the internet. I'm flogging a dead horse here. Someone has just booked an appointment with him via his ad in the local parish magazine instead. Much more appropriate.

Meanwhile Ex has asked me to use my SEO skills to get him up the order if you Google 'Consultant in Leadership'. Well I can't achieve that! This would mean pitting one private individual against multi-corporate-global-conglomerates' entire professional IT departments!

On the other hand, if you put "What can I do about my teenager?" into Google's search engine, up comes nothing. NOTHING!! I am fascinated by this. Just a few extracts from books. No one offering personal or professional help, not even qualified children's psychologists! I mean what an opportunity! Years ago Ex and I investigated this area, as he's so wonderful at communicating with/helping troubled children. We thought we would aim our service at super-rich people like Madonna. But how to find/approach them? Well, through Google it would now be a complete doddle!

Likewise, I've another friend who provides the ultimate service in helping couples through marital bust-up, to emerge the other end having escaped the court process, vaguely satisfied with the financial outcome, and sharing a genuine and mutual, if somewhat rueful, respect and friendship. I know this because he did it for Ex and me. This chap thinks that, without years of training, ideally as a solicitor with subsequent experience, there is no opening for him in offering this kind of mentoring/mediating as a professional service. But through Google I think there is.

You could test the waters using a fake name and making up an identity - just to see if there's a demand. If no one is interested, you haven't really lost anything. There must be millions of other ideas out there. Soooooooooo exciting! The potential! The possibilities!

Meanwhile, still smug and complacent as you like with my Number 1 positioning, if you Google 'Luxury Dartmoor B&B', the implication is that this will create so much demand that I can probably finally afford to dispense with the 15% +VAT commission required by booking agents. I should now be able to go it alone for free, thanks to a wonderful combination of Google and TripAdvisor. So very many thanks to all of you who have put such nice things about me, my family, dog and home on TripAdvisor. Sometimes I am so touched by what you write that I almost shed a tear - certainly my eyes water!

So, yes - I am absolutely so great at all of this that I haven't had a B&B customer for a month, and Wydemeet remains free to be rented as a whole for all of its four 2014 slots. What on earth am I feeling so smug about?

Grumpy Old Woman

19/01/2014

My phone's been down for over two weeks now.

I have sued BT twice before, and won both times - £3000 altogether. It's cheaper for them to give in and pay the fine than to cover the fees of a solicitor to face me in court.

My satellite broadband has come into its own bigtime. Not only have I been able to download or stream or whatever you call it Christmas Day's Downton, but also it has meant that despite BT's best efforts, I still have internet access, retaining both my sanity and, hopefully, an acceptable route by which potential guests can reach me.

However, I am shortly going to lose my temper.

They told me it would be mended last Tuesday, but that day they mended everyone else in Hexworthy but me. So then they accused me of an internal fault which would set me back £130. Funny coincidence, that. Then they kept telling me to phone them to confirm an engineer's visit tomorrow. How can I, Dear Liza - my phone's down! They sent seven texts to this effect, and then an eighth saying that actually they're coming on Wednesday. And then a ninth to say actually they're coming on Monday. All communication via some chap in a call centre in India called Edwin.

If I lose my temper, I've discovered a new way of causing trouble, which is much simpler than going through all the Small Claims hoops. You just condense the story into however many words and stick it on Twitter. I've already tried this with great success with Hertz, who refused to answer my emails. They got back to me within 30 minutes!

My next victim is likely to be Tesco's.

Tesco has advised me that they are automatically going to take £504 out of my account to re-insure Marvin, my Ford Focus. Well a quick check on Go-Compare reveals that I could insure with Tesco again for literally half that amount direct on-line, or with Swift Cover for £245.

I think this automatic re-insuring for twice the market rate thing is a racket.

So I've paid Swift, but, without a phone, how do I prevent Tesco from going ahead and gnabbing £504 off me? There is no email contact address anywhere on their banking/insurance site, and if I post a letter it will arrive too late.

So I emailed the Tesco Beds & Linens department advising them of the situation and requesting them to forward my email to the correct people. They've refused, citing financial directives or something. Well you can email any other insurance business. So I've told them no wonder everyone's turning against Tesco, and I'm feeling another Twitter coming on. I just need to ask Miriam, my ex-policewoman friend, to remind me of the procedure. I've already forgotten how to work Twitter.

Taxi Service in Jaipur

19/01/2014

Very occasionally I receive a comment on the endless drivel I write on this site, which I find very exciting!

The other day, I clicked on each of the comments, to find out who of my friends had been supporting me with lovely uplifting responses to my various observations.

I discovered that every single one was simply an ad for a taxi service in Jaipur. So I have deleted them all. Dejected of Wydemeet.

Bored and Mischievous

21/01/2014

Oh dear. I need some more guests. I've got time on my hands and I can feel myself about to get into trouble again.

Malcolm and I, after a very happy three years together, have mutually, and somewhat ruefully, agreed to go our separate ways, in order for us both to find someone a little more compatible and hopefully long term.

So I'm back on the dating game again. And this time, out of sheer curiosity, I've logged myself in as a bloke - to find out what the competition is like - how women on the hunt behave and present themselves. I've called myself DarcyEatYourHeartOut, described myself as 'tall, brooding and loaded'; and written some copy which I think will appeal to women like me - including that I am widowed, that I live in a too large house by the moors and sea, play squash and swim to keep fit, my children have left, and now I only have my dog left to love. No pic included, obviously.

I was prompted to do this because I noticed that some hunk calling himself Carbon56 from Blandford, put up pics of himself hugging his dog, bike and surfboard, and, despite not bothering to write anything, went straight to No 1 in the Encounters Lonely Hearts Top 20! Honestly - I despair of woman.

Having completed my bloke's profile I went searching on the site for the 'matching profiles' of women the computer thought I might suit, and bumped straight into one of my good girlfriends who happens to be already married!

Well my faceless profile has been up for literally two minutes, and I've already got two fans, who have given me open access to their private pics!!

Perhaps life would be easier if I became a lezzer!

Who Hates BT The Most?

04/02/2014

BT has seen fit to leave us with no landline service now for over four weeks.

No less than three of my 'charm' of men-mates have been shouting at them, all thwarted by nice ineffectual chaps from India, who continually send me texts with conflicting messages that I can't get because there's no mobile signal here. Various representatives from BT also try calling me almost daily, surprised to find that no one answers the mobile - because there's no signal. As they have been told on so many occasions. You can't return any calls, as there's no way of leaving a message, even if you had a line.

No one from BT has turned up for three appointments now. One text that I eventually receive, from driving through the elements up to the cattle grid, tells me it's an internal fault, the next that it's an external fault which will be mended within a couple of days, and the next that it is an external fault which requires planning permission, is affecting a lot of people, and there is no date given for repair. On one occasion I received 45 identical computerised texts running, acknowledging receipt of one of mine.

Funny how BT or Open Reach or whoever they are, have managed to mend Neighbours' phone (they live at the end of the line) twice, the van driving straight past my gate, while all this has been going on.

Thank goodness for my satellite broadband which battles on through the gales, snow and hail, and allows you to contact me without too much trouble.

Everything else, apart from the electric gate, is withstanding the worst weather that Dartmoor has thrown at Wydemeet in the 20 years that I have lived here, really rather well. A part of me is pleased and relieved, and a lot of me is delighted while Faye and I snuggle down to watch telly in front of the fire in the cosy sitting room, as the rain lashes against the window.

There was snow on the way to school this morning, it's just finished hailing, and now the sun's out, with a chill wind.

I couldn't face my regular Tuesday ride, and am preparing for this weekend's guests instead. They will be ably looked after for a couple of nights by Faye (11), her Dad, and Twiglet, while I see my seven best friends from university in Somerset. How grown up and civilised have we all become?!

We've Won an Award!

04/02/2014

Faye and I have won a prize in the Scoot Headline Awards!

We are to be presented with our trophy and certificate by someone famous called Ebony Feare at a glittering ceremony on April 28th at Milbank. And if we attend that ceremony, we qualify to win another award for 'National Business Leaders', and go to another presentation, as well as getting our entry included on a CD!

We were very excited at the prospect of going up to London for a sit-down dinner surrounded by lots of other successful and knowledgeable B&Bers, all dressed in their best lounge suits and frocks. We thought we'd pick up even more tips than we have already from watching Four In A Bed!

But then I realised that, as far as I am aware, no one from Scoot has ever visited Wydemeet to check us out, nor, I don't think, has anyone ever booked Wydemeet through them.

What I do know is that I enjoyed completing their competition form in my best PR speak, and that appears to have done the trick! Hurray!

We thought we'd still go, until I read that, as far as I can gather, the event just offers light refreshments, and it's during a school day, and it costs £150 + VAT for two, so we thought we'd give up and let them post us our award instead.

I'm still wondering what we've actually won it for?

£5000?

05/02/2014

Last night I sued BT again, for the third time, on this occasion for £5000.

It takes about five minutes to sue someone, if you go through the on-line small claims arrangement. You're allowed 1000 characters to describe what's happened and why the defendant owes you however much you're asking for. I need 1000 pages to list all my grievances against BT! The stupid computer wouldn't let me send my completed form through for ages, and eventually I discovered this was because you're not allowed to use a '&' in your copy. So I changed it to 'B and B' but the finished version came out as 'Band B' so I hope they don't think I'm a rock group.

I claimed for pain and suffering - the worry that I have been through, and the misery Ex has suffered, unable to make his daily night-night call to Faye; lost earnings and reputation for my B&B business, the cost of my satellite broadband dish, my HTC Orange mobile with its special built-in Signal Boost app, wages for Sashka to wait around while BT failed to keep its appointments, and an Orange 'Signal Box' which I'm going to be forced to buy at this rate. Trouble is - I can't call anyone at Orange, or what's now called ee for some reason - to ask them whether their new Signal Box thing will work here.

The summons gets sent direct from the Court to BT's head office in London. This exercise has cost me £100. Even if I don't win anything, it will have been worth doing, just for the satisfaction of knowing that I have caused them some inconvenience!

Tree Down

05/02/2014

Wydemeet is probably the most remote B&B on Dartmoor.

At least that's what I have written in my advertising blurb. I expect it is - we're at the end of a 3/4 mile dead-end lane which looks private, but which is actually public. Occasionally snow ploughs with 'Motorway Maintenance' written on the side can be seen making their way along it, just outside our gate. I think uniquely, we have footpaths and bridleways stretching in every direction from our house, and we're 800 feet or metres (I forget which, but high enough to be bleak and cold) above sea level.

The school run to Faye's place of learning, just outside Tavistock, is a twice daily, 26 mile round trip of absolute pleasure. We start by going up a steep hill, and then we go down an even steeper, very windy one, over a bridge, and after a couple of miles we meet the main Dartmoor B-road that crosses the moor.

This is primarily used by prison officers who fly up and down along it at 100mph, even though it's got '40' written and circled in white at regular intervals on the tarmac, bright enough to make the horses shy and refuse to tread on it.

So I need to have a 4-wheel drive in case of ice, hence Bill.

I have never seen anything like this weather, and have been out digging ditches in the field to divert the water and preserve what's left of my drive; thrusting my arm down pipes and gutters, pulling out gunk and leaves, to stop the water flooding over into bits where it's not supposed to go.

This morning Faye and I nearly reached Huccaby Bridge, to find a tree fallen across the power lines and over the road. This resulted in a 30 minute diversion to the next bridge available, and meant for the second time Faye was unable to be presented by the headmaster I mean head teacher with her certificate for 'Musician of the Week' in Morning Assembly.

The phone, obviously, remains down, but so far broadband, oil and electric power are intact. We have a couple from Norfolk arriving to stay tomorrow. They are bringing wellies and macs. I'm hoping they're not going to need torches and a gas burner as well! In the event that we do lose power, ironically we will have no water (it's electronically pumped up from a borehole and pure enough to sell!) so I expect I will have to find us all alternative accommodation.

Fingers and toes crossed!

Two and a Half out of Ten

19/02/2014

We've just received a score of 2.5 out of 10 for 'service', on Booking.com.

That would have been the couple who booked Hexworthy at 1pm, for a 4pm arrival the same day. Hexworthy is our most luxurious room, costing £130 per night, worth it, I hope, because of the comfort and spaciousness of both bedroom and bathroom.

I have been personally using Hexworthy for months now, so it needed a very urgent deep clean, which normally takes me three hours. Without the use of the phone, with minutes to spare, using my clever HTC app, I succeeded in arranging by text for some neighbours, who are also in the B&B game and therefore understand the problems, to kindly collect Faye from school while I did battle with my Marigolds.

So my guests arrived to no phone. No mobile signal. No electric gate. Weak Wi-Fi. And then to cap it all, Tesco's, with various ingredients of my guests' vegetarian breakfast on board, came and went without delivering anything, neglecting to ring the bell (the battery had expired) or shouting, despite the fact that there were three cars parked outside the house, and three people in it.

Through the window I caught sight of the Tesco van slowly disappearing out of the gate in the rain, and Tesco (who I couldn't phone) ignored the urgent email I sent, imploring them to send it back.

So fair do's. Sometimes you are just jinxed, especially living out in the wilds of woolly Dartmoor. Incidentally, my guests did describe their visit as "Welcoming, homely, awesome location, really quiet, would go again" so it can't have been all bad. I'm just relieved they wrote their review on Booking.com's site (we still rate '9.1 Superb') rather than on TripAdvisor, where we have slowly climbed to the No 14 Slot and rising, out of all 182 B&Bs on Dartmoor.

Phone Back!

19/02/2014

"BT's here!" shouted Faye. Odd. They hadn't made an appointment as far as I was aware.

Hey Baby I'm the Telephone Man popped out of the driver's door.

"You've taken your time," I said rudely, and offered him a cup of tea.

It turned out that he's visited Wydemeet many times over the years, and knew exactly where all the boxes are. He solved both problems in a jiffy - a blown socket and two burnt out wires, caused by lightning on January 4th.

Meanwhile Neighbours next door have now enjoyed three visits from 'Open Reach' or whoever, who could easily have popped by and sorted us out, and all this nonsense about broken telegraph poles requiring planning permission with an open ended date given was just clap-trap sent in an automated message to us from a BT computer in India.

So now I was able to hear all twenty messages left on 1571 in the first week of January, one of which was a potential booking of the entire house for a week in the summer, sum total: £2500. I called the lady back and they've booked somewhere else now, no surprises.

Anyway, so now I am finally able to book an appointment at the hairdressers.

Hurray!

Broken

19/02/2014

It's half term, with lots of lovely horsey events booked for Faye at the pony club.

On the last school day, I drive home and just as I reach the garden gate there's a terrible stench and smoke pours out of the front of Bill, the Shogun. I leap out before he explodes - he's petrol so he'll go up big and fast. The nice man from the AA joins us for breakfast and follows me to Super Sexy Dick's garage, where the problem turns out to be simple – a stuck brake.

The next day, Faye is entered for the Intermediate Trec competition, which includes some people who represent Great Britain. I've put her in this grown ups' class so that our slots are at about the same time, for efficiency.

Faye comes fourth out of six - not bad! We also enter the Pairs together - it is a very special thing to be able to participate in the same sport as your offspring. The weather has an extraordinary window and it is just beautiful riding across Woodborough Common.

The next day is a fun ride and another early start. While I cook our guests' breakfast, Sashka prepares the horses for Lady Muck (me) and my daughter. We are just about to set out through the horizontal lashing rain, to discover the trailer has a puncture. Ever resourceful Sashka swaps the wheel, and we are still early for the start. Faye's pony, Warrior, decides he is in charge, and he'll go wherever he likes, at his own pace - the gallop. On a scale of 1 - 10, one being a disaster and ten being brilliant, the day scores three.

After that is a show jumping lesson, oversubscribed and booked three months ago for £20. Bill overheats at the top of the hill and Faye has to ride home, while I am visited by the AA man again. This time it is a simple leaking radiator.

On the fifth day we have a Fun Ride of around eighty horses scheduled. I have been looking forward to this for months. I'm all dressed up and ready to go, to find that my wonderful mare, Panda, has lost a shoe, so that's the end of that idea.

Instead I drive to Newton Abbot to collect Will from the station after his daily parties of sex, drugs and rocknroll, or whatever they do instead these days, and Bill hardly moves, going through half a tank of petrol, and overheating again on the hills, as a funny orange light flashes. I limp into Super Sexy Dick's again and swap Bill for Marvin, who is still without a clutch.

So much for Faye's next horsey event booked for tomorrow. We'll never get there now. I hope it pours.

Next time I might buy a new car.

So that is why I suddenly have time to contribute to my blog.

Schadenfreude

22/02/2014

Wow! You know how Four in a Bed - the programme where lots of B&Bers get together and make each other cry - is my favourite, after Downton?

Well I've just received a very polite email inviting me to be on it!! I am absolutely chuffed to bits that they've found and targeted Wydemeet, out of all the millions and trillions of B&Bs that are out there, especially since we're not on any official lists except for TripAdvisor.

I have often daydreamed about what being on Four in a Bed might be like, as I embark on my fourth pre-recorded episode of an evening, once my guests are all cosily tucked up in bed upstairs. And now the offer has come direct!

As a professional PR, my advice to me would be that going anywhere near it would be complete madness. The only reason ever to get involved with the media is if you think they might be able to help you in some way, eg marketing something for you that you want to sell.

Well call me complacent - but judging by last year I will already have sufficient demand for B&B this summer. So why would I proactively wish for the humiliation endured by every B&Ber who goes on that programme, purely for the entertainment of the great unwashed, as they get a buzz out of my distress? Schadenfreude, my clever 15 year old son Will called it, as he bent over his congealed baked beans at lunchtime earlier today.

Because I'm a show-off, and it's a long time since I was last on telly, are the reasons. Also I would be very interested in watching the process of making the TV programme, and finally, hopefully, there might be some money to be made afterwards.

So I've emailed them back, questioning their assertion that Four in a Bed 'Celebrates the Great British Bed & Breakfast and its owners' drawing their attention to all of the above observations, and we'll see what happens. I think the idea of a fat Blackpool landlady visiting Wydemeet, falling off stepping stones into the river, and off tussocks into bogs, will be too tempting for them to resist.

I will probably live to regret this, but at the moment Faye and I think it will be a great wheeze, and hopefully hardly anyone we know watches the programme anyway.

Oil at the Weekend

21/03/2014

My Mum is the most supportive Granny in Faye's year group.

Funny. When I was at school she only came once, to watch me in the swimming team, but she arrived late and missed my 13.2 seconds of fame as I won the 25 yards U13s Freestyle, battling my way through the icebergs floating around in our unheated school swimming pool.

But now, even though she lives 1 1/2 hrs away in West Dorset - call that two if it's her driving - she attends lots of Faye's events, and it is a real pleasure to see her there.

So we drove home in convoy after Friday night's Evensong, and as we entered the house I growled - "No one make any mess. We've got visitors arriving on Sunday, the house has been cleaned at vast expense, and we have no Sashka coming between now and then." Within five minutes, dear Granny had walked a splodge of mud at repeated intervals, starting at the outside door, across the hall carpet, up the stairs, and all the way along the landing carpet to 'Bellever' at the far end of the house, where she was sleeping.

I made myself scarce to a place in which to quietly lose my temper, while Faye somehow made the mess disappear.

I thought the kitchen was smelling increasingly of oil, while Granny and I caught up with each other's news over turkey breasts in white wine and grapes - a signature dish I copied off Bridget Jones.

And by the morning my worst fears were confirmed. Both Aga and boiler were out of oil.

No oil means no hot water, no heating, no cooking facilities = no guests.

I have something called a Top Up System with the local oil suppliers, which I assume means they top up the tank every time they visit.

Apparently not.

Poor Granny had, again, to see the worst side of her middle child, as the air turned blue with my anguish. She gave up and went home.

This has happened once before, last time on Christmas Eve when the house was full of family, so I already knew that putting things right was not going to be easy. The oil supplier has no emergency number. There are no other local companies on the internet who supply oil during the weekend.

I called Malcolm, who said there might be a drop of oil in the second tank that I could run through to the first. Guided by his instructions, Ex dropped in to B&Q on his way down to Devon, after watching Will playing hockey, to buy some special spanners to bleed the system, but all to no avail.

Astonishingly, at 6.30pm on Saturday night, I tracked down a plumber new to the West Country, who came round to bleed the system at 8.30 on Sunday morning. £150 later - Bingo! Lucky I dye my hair, or you would have noticed it turning grey as we speak.

Angry of Wydemeet (not again)

21/03/2014

I had a brilliant idea of how to get my own back on BT today.

In response to my £5000 small claim, they sent me a forty-ish page legal document, direct from their team of specialist lawyers, which was enough to scare the living daylights out of anyone, even me!

I am reluctant to travel all the way to Northampton to face these professionals in court, when I have every reason to believe that BT's Terms and Conditions cover them for every complaint I have made, not helped by the fact that mine is a residential, not a business, line.

Did you know, for instance, that if you fail to be at home for an appointment with them, they will fine you £139, whereas if they fail to attend the appointment, with or without advising you, you can only reclaim £10? How fair is that?? Anyway, I really don't want to be bothered to read through all the blurb to check the various ins and outs - as I expect there's nothing we can do about them. I bet BT and all the other Big Boys rely on all of their customers being equally lazy, and anyhow, what alternative supplier do we have?

But I was impressed by how spending £100 on suing BT finally, finally brought out their engineer straightaway.

So I have written to Sean Poulter, Consumer Editor of the Daily Mail. He must have been at the paper for practically thirty years, as he was on my contacts list when I used to do a proper job - PR for sunglasses, skis, sports watches, you name it - back in the days when I was a yuppie with a red golf GTi, living in Fulham. I suggested to him that my plight might strike a chord with many of his readers, and that we are all bullied by the Big Boys and helpless in the face of a near monopoly supplying a necessary product which is not fit for purpose. That a normal person can't begin to understand the gobbledegook that comes back from their legal department if you try having a go at them; eg "The Defendant therefore seeks that the Court exercise its case management powers in striking out the claim pursuant to Parts 3.4(a) and (c) of the Civil Procedure Rules", but that these big corporates all start grinding into action if we invest a little in suing them through the small claims on or off-line.

I haven't sent the letter, but have forwarded it to BT News Office (who haven't replied yet) suggesting that we settle out of court rather than going to any further trouble and expense over the matter. Included in my email were links to two recentish articles remarkably identical to the one I am proposing Mr Poulter might run, if BT doesn't play ball. They are:

www.theguardian.com/money/2012/jun/01/get-bt-listening-visit-hq#start-of-comments;

and

www.theguardian.com/money/2013/oct/13/bt-openreach-broadband-phone-fault?INTCMP=ILCNETTXT3487.

I'm feeling a bit nervous now, as it's possible I might have broken some law(s) over this, but what will they do to me? Fine me? Caution me? Or send me to prison? I've always thought it might be interesting to go to prison if I wasn't incarcerated for too long. Better than girls boarding school anyway. Free heating, ensuite facilities, food cooked for you, and the washing up done. And I bet there are some other inmates in there who would be all too happy to join me in a moan about BT.

Bags I Lidl

21/03/2014

The people I bump into most often at Lidl are my fellow local Dartmoor B&B proprietors. Don't tell anybody!

I generally use Lidl to stock up on chocolate, scent (it's called 'Suddenly' and at £3.99 for a bottle was highly recommended by the Daily Mail recently), smoked salmon, gravadlax, individual steamed haddock with broccoli dinners, frozen paella, kangaroo steaks and stuffed duck.

But the best moment of any Lidl visit, is if I succeed in accurately guessing the number of bags I've got to buy in advance at 4p each, to pack away all my goodies in. Four were enough to carry £120 worth of groceries, as well as a broom and a rake, last visit.

Queen of the Road

21/03/2014

Sometimes it feels as though everywhere I look, just nothing, absolutely nothing, works.

I've had six weeks of no telephone landline; all four 'new' handsets bought off eBay turned out to be faulty; three months of no electric gate; outside lights with minds of their own; no oil, pipes requiring bleeding; leaking overflow causing mildew; blocked macerator; stupid shower, leaks under the bath; the electric plug has come off the horse trailer which also has yet another puncture; Marvin the Focus needing a new clutch; and Bill the Shogun seems to be on his last wheels, so that despite the fact I own two cars, I am stranded. I did actually begin to shed a few tears about all of this, which isn't like me at all.

And then a little glimmer of light began to twinkle in the distance.

The first amazing thing was that the Princetown Mower man came and collected my mower and strimmer the day after I asked him to, and a couple of days later brought them both back, fully serviced! That's a first! The landline eventually got sorted out (it went down again last Sunday, but one look at my file and BT fixed it again within hours!); I bought a fifth handset for £7 - a Binatone for deaf and blind people which has big buttons, and is very loud; the gateman is here right now; Godfrey has replaced the bulb in the outside light; Super Sexy Dick's son, plumber George fixed all the bathroom things, and Super Sexy Dick himself has just brought Marvin back £550 later as good as new, sorted out the trailer; and best of all, Bill *isn't* mended and is sitting at a garage outside Okehampton!

Instead, I am Queen of the Road, driving 'The Beast' - all 4.2 litre engine of it, at a stately pace all over the moor, averaging 28mph whilst consuming 22.3mpg of diesel, that they've given me as a courtesy car. Desperate to get Faye to her horsey events, I rang all round Devon in an attempt to hire a 4x4. Nothing nearer than Exeter at £200pw. And then I found this garage where they offered to mend Bill while lending me a 2004 Toyota Landcruiser Amazon!! Well I asked them to take as long as possible over Bill, and they've still got him, over a week later. I am chuffed to bits with my fantastic alternative. I looked it up on Auto Trader and it's worth around £20,000! I rang the garage up and implored them not to hurry with Bill and kindly, they still haven't started work on him!

Things are looking up!

Are You a Clamp Silage Man?

23/03/2014

Sometimes my B&B guests very kindly give me presents. Occasionally tips even - that's particularly nice!

But last week I was given something much more valuable than that. £750 worth of chemicals for making silage with! Packed in little silver foil pouches.

So I immediately offered them to Neighbours, expecting to win lots of brownie points. But unfortunately they make the wrong of silage. It has to be clamp silage. I tried my next neighbouring farmers, but the same story.

So the little foil pouches continue to take up space (and I think they're supposed to be refrigerated) on the 'this needs to go elsewhere' table by the back door. Do you know anyone who makes clamp silage that I can offer them to?

Twiglet in the Dark

07/04/2014

"I wonder how airlines deal with changing of the clocks?" I mused out loud to Faye. Our flight was leaving at 6am, and we had to catch the coach to the airport from Faye's school at one-in-the-morning.

She and I were enjoying a typically disgusting unhealthy lunch prior to a swim at my awful health club, now that term was over, to commiserate the fact that after all our efforts, she hadn't made it into the school's music competition final. Which, incidentally, was won by an excellent cellist, aged eight, playing a Grade 1 piece immaculately. Meanwhile the school's top music scholar went home with nothing, despite a particularly impressive advanced performance on her violin.

But who am I to judge.

"The flight's tonight - the clocks go back tomorrow," Faye casually replied, finishing off her microscopic 'for adult tums' spag bol, ordered off the kids' menu.

"No, it's tomorrow," I said.

"No, it's tonight," she said.

"Well I'm going for a swim and we'll find out when we get home," I said calmly, rattled.

And so it was that I found myself driving around central Dartmoor at 10pm, with the dog and his food and cage, mobile in hand, desperate for a signal, running out of petrol, trying to find someone prepared to look after him for a week, to whom I could deliver him immediately, two hours to go before we had to catch the coach booked to take us away on our school ski trip. My landline down again, thanks to my old mates, BT.

Gloves Off

07/04/2014

"My ski gloves are older than Malcolm is," I declare.

Malcolm is one of the teachers running the school ski trip. He is twenty-eight. My gloves are twenty-nine and still white(ish). They still work too.

The school ski trip comprises 32 children and nine adults. I have been clear throughout the planning of it, that I am not here to look after children, and all promises have been kept to, rigorously. I have nothing to

do but be told when and where to go. No decisions to make. No responsibility. I don't care what the weather's like, what the hotel's like, what the skiing's like. It is just heaven being able to relax for a week.
 Even though it feels odd that there's been no break between attending the school music competition, swimming at the unhealthclub, finding a home for Twiglet, coach, plane, coach, hotel, ski-hire place and revolting supper in the very basic hotel's very basic dining room somewhere in Italy, surrounded by eight year olds who've also been awake for 48 hours. I've rarely been happier.

Dancing on the Bar

07/04/2014

Eleven year old Douglas's parents, who live in France, arrive to find all the grown-ups gyrating on the bar, enthusiastically 'moving like Jagger' in the routine some of them put together last night over a few bottles of Prosecco, while the rest of us were engaged on a galati hunt with 32 children, two of whom are acutely allergic to nuts.

Soon Douglas's big brother joins him on the dance floor, to demonstrate 'Gangnam style', while ten year old Wilbur does an Irish jig to 'I am Happy". And we all are. This eclectic mix of adults and kiddies have bonded so well that no one cares who they find themselves sitting next to over the unremitting daily supper of rock-hard white rolls, cos lettuce, radicchio, olives, and tinned chopped carrots.

Prior to supper, evenings comprise two lines of adults and children sitting on their bums, back to the wall, legs in everybody's way, in the hotel passage, gaming, running their businesses, gambling, or checking out the talent on Encounters, as the free Wi-Fi doesn't work in our rooms.

Days involve forty-one Brits racing around the mountains on skis, from the first chair-lift up, to the last chair-lift down. It is extraordinary that every single child appears to be mad about skiing, however much crying takes place in between runs. Meanwhile the adults oversee the action from the centrally located mountain cafe, tucking into something called Bombardino - an orange kind of advocat that you mix with coffee and cream - discussing children and parenting.

'Benevolent Neglect' appears to be our most favoured approach to the bringing up of our little loved ones.

The sun is hot, the sky is blue, the snow is perfect, the runs are virgin, there's no one else here. The mountain is our very own.

On the last day we are all such experts that we ski to France. Here we find noise. Hundreds of English people clogging up the chairlifts, all colour coordinated. Some wear orange caps, lots of tiddlies are crying, some young teenagers sport purple sweatshirts, others have sky blue ski jackets, all with the names of their schools emblazoned on the back. School ski trips have clearly become big business. The Bombardino's cost nearly double over here. We are glad to get back to the peace of Italy, where even the first-timer seven year-olds are now leaving me behind, as they ski their bittersweet last run, after a week of universal hilarity and joy.

It Never Stops

07/04/2014

My son Will has just broken his thumb, by punching someone.

The game is called 'Bum'. You form two lines opposite each other, and then individual children run down between the lines, as the others punch them as hard as they can. The modern version of 'Strip the Willow'. The kind of thing you expect your children to learn, if you are stupid enough to pay for them to attend private school.

This is bad luck because Will has been playing rugby all season at regional level, and is now engaged on an outward bound adventure course outside Barnstaple, which is clearly being run with all the ElfandSafety small print crossed, ticked and dotted, but the small print clearly doesn't cover the playing of Bum.

And now he's gone and punched someone in the hip, broken his thumb joint and so can't go skiing. Which means neither can his father nor his two friends, one of whom, it turns out, isn't insured. That's £1000 wasted for his poor mother.

So while I'm living it up in Italy with Faye; Will and and his Dad Ex have moved into Wydemeet, which, frustratingly, I have failed to let out either for my skiing week, nor for Easter. The result? No £2,500, and no B&Bers booked in either.

It is an odd thought - having Ex back living in what is now my home, while I'm away. Where will he sleep? Will, now fifteen, refuses to sleep in his own attic bed, as we found a spider on his lampshade in there last week, and he's not fond of spiders. So he is currently in Bellever. No one is allowed in Dartmeet as it's made up all clean and ready, by Sashka, for our next visitors. I don't suppose Ex will want to go back into my luxurious, rather pink, bedroom, 'Hexworthy', but I'm not too bothered if he does.

Also odd is that I have had more communication with Ex during my Italy stay, than with anyone else. First he is organising for the puncture in my courtesy car to be mended, then the third puncture on my trailer; then the dishwasher blows up and needs to be repaired; the landline goes down again twice more, and Twiglet is retrieved from the couple who took him in with a smile with one minute's notice at dead of night for a fiver. Meanwhile both Will and Ex are clearly quite ill, with colds bordering on flu. In the end it becomes apparent that they have had a very happy week, chatting, bonding and relaxing; finally leaving me a bottle of Premier Cru Chablis and an immaculate home with everything working in it again.

So Much Fun

07/04/2014

We arrive at Grenoble Airport three hours prior to our flight home, to ensure there is plenty of time for a party of 41 to check in.

We discover that our plane hasn't even left England yet, and will probably be delayed by around four hours.

I don't care. I am still in a state of bliss. No decisions, no responsibilities, I will just do and go and be wherever, and whenever I am told. I am a remarkably obedient person for someone who is so cussed.

The airport is entirely choked with school skiing parties. 'Unicorn School' seems to have nearly fifty children, all in matching brightest blue.

The people at check-in are clearly like the ones in 'Airplane', enjoying mixing up and matchmaking the children from the different schools. Our coolest kid, Jonny, who went from nought to skiing helicopter turns in the air in just one week, is horrified to find himself seated between the window and a strange 13 year old girl from another school. He can't sit down, crouching against the wall of the plane, his mouth open in abject terror, until a teacher takes pity on him and swaps some children around, and he is next to a boy he already knows.

We are finally dropped back at school in a pitch black gale of horizontal rain at 4am, to find our cars without the aid of a torch or an umbrella.

Up again at 9am to prepare a picnic to rival and beat that of Nemesis, the woman who stole my husband four years ago, and off to the annual football match of 21 of Will's friends from his old prep school, on its exposed cliff outside Boscastle. The rain, as last year, is bucketing down and I have never seen the West Dart more torrential.

As it happens, it doesn't really matter what the picnic comprises, because Will is captain of his side, broken thumb and all, and his friends crowd around him at the back of my cool courtesy car anyway. Will's team, "Twiglet Hotspurs", has won again, for the fourth year running, and this year, I promise Nicola, the organising Mum, that I will definitely get the huge silver cup, lovingly polished by Ex, engraved. The adults hover around, quaffing plastic cups of chilly Cava, as their hair sticks to their heads in the downpour, and the hard-core, which this year turns out to be only Nemesis (Bevan appears to be history already) and me, repairs back to Nicola's house for more.

Racing home again we still haven't unpacked, done the post, nor replied properly to B&B enquiries, risking the disaster of double-booking. But no, we can hardly sit down before it's the next morning and Faye's first official ride on Perfect Panda, my wonderful horse, in thick fog, high winds (you only get both at the same time on Dartmoor) and rain so heavy it's as if God is pouring an endless giant bucket of water over the whole of Devon.

I have given myself a couple of days' grace from the B&B to squeeze in some fun – even more riding scheduled for tomorrow - and then it's back to work.

Hopefully I will have a shower that works properly installed before our next guests arrive on Thursday.

Vicarious Love

15/04/2014

"If you write about me on that blog of yours, I'll never speak to you again," warns my friend Stephen. As it happens, Stephen is, after all, still speaking to me, because that is not his real name.

I have to be careful what I put on here - I mean anybody could be reading this!

To try and keep myself in check, I always imagine my Mum is perching on my shoulder, telling me off, or Uncle Jock, ex-CEO of the AA, who once thundered at me: "I can't think why you want to tell the whole world about your sex-life!" after I'd written an article for Harpers & Queen about blind dating people from Private Eye. That was back in the '80s.

The other thing is, of course, that I don't want my guests to think that they're going to be written about, and therefore not want to come here. So I try to keep things vague.

But I can't help writing today. I am living vicariously off other people's love.

Wydemeet is a house of love. 99% of people who stay, come as a couple.

We've had our first engagement here, by the stepping stones, as regular readers will know; we've had couples who've been married 40+ years, couples celebrating wedding anniversaries, and now we have a young couple on a 'MiniMoon', who got married on Saturday, which, much to her delight, was Faye's twelfth birthday.

I would want to come here if I were part of a couple. It's terribly romantic, the rooms are spacious, soft and comfortable, you can sit in a hot tub together under the stars, or lounge around together in front of the log fire in the cosy sitting room, you have breakfast side by side, in your pyjamas if you want, looking out at the trees in the garden outside, you can go back to your room for the rest of the day if you like, the walks along the rivers and across the moors are private and spectacular. It's all a bit like Steve Wright's Sunday Love Songs - it gives me faith that deep love and affection still exist in spades.

∞

Serial On-Line Dater

∞

Love Life - Lack Of

15/04/2014

I just got dumped.

By email.

After what has been a four month, sort-of, relationship.

He had turned up on Encounters, just thirty minutes after Malcolm and I went our separate ways. It was all too surprising and extraordinary. The perfect man for me. I was so excited I wanted to shout "I love him!" from a mountain top!

But it turned out to be very stop-start. He was receiving a lot of grief from his ex-monster-wife, and experiencing a great deal of trouble and worry sorting out a reliable routine for his handicapped son.

But really. Email. After all that. Not impressed. So being me, I rang him up and said so.

And now I'm back on the old Encounters again. Maybe I'll give Guardian Soulmates a go too. It's possible the people on that are more thoughtful and interesting, but the minute they hear I read the Daily Mail for its coverage of Britain's Got Talent (the whole of Page 3 was devoted to a performing Eagle Owl yesterday), they'll run away from me, howling in anguish.

I am a woman of substance. I have a beautiful large home, a thriving business, financial security, two well-balanced (at the moment anyway) children at private school, land, an income, loads of friends, functional loving family, cordial relationship with Ex, hardly any baggage, hardly any bitterness, I am tall, fit, good looking (I hope anyway, can't really tell), friendly, funny and independent.

If I were a man on that site, I would be eaten alive. But because I'm not, it's a very different kettle of fish. I am insufficiently vulnerable.

Zoe Ball has just played a song on Radio 2 called "I'm coming back as a Man". I'm off to download it onto my iPod.

Publicity - that old chestnut

15/04/2014

Last night I indulged myself with two episodes of 'Four In a Bed', the reality show featuring competing B&Bs.

Loyal readers will remember that the show asked me to be on it, and I haven't told you what happened next.

Well, having initially said I'd do it, I then changed my mind, because they wouldn't allow Faye (now 12) to come with me on the visits to other B&Bs, due to legal restraints, requirements for carers, nannies, bodyguards, licensing, restricted hours, etc etc etc. Bummer! So I'm not doing it, which is a great shame, as it would have been a real laugh and a very interesting experience.

The outcome might prove fascinating too. Malcolm told me that 'Probably the Cheapest B&B in Falmouth' where he is a regular, received 62,000 hits on its website after it was featured on 'The Hotel Inspector'! Well I wouldn't want that - it would be a nightmare! I've got the perfect number of guests already!

But hark! I hear a car arriving. My next guests are here. I must go and welcome them...

Weirdos

16/04/2014

"Only VERY bossy ladies please" requests 'Totdevoted' on Encounters. I immediately sign him up as one of my 'favourites', and he returns the favour.

I scroll down to find out more about him.

"I work in the City and I am smart, successful and driven at work," he says.

"I am well-travelled and very well educated, cultured and well-read. I am seeking a long term relationship and REAL commitment - so no flings please." How exciting!

Skipping a bit, I get to, "I seek the kind of woman who demands worship and pampering and obedience from her man." FANTASTIC! blah blah "I do hope this piques your interest - if you understand how a man can adore worship and obey his diva Goddess... " errrrrr

For his ideal match: "I mean REALLY bossy and demanding."

"Body type: A few extra pounds; Curvaceous; Full figured."

I consider messaging back saying "I'm afraid I'm too thin." But it's all too weird. Steer clear.

I don't know whether this internet dating stuff is evil, or a force for real good. Both I suppose. What I do know is that it is extremely time-consuming, addictive and brutal.

Even if you've ceased subscribing, they keep your details up online, unless you ask them not to, and every couple of days send you a selection of 'matches', who are usually short, fat, bald, broke, and live at least 100 miles away.

I am constantly experimenting with the thing - you can check out who has looked at your 'profile'; and there's a 'Top 20' featuring the most favourited or messaged people who've signed up with them. The women look gorgeous and young, and their photos are often professionally posed and airbrushed, while the men are mostly hideous. Some people 'favourite' everyone they can, hoping to get 'favourited' back again and thus into the Top 20. I haven't tried this yet but I wouldn't put it past me.

I don't think many people are deliberately dishonest, but some of my pics are nearly five years old simply because nobody's taken any of me recently, not because I was nearly two stone lighter in those days!

Anyhow - hold onto your seat... and watch this space! It's going to be a rough old ride!

Scary Boiled Eggs

16/04/2014

How many ways are there of cooking an egg?

This morning I did my first omelette, complete with bacon bits and cheese. It worked fine, thank goodness, despite my little non-stick pan feeling rough after I've used it for lots of poached eggs. I have just ordered another, off my mate's highly successful www.onestopcookshop.co.uk.

Yesterday I prepared Eggs Royale - toasted muffins with smoked salmon, poached eggs and hollandaise. I also offer Eggs Florentine (with spinach) but not Benedict, as I don't always have ham to hand.

Another speciality on our menu is the 'Wydemeet Special' - one egg made as an omelette, the other broken into it like a poached egg. Nobody has asked for this yet, which is a shame, because it's a lot easier to prepare than it looks.

Most people ask for fried, poached or scrambled, even though I encourage everyone to ask for anything they can think of.

One of my guests, who was Thai/German/American, made a special request that I cooked his scrambled eggs 'properly'. I was a touch insulted but didn't say anything. The next morning I served him up what I considered properly cooked scrambled - soft and rich - and of course I had totally misunderstood him. He meant 'well done'; and ordered 'hard easy-over' for the next morning. I had to look that one up on Google.

Oddly, the most demanding thing anyone can order for breakfast is a boiled egg. Did you see that episode of Gordon Ramsay laying into a chef, yelling: "You couldn't even cook a f..........g boiled egg!!" Well poor bloke. They are very difficult to get right. Especially here, because I cook on an Aga. One plate is too hot to simmer water, and the other one is too cold. So I have to keep moving the pan around, which means that one minute it's boiling its head off and cracking the shell, and the next it's not boiling at all.

I have invested in various gadgets, including that pin-thing to let the air out, and a plastic oval thing which supposedly tells you whether the egg's inside is soft, medium or hard; but the main problem is that you simply can't *see*. I get butterflies every time I have to serve one, wondering what my guest is going to discover when they crack it open.

I have been conducting 'taste tests' for best eggs over the past few months; involving eggs from down the road, eggs from up the road, eggs from Mr Dumped-Me-By-Email, and eggs from Mum's neighbouring farmer. For size, taste and value, I couldn't fault Mr Dumper's contributions, but now that he's history, Neighbour's eggs are proving to be my mainstay. They are large, rich, orange, and very fresh. No one can fail with such eggs.

I have a lot of guests who say they can't make poached eggs, but they're easy if the eggs are fresh enough. My ultimate goal is to produce poached and fried eggs so perfect that, every time, they look like pretend plastic ones.

Coming Back as a Dog

20/04/2014

"I'm Coming Back as a Man" may be on Radio 2's current playlists, but upon further reflection, I think I'd like most of all to come back as a dog.

This thought first crossed my mind when I heard that I had been accused of treating Ex like a dog. "Lucky him," I said to myself. Every need catered for, unconditional love.

Then, when I first met Mr Dumped-Me-By-Email, and an ancient, crippled black Labrador hobbled out of the back of his Subaru Legacy, to tender encouragement and soppy tones of endearment, I thought, "That's how I want him to speak to me too." Alas, it was never to be.

So, on to my next crazy adventure...

"That's the best possible reason for taking part in Four in a Bed," wrote charming Jackie - one of the reality show's producers. I received this potentially life-changing email 30 minutes before I was due to host a fancy dress party for 20 x 12 year old girls, after preparing B&B breakfast for four, and taking Faye to a Pony Club Rally. An Easter Egg Hunt, Fashion Show, Quiz, Jacuzzi, Dancing, Supper and Sleepover in Will's joss-stick/tobacco reeking, teenage den of horrors, complete with semi-naked calendar of Kelly Brooks, lava lamp and flashing fairy lights, all still to be prepared.

I had written to Four in a Bed wondering whether it would be too late to change my mind back again, and whether they still had availability for Wydemeet to be featured on it, as I had a new objective in mind. I had been in touch with a previous contestant who I liked the look of. I had emailed him asking him whether he might be gay, and we had subsequently had a nice chat and discovered we were both on internet dating sites. I looked him up after our phone conversation and found that he was 48, looking for (female) partners aged 26 - 46. Not me then. I'm 54. But lying in the bath afterwards I came up with my cunning plan. Encounters appears to be replete with fat, old, bald, dull men, whose lifestyles I have almost nothing in common with and who live 100s of miles away. I'm fed up with it.

What about giving up on that, and putting myself on Four in a Bed instead, and see what happens?

So I jumped out of the bath, sent off my email explaining my reasons for changing my mind, and hey presto! They like it!

So maybe I'm going to be famous again! The last time I was on telly was 25 years ago, on a show hosted by the emerging Carol Vorderman, when she was testing my ability as a graphologist, but that is another story.

Moist

30/04/2014

Encounters has gone mental!

"Wot a Kisser!" my friend Judith emailed me excitedly the other day. She is also signed up, as is every single single person I know.

She is so thrilled by her result, after months of nothing happening, that when I went to stay with her last week, after a bottle of red wine she started 'messaging' about 1,000 people (including one or two girls) on my behalf, whom I would never have dreamed of contacting myself. Eg she contacted lots of good looking men from the Top 20 who live miles away and will already be receiving 200 messages daily; and then a whole load of people simply because the site informed us that they were logged in at the time.

The next day I was inundated with replies. Despite the fact that Judith's computer hadn't worked properly, so the funny, charming, loving messages she had sent out had been turned into gobbledegook.

So since then I have been very busy practising my amateur writing skills, bantering, if there is such a verb, with all my new admirers dotted around the country, instead of adding to this blog.

My favourite is a journalist who lives in an eco-house near Chippers (Chipping Norton to you and me), who is game to play footsie at Faye's Prep School Quiz Night next week. He is a motoring correspondent and is going to drive me there in the latest Maserati. (He is not Jezza Clarkson, before you get any ideas.) We'll believe all that in the unlikely event of it ever happening. His writing skills are such that, even without a picture, at one stage he made it to Number 2 in the Encounters Most Popular List. I am very impressed. I have yet to make it onto the List at all, but I will keep on trying.

Anyway, he has challenged me to use the word 'moist' in my next blog. So I have. There it is. Moist. Three times now!

B&B For Everyone!

30/04/2014

"Do it! Do it! Do it!" is what I seem to have been saying for the past 24 hours.

Over a year ago I went to look at a friend's B&B nearby, and came away totally depressed by how impossible it would be for me ever to aspire to his standards. The result was a toss-up as to whether I should stay here, with my house crumbling around my ears, and two children who never venture out of the garden gate onto the moor, or downsize into something draught-free and comfortable, where everything works, near a bus-stop and a Costa's.

I can't remember what persuaded me to stay. It may have been Will saying how much he loves coming home to relax, turn his music up to full volume, and proudly entertain his privileged school friends in his dreaded 'Bothy'; or Faye becoming increasingly involved with the local pony club; or simple inertia.

But I recently attended a hunt meet at my friends' hotel down the road, to discover I knew and felt welcomed by over half the people there. A result of living here for nearly twenty years and becoming a part of the community, I suppose. However bonkers they may all think I am, it doesn't really matter. It is a scenario that I will never be able to recreate anywhere else, and I treasure that feeling of belonging.

Last night my friend with the B&B came to dinner. He and his wife arrived at the same time as my latest guests, and were immediately enthusiastically immersed in discussions about where to go and what to see around Dartmoor, looking at maps together, and admiring the evening sun setting behind the hill. My friends are absolute natural B&Bers. Their home is well located outside the most desirable village on Dartmoor, it's beautiful, their garden is outstanding, all is pristine, tasteful, comfortable, and works. But they're not marketing themselves properly, so are not getting the bookings. They're tired, are losing their nerve, and concentrating on other things which are less profitable, more time-consuming, and more exhausting.

"You need more rooms," (they only rent out one) I advised, "get yourselves properly SEO'd on Google - you can do it yourselves; rent the house out when you're not in it (they're off to Greece for two weeks); and charge double for more weddings. Bingo." (I'm not bossy, smug or complacent at all.)

Then this afternoon one of the school Mums came over to ask me about B&B-ing.

"You're in the middle of the moor, while we're nowhere, really," she said. "We're about equidistant between Dartmoor and Bodmin moor, and quite near to lots of beaches on both the north and the south coasts, only about 10 minutes from the A30," she continued. Well - there you have it. Centre of the South West.

Running a B&B is so much fun, and gives you such a feeling of achievement. The guests are so nice - I've never had a dud - and there is nothing more enjoyable than hearing people admiring your home and knowing that in effect you are getting paid to make it attractive. I feel I've turned full circle - from chambermaid to graduate, to yuppie, to professional, and now I'm back to cleaning loos again. But at least they're my own.

Anyway - the proof of my particular pudding will presumably go public on Four In A Bed. They're coming to visit tomorrow afternoon to check me out. If they decide to feature Wydemeet, I think it's going to be soon! Eeek!

Be Careful Who You Meet!

06/05/2014

A transgender hip replacement surgeon was the first person Mr Dumped-Me-By-Email and I realised that we both knew in common. The surgeon's name used to be John, and now it is Jennifer. My sister, who was operated on by him/her, did comment that Jennifer looked a bit 'manly'.

Strongest man in the world, also ex-president of the Budgerigar Society, Geoff Capes, turns out to be the mutual point of contact between my new journalist friend and me. I once employed Capes to judge a "Bravest Little Boy" competition when I was doing PR for Tonka Trucks. Cape wouldn't do anything I asked, so I had to issue instructions via my photographer who was a bloke.

Malcolm and I discovered that we had been at the same skating party in Suffolk when I was six. And now my Nemesis, 'She', has embarked on an affair with his first cousin, who's a Duke. Grrrr.

Another blind date I was recently set up with remembered meeting someone like me 30 years ago, at a party full of Exeter University undergraduates. He arranged to see her the following day, but he arrived four hours late and missed her. It turned out that that person was me. He drove a Ferrari at the time, and had a pet parrot too. What did I miss?!

Who's Brainier?

10/05/2014

Frederic Chopin wrote the "Minute Waltz". I know the piece quite well, because I've timed myself playing it. Unfortunately it takes me five minutes to finish (including repeats) so anyone trying to waltz to it with me at the piano would probably fall over.

"Who wrote the Minute Waltz?" was the only question, out of 166, that I could answer last night, at Faye's School Quiz.

Normally I win quiz nights, but last night my team "Snowflakes Plus", comprising three members of the school ski trip and some ringers, came sixth out of seven.

When I say "I don't know anything about anything" this is not false modesty. It's entirely true. Despite my having benefitted from (allegedly) the best education in the land, I can't remember anything whatsoever. My method of winning quiz nights is an innate attraction to highly intelligent people - I am drawn to them like a magnet. I then ask if I can be on their team and sit there, open mouthed at the things that they know, contributing nothing at all, or possibly buying the drinks.

Ever since studying graphology (handwriting analysis), I have been particularly interested in different kinds of intelligence. Graphologists tend to look at four: memory retention, practical, original, and planning.

Once upon a time I would have felt highly inadequate after an evening like last night's. Even though we only came sixth, I still thought that every member of our team was intellectually electric! I was stunned by their Encyclopaedic brains!

But I wondered how many of them would succeed commercially on their own. To run a small, efficient, successful entrepreneurial business such as a B&B, I would say that you need common sense, concentration, energy, a sense of prioritising, more common sense, and charm.

So I don't feel too humble in the presence of brainboxes anymore. I just gaze at them in affectionate awe.

Gold Winner Scoot Headline Award

14/05/2014

Something new to put on the wall in the downstairs lavatory - my 'Certificate of Achievement' for winning the 'Scoot Headline Award' arrived in the post today.

A couple of days ago, I received a letter from them, informing me that the plastic plinths that the certificates were originally presented in kept breaking in the post, so they were sure we would understand why our certificates were now being sent out just in paper form. Hmmmmmm. And who is this 'famous actress, Ebony Feare', who presented the awards at their ceremony in London? As you, a loyal follower, are already aware, I don't know anything or anyone, so she's probably really well known, but I've never heard of her.

Meanwhile, a few days ago, Four in a Bed's delightful Jackie drove down and interviewed me on camera. She felt like an instant friend. The most dangerous kind of media person! I trusted her absolutely and told her all sorts of things that I shouldn't have, I am sure. She feigned such interest in me and my B&B that I fed into her hand, giving her such an endless monologue that I started boring myself, quite apart from her, let alone her bosses who will ultimately be judging whether I am interesting enough for their programme or not.

So will we be on it? I have no idea. Jackie's footage was delivered for her bosses' summit meeting last Friday. After that, it is down to working out who will match best with whom, and whose locations and available dates fit in with everyone else's.

Having watched another old episode last night, in which there was a posh lady with an immaculate home in Nottingham or somewhere, I yet again feel massively inadequate. If they film me, I am going to be in so much trouble for my plumbing that it doesn't bear thinking about.

Value for Money?

14/05/2014

Am I? Value for money I mean.

On last night's recording of Four In a Bed, a dour bloke from Yorkshire, whose B&B features flowery purple wallpaper, maroon sheets and red bedspreads, said, "No B&B room in this world could ever be worth £130."

Oh dear. If I ever get to be in it, that'll be me then.

The B&B that this chap was referring to, that charged £130 a night for a glorious room with a wonderful four poster, was absolutely gorgeous. It had an immaculately painted grey front door with polished knockers and stuff. Then inside all was proper quality interlined thick curtains, real antiques, but, worst of all, light coloured, plain carpets with no stains. It was clear to me that the owner, who looks as though she's a real hoot and I would love to meet her, speaking like Princess Anne and all and everything 'ghastly' gives her 'the heaves', has never had children nor dogs around.

Over a decade ago our nanny's two year old toddler spilled an entire bottle of black Indian ink over our brand new coral coloured deep pile sitting room carpet. We laughed at the time (she was on the verge of tears) and have finally nearly managed to get rid of the stains, but we never replaced it. Perhaps we should. I prefer to cover the grey areas still left with rugs, and hope for the best.

Similarly with some of the bedrooms. Do you really have to replace a whole carpet the minute a guest spills a cup of coffee on it?

And the plumbing. If I go on Four in a Bed I am going to get crucified for the plumbing! Each time I hear a guest turn on a tap upstairs my heart starts thumping.

There is not one tap, one shower, one loo flush or one over-flow which has not gone wrong at least once since they were fitted not long ago.

But my real terror lies with the lurking macerator - otherwise known as 'Mazza-rater' - a joyful play on my name. Whenever the Dartmeet loo is flushed, this potentially lethal monster gives off three grinding explosions and sends the effluent slooshing down a pipe which runs along the side of a thin wooden partition wall, past the sleeping heads of any B&Bers in Hexworthy, the room next door.

Throughout the house are pictures and photos of family, ancestors, friends and pets; and ski clothes, old lipsticks etc are stored in various drawers. The tellies need someone with a Mensa-level IQ to turn on.

All this, yet I charge more than anyone else on Dartmoor.

Because my guests are paying for our extraordinary, unique location. Possibly the most remote B&B in Southern England, with footpaths and bridleways stretching in every direction from our garden gate. And for my amazing chat. And for Faye's general loveliness. And for the honour of taking Twiglet out for walks, of course. But the Four In A Bed contestants won't know any of that. And anyhow, the score sheets don't cover that kind of thing.

The other day a couple of Lithuanian shop fitters arrived for breakfast with beer, at 9am, slept through the day in Dartmeet, then had breakfast again at tea-time, and went off to re-fit a fast-food cafe during Plymouth's annual International Fireworks Extravaganza. They were brothers. One was covered in tattoos and spoke no English, while the other is a keen fisherman and says he's going to come back with his family for a fishing holiday. Anyway. This unusual arrangement caused us no problem at all. And then they paid me what I'd normally charge for a two night stay. Result!

These days I'm receptionist, chambermaid, front of house, marketing person, gardener, waitress and chef. A Lady Who Lunches, rides, and swims, a chauffeur, serial on-line dater, single Mum, and now an author too! No wonder I suffer from IBS and a juddering left eyelid!

So, going back to this skinflint publican of a Yorkshire man with a questionable taste in interior design - he thinks B&B people twiddle their thumbs during the afternoon.

Well he's wrong. I'm jolly busy doing lengths at the health club, while Sashka, my right arm, left arm and both legs, does all my work for me.

And one of the plusses of staying at not-so-immaculate Wydemeet is that you can break a chair, knock over your tea, leave mud on the stairs, and I won't blow a gasket if I'm in a good mood. Wydemeet is a place to sit back and relax in.

Which is not necessarily what the Four In A Bed contestants are looking for. I'm beginning to feel just a tad nervous!

I've Got a Little List

19/05/2014

"I think I'm going to be featured on Four in a Bed," I said.

"Oh I don't think you should do that," my Australian guest replied, and he meant it. He and his wife are celebrating their 40th wedding anniversary by going on a tour of all the places in the world they want to visit most, and are investigating his Dartmoor heritage. They have stayed in ten different hotels and B&Bs so far, so they jolly well know what they're talking about.

"Would you like us to provide you with a list of all the things you might need to do before going on television?" queried his wife.

"Errrr, ummmm, yes, it would be useful to have a friendly, objective view," I said. "One can get too close to it all."

The macerator and the gurgling of its effluent seemed to have been particularly noisy that day, and the telly especially difficult to turn on. I hoped they would forget their offer, and I thought that they had. But when it was time to say goodbye, his wife said,

"Would you like that list then? Do treat it with a pinch of salt."

I said that that would be very kind, and she handed it over. It was two pages long. My heart sank down to my Ugg boots.

Sashka and I went into the garden with a fag and a cup of coffee each, taking the list with us, filled with dread. Sashka read it out slowly, point by point.

"Take the staples out of the new rug; provide tissues; a mug for toothbrushes; instructions for the TV, ensure the kettle's flex reaches the plug without having to put it on the floor; replace the too large, wobbly table lamps (these were a sentimental wedding present from my graphology mentor); replace the towels daily ("We always used to do that at the Forest Inn anyway," commented Sashka); and a couple of other minor comments.

Well. All eminently do-able. And probably obvious. Incredibly helpful. I am massively grateful, and immediately emailed the couple saying so. I wish they could come back and do the same for another room!

Meanwhile I am going to bite the bullet and put soundproofing in the party wall between Dartmeet's bathroom and Hexworthy, so at least I can sleep guilt-free at night, knowing that I've tried, whether my efforts cure the problem or not!

And bloody Hell – I'm clearly going to have to buy a whole load more towels.

Ein wahr gewordenes Märchen

09/06/2014

Well I haven't a clue what it means, but I think whatever my latest lovely, review says, it must be nice, because as a result we've finally made it! We're in TripAdvisor's 'Dartmoor National Park B&Bs' Top 10! Out of 183! Hurray! At last! Thank you so very, very much everybody who has helped Wydemeet along in this journey!

The significance is enormous. I am massively excited, not just because now I can preen myself at my brilliance as a B&B hostess. It's mostly so that I can kick the expensive agents into touch, which means that my booking process is massively simplified and streamlined.

My goal is to run Wydemeet in the most efficient way possible, whilst not skimping on anything. Except marketing costs.

The agents nearly all charge B&Bs a commission of 15% plus VAT. By achieving this high placing on TripAdvisor, I'm hoping that potential guests will be sufficiently interested to find this website, and book direct on my 'Freetobook' form.

The downside is, of course, that every time someone comes to stay, I feel as if I'm being judged for an exam. It's critical that all my TripAdvisor reviews are lovely or I'll slip down the league again, and out of sight. How exhausting!

I quite approve of all this reviewing stuff that the social media is/are? so keen on though. I think it works for raised standards all round.

This weekend we had eleven people and two dogs sleeping in the house. You would never have known, as I tiptoed down three flights of stairs for a glass of water at 3 o'clock in the morning. All was completely silent, bar the occasional snoring of a slumbering guest.

The three rooms were all booked out, as they were last weekend, next weekend and several more times over the summer, leaving nowhere for me to sleep.

Faye and I found ourselves in Will's room in the attic, Ex slept in Faye's room, and Will (currently otherwise known as 'Tank'), and his friend, ('Little Man') both aged 15, slept outside in the teenagers' Den of Iniquity - all of us sharing the downstairs loo, which has no shower. Faye hasn't washed her lustrous golden locks for very nearly three weeks!

Faye spent the night thrashing around scratching her eczema, while countless enormous spiders, kept landing 'thump!' by my head on the pillow. So the morning's order of three Eggs Royale, three Eggs Florentine, two poached eggs on muffins with smoked salmon but no hollandaise, and two full English breakfasts, all at once at 8.30am on a Sunday morning, while Claire Balding discussed her faith with Rhydian on

Radio 2, did my head in. I found myself sweating over the Aga, rather unattractively.

So I've made a major decision. Today I have booked out my smallest room, Bellever, for the whole of the rest of the summer, for ME! (except for those nights when it's already been pre-booked).

How much is this going to cost me? Do I know? Do I care? What sort of a life is it when I'm moving around my own home living out of a Tesco's crate with no bathroom to call my own? So I've 'closed' out Bellever on my Freetobook form and now I am going to get some sleep.

And also, to preserve my sanity, I'm going to say 'non' to dogs, which are a total pain whining away when everybody else is trying to enjoy breakfast; and sticky fingered children who leave sticky patches on my mahogany table, and hot chocolate stains on my new chairs.

Will anybody ever book again?

The White Company

10/06/2014

'Added Value'. That's what I do. It's the most fun and efficient way of earning as much money as possible in the shortest possible time. Stack it high, sell it cheap, is not for me. Sounds like much too hard work, for ingratiates.

Non. The fewer customers the better, paying as much as I dare charge, means less work for yours truly. And happier, nicer customers too, don't ask me why.

I love The White Company's products - they're very added value. When first setting up, I spent a long time trying to source their specialist trade B&B toiletries on the internet, getting nowhere.

After fruitless hours, I finally tracked them down, under the umbrella of a distribution channel called Pacific Direct, which also represents Asprey, Conran, Floris, Elemis and Penhaligon's. But they wouldn't let me become a customer! Not good enough for them eh? What a bloody nerve!

Anyhow, last week I called them again, and now I'm allowed to stock their high fallutin' products! Hurray! I've clearly Arrived!

So I'm sitting here in my attic office, buried under 100s of titchy bottles of shampoo, conditioner and soaps. It smells fantastic!

The odd thing is, though, that however gorgeous I think the stuff is that I provide, most of my guests still use their own, and no one ever takes my lovely freebies home. How come? If I stay anywhere nice (those were the days) I throw everything available into my suitcase. OK sometimes I leave behind a dressing gown, or a sheet. I turn up the heating, open the windows, leave all the lights and the telly on, and throw the damp towels with their mascara stains on the floor.

Wake up call Mary. My guests are so tidy that sometimes it's difficult to know quite how to 'refresh' their rooms! "Leave a rose on the bed," they said.

Anyhow, my guests get proper fresh orange juice with bits in, unpasteurised so it only has a three day shelf-life and it doesn't freeze properly, at £2.49 a bottle.

Their Christy's bath sheets (not mere towels) weigh 650gsm (no idea what that means, but it sounds good). Sausages come from my mate's down the road and she feeds her pigs on leftovers from the Princetown brewery. My bread is artisan, and looks home-made. The other day I spent £40 at the local fete's cake stall, on five home-made cakes and six pots of strawberry jam.

I don't want to do the sums but with laundrette bills, shop-flowers, Sashka's hours, heat, loads of hot water etc I guess everything adds up to quite a lot. But so what. It's still nothing compared with the agents' bills!

Even so, a particularly jolly Russian couple who stayed last week, have just described Wydemeet as 'rustic' in their TripAdvisor review.

Death on Dartmoor

10/06/2014

We're going to be famous!

Faye and her friend Julia are in a film, being shot this afternoon! A proper feature film - not just an episode for telly!

It's called 'Dartmoor Killing' and is the baby of our mate, Peter Nicholson, who has won a Bafta, as has his co-writer, Isabelle Grey, whilst his producer Jayne Chard and production designer Amanda Bernstein from Star Wars are both Bafta-nominated. Wow!

They're the ones who first used Wydemeet as a B&B a year ago, and shot their promo-film here. They've got the funds together to make the movie proper now! Hurray! I hope it's a block-buster!

I think Faye and Julia might be playing two friends who are 'led into a web of mind games, sexual deceit and betrayal, on a weekend trip to Dartmoor.' I suppose we'll find out if this is the case, on location later on today at Poundsgate, at 5.30pm. We'll drive there direct from today's school Rounders Match.

Yesterday I had to pop into Tesco to see if I could find a pair of '90s looking jeans for Faye to wear for the film. I discovered that Tesco stocks 'skinnies', 'very skinnies', 'boyfriend' (severely oikish), 'cut-offs', 'bootleg', and 'flared'. I was forced to buy flared (at £16!), as bootleg wasn't available in a Size 10, so Faye will look as though she's from the 70s, not the 90s.

And in the meantime, Four in a Bed has raised its head again. Only this time it might be Three in a Bed. During the time slot I gave them that we could do it, they're going to be filming in Scotland. However, they have now emailed to say that 'they all like me' and could I be in their new series in early Autumn?

Well their new series is changing back to the old format: three B&Bs competing against each other, to be screened in a one hour slot at 8pm - peak viewing time - on Channel 4.

So that's much better. I was beginning to panic at the thought of providing six breakfasts at once, to people who will be determined to test my mediocre, amateur, limited cooking ability to its limits. And envisaging deep-cleaning three bedrooms to such a degree that we could guarantee not a single 'curly' inside or outside a mattress protector, nor bog brush, nor underside of a plug-fitting, was filling me with dread. And where would I sleep with all my immaculate bedrooms full? Back in Will's attic room I suppose.

Meanwhile, my romantic life isn't going very well. In fact it's pants. So my being featured on telly could give that side of things a boost.

At the moment, there's a lovely, good-looking, tall bloke from Encounters with a small sports car, who has taken me out for fantastic lunches twice, who understands a wine list, and who pays. That is a most exciting start, but he doesn't want a relationship. Then there's someone from Taunton who writes so well that I've paid £14 to join matches.com in order to be in contact with him.

And then there's my last, final, forlorn and expensive hope - I've booked a Nielson sailing beach resort holiday in Turkey for us all, a week in July, when I may bump into the solvent single Dad of my dreams! But that will only happen if our passports get back in time. It's tight.

Don't Get Divorced!

10/06/2014

Just don't get divorced if you can possibly help it, OK?

The grass isn't greener - just different.

Go through your Christmas card list. How many 'happily married' couples' lives are you jealous of? Nobody's probably. So don't wreck things and then regret it.

My experience of the last five years has led me to believe that most people you could end up with are neither better nor worse than anyone else, really.

Whatever happens, if you get divorced, you will be poorer. And you will make your children cry. And you will never truly enjoy Christmas again.

If one of you goes off with someone else, beware! The someone else is consciously helping bust up a family. Not kind!

We have such a lovely time when Ex comes to see Faye, often picking up Will from boarding school on the way. This weekend, Ex, Faye and I went riding. Well Faye and I rode, Ex was on a bike.

Steak, ducks legs, macaroni cheese. I cooked everybody's favourite things. And then we did the 'Man vs Horse vs Bicycle' race, to Princetown.

Man - ie Ex; wins, easily.

Bicycles - last, by half-an-hour, just avoiding getting electrocuted in a lightning storm.

And then after all the fun, everybody has to go back to wherever they came from.

Why?

12/06/2014

... do I bother? Spending (wasting?) so much time with this blogging business? Risking alienating potential guests, offending friends and family, and probably ending up in some lawsuit?

1) Because the blurb says that if you update your website it improves its SEO - Search Engine Optimisation, ie it makes the website come up first when googled.

2) Because post-divorce, one of my many money-making ideas was to write a book, to be called 'Surviving Solo'. And another was to have a go at becoming a columnist. With the blog it's possible that I might eventually be able to amalgamate both, along the lines of, say, "A Year in Provence", only less well written and less about France. The trouble is, books need shape: a beginning, a middle, and an end. Hence my remorseless search for the perfect man.

Once I've found him, I can give up the blog, as the fairy tale will finally end: "So then they got married and lived happily ever after."

3) Because it's the perfect excuse to go on, and on, and on, and on, and on, and on.. about me. My favourite subject.

Taking on Babington

16/06/2014

Yesterday I bid for three Nespresso machines on eBay.

Guess how many I won? Three. Oh dear - where shall I put them all? And I don't even like espresso coffee that much.

They are called 'Pixies'. Two are Krups, and one is a Magimix, and I got them for around £50 each, instead of the £100+ charged for new ones by companies such as Lakeland Plastics.

These machines are part of my drive to improve the 'product', or 'offering' of my B&B, in advance of the Four in a Bed debacle.

I have been looking at pictures of Babington House on their website, so that I can copy what they provide. Babbers, near Frome in Somerset, is where the pop stars go, or used to go, to pretend they were enjoying a country break, complete with borrowed wellies. It costs up to £400 a night without breakfast, and I am hoping to meet someone via Encounters who would like to take me back there. It's my favourite hotel, and it's been many years since I was lucky enough to be able to visit it.

So, in my bid to emulate, or, of course, to outdo them, in addition to the Nespresso machines, I have also bought three white candles from Morrison's, some cotton wool balls, and a really nice little box to hide the tissues under.

A see-through bath in the middle of the room, and a TV the size of a garage, complete with Dolby surround sound, remain beyond my means at present.

The 24 Hour Rule

16/06/2014

Last week, two Mums fought each other in the car park of Faye's posh school.

Not literally. I exaggerate, to catch your attention.

In actual fact, they shouted at each other, and one broke down in tears and called the other a nasty name.

I was sad because I know both of them and they are both nice. And they both had a point, but the environment was not conducive to rational thought or discussion, as we all stood out in the rain and wind, waiting for a summit meeting in which to discuss the school's future.

With around 100 pupils, Faye's school achieves places, and often scholarships, for children going to Eton, Harrow and Winchester. A mad proportion end up in Oxbridge. Every year its children win academic, music, art and all-rounder scholarships worth £100,000s to all the best schools in the South West. This year, so far, 13 pupils have won a total of 16 scholarships, and the entire top year group has passed Common Entrance.

Over the last six months, just some of the highlights include the school *winning* the *national* prep schools' Rugby 7s at Oundle, winning a national IAPS team trampolining competition in Croydon, best school in all three age-groups and both genders of the Devon and Cornwall athletics championships, county players in hockey and cricket, national diving champions, and it came 6th in the U14s national schools show-jumping in Buckinghamshire, with two of its four team members on their titchy ponies, aged just eight.

Yet, like so many other rural prep schools, its numbers have halved over the past few years, and the governors have told us that we are to merge with the less expensive, less successful, less beautiful school across the river, which isn't geared towards its leavers going on to posh boarding schools. There are simply not enough children in the area to fill up both.

Feelings are running high.

One group of parents is so rich that they want to buy the school outright.

Some of the unsolicited emails I'm being sent are extraordinarily vitriolic. If their authors had gone through a divorce, they would have learned the 24 hour rule. Never press 'send' til you've read the thing again a day later.

I am sooooooooooo tempted to get involved. Down girl!

Old Friends

22/06/2014

Last week I spotted a small sign outside a neighbouring farmer's gate saying 'Barn Dance'. On the other side of the notice it said 'Open to All', June 21st. That was yesterday, for those of you who didn't notice how long the day lasted.

So I was faintly appalled that I knew nothing about it, and was not aware of anyone I knew going to it. No one had mentioned it.

Neighbour, bringing round yet more delicious eggs for my B&Bers, clearly was aware of it after all, telling me that it had been organised to raise funds for my children's old village primary school.

I've mentioned before - I'm a bit of a pariah around here. It must look a bit odd - this woman keeping going, running this large house in the middle of nowhere, alone with just her young daughter for company.

I don't really care if people think I'm Mad Mary of the Moor, but I do find it hard to attend these social gatherings full of indigenous local people, all of whom have partners, and most of whom are related to each other. I've been here nearly twenty years now, but I'm not part of the soil. Not even rural really - I still don't know the names of the fields, tors nor birds. And you're more likely to catch me going for a walk in a swimming costume, sarong and flip-flops, than boots and those stupid sticks that scratch the roads and mess up the moor. Anyway - that's why I have horses. So you can sit down going uphill.

Faye didn't really want to go to the dance either. She hasn't seen her local friends since last year at Widecombe Fair, when they sweetly came up to say hello, and she rushed off to the dog show, looking and sounding like a posh girl, when in fact she was just suffering from an eleven-year-old shy-on.

"We're Hadows" - I said. "Best foot forward. We're good at this sort of thing." So we went. And thank God that we made ourselves do it. I would have died to have heard about it afterwards, and to have missed it.

This part of Dartmoor still holds events verging on the celestial from time to time.

There's an annual Cricket Match, Widecombe vs Poundsgate; the first match of the day is played by women and children, and the second by the men. Ex once hit heads with a jockey while fielding, got severely concussed and ended up in hospital. It's held in a natural amphitheatre with views towards the sea; everyone wears whites, drinks beer and wine, and brings barbeques, garden chairs and tables, even gazebos, marquees and hammocks! It's like Dartmoor's version of Henley.

Well this Barn Dance last night was held in Near Neighbouring Farmer's field and barn. His son is in his last year at the primary school. The large field was newly mown, and lit by the fading evening sunlight were a bucking bronco and several bouncy castles. The barn was huge and immaculate - about 100 metres long, featuring local jazz, soul, blues and rock bands, and even local children, playing and singing to us all.

The young were everywhere, and almost everyone I've met in my twenty moorland years was there. I'm clearly still a part of it all, however vicariously.

After a shaky start, and a little word in a few little girls' ears from me, Faye ended the evening happily sitting in the family car of her best old friend from her old school, turning elastic bands into hair attire. It was as if they had never been separated.

It was the most perfect evening imaginable.

Rationalisation

27/06/2014

Hmmm. I might have made an error. In my extreme efforts at rationalising the marketing of my burgeoning new business, I appear now to be empty for most of July. That wasn't exactly the plan.

Having closed out 'Bellever' so that I can sleep there myself, this leaves just the two larger, more expensive rooms available: 'Hexworthy' with its morning sun, huge bathroom, private shower cubicle, bidet and trouser press; and 'Dartmeet' - evening sun, twin option, and lovely private view across the garden to the moor.

I've sacked all the agents – and now this seems to be proving a bit serious.

But I did it because with their 15% commission plus VAT, if you book Dartmeet for a week, say, they'll take a whopping £150! That's completely ridiculous compared with all my other overheads put together!

PLUS; guests booking via the agents just don't always seem to quite 'get' what Wydemeet offers. Not surprising really, considering the main agent is based in Amsterdam or somewhere, and it's staffed by people who have never heard of Dartmoor. I keep being sent extremely nice Germans who erroneously believe we are a convenient central point for exploring the West Country, and are surprised and a bit concerned that there are no signs to the B&B, and that we don't have things such as wardrobes, and that our albeit satellite broadband is nevertheless still rubbish and only works in half the house.

The next most expensive items after the agents are Sashka's hours, and laundry, which come to half what the agents charge, and are absolutely vital for my sanity, or at the very least to keep me in a good mood.

TripAdvisor's doing its best, but it's a challenge to stay in the Top Ten when you've only got two room-fulls of guests writing up-to-date five-blob reviews.

And I also need to keep coming up first in the Google Search Engines.

On top of all of this, what with originally 'closing out' much of July in an attempt to let out the entire house, and banning large bouncy dogs and sticky-fingered children, perhaps I've gone too far!

So I've just re-opened lots of July, typed this up to help with SEO optimisation, and crossed my fingers. Do come! It's fab!

How the Hell Does She Do It?

30/06/2014

Help!

My rationalisation has definitely gone too far! I am STILL empty for the whole of July! Now I'm panicking!

OK - I have let the house out for the week of July 26th which means closing the B&B for a couple of days either side. And until three days ago I had shut myself down for the first week in case Four in a Bed came, and the second week hopefully for another rental which hasn't transpired.

But I had thought that my marketing expertise was so splendid that my two glorious, luxurious rooms would fill up with last-minuters. Wrong. Nothing. Not a squeak.

But meanwhile, I am really, really tired after a frantically busy June. I might get a lie-in on Friday morning when Faye is boarding overnight. That will be my first, including weekends, in probably a month. So it's odd having our house suddenly back to ourselves after such an ongoing round of guests, especially with my lovely huge sunny Hexworthy room empty, waiting for someone else, instead of having me in it. Yesterday I lay for an hour in our hot tub, which has been completely renovated at vast expense. As a result, today my ancient skin is even more dry and wrinkly than usual. Faye didn't even bother getting dressed all day. And we forgot to feed the horses.

I guess business is bound to pick up soon. We have been given yet another cry-worthy fantastically fantastic review on TripAdvisor so we retain our place in the Top Ten, and now I've fixed it so that you can book us direct via TripAdvisor too.

I'm not sure how much that will cost, but I'm very interested to find out.

Tonight it's "I Can't Believe That She Does It" or whatever the name is of the book by Allison Pearson, on telly. Ms Pearson once met Ex at some talk, and sent him home with a copy of her book for me, with a message in it saying "I can't believe how you do it."

Three years later she was speaking about her sequel - a book about her teenage crush on David Cassidy - at Dartington 'Ways with Words' literature festival, which is one of the highlights of my year - it's so beautiful. So I went to see her, and told her that I hadn't managed to 'do it' after all. She commiserated, and she wrote another lovely message, such as "All men are bastards" or something, for me on the inside cover of the David Cassidy book.

Actually I've checked, and she's much too nice to have penned such a thing. In fact she wrote "I think I love you" (with the 'think' crossed out and changed to 'know') "Better Luck Next Time."

Anyway - they're showing the film of "I Don't Know How She Does It" tonight on ITV2, and I must catch it. I'm fed up with all the channels showing the most boring acts taking place at Glastonbury. I'm sure there must be some better ones going on, on different stages, that we don't get to see.

But in the meantime, I've just realised why I appear to myself, and probably everybody else, to be so obsessed with this internet dating thing. It's because I'm a Virgo, and I just can't rest until I've properly completed the job in hand, whatever it is, to the best of my ability.

Which, as it happens, I've just arranged.

I have now got profiles up on three sites: Encounters, Guardian Soulmates, and match.com; and can't do much more. I've told my various audiences exactly who I am, whom I would like to meet, and then made up a sort of TripAdvisor Review about myself, written by a fictitious first date. I think all internet dating sites should carry reviews, just like hotel sites do. I've given myself five blobs, naturally, and described myself as 'an extremely attractive woman'. I wonder if it will work?

Nothing else has, so I can't lose. The trouble is, looking at all the men available on the sites, I'm not sure if I'd want any of them anyway.

Poison

02/07/2014

This morning I looked like one of those characters in a cartoon where water streams out of its eyes in a gush.

I don't remember ever crying so hard - not ever. Except when our first dog died, when I was seven.

Last month I poisoned Twiglet, our wonder-dog, by giving him an ibuprofen after Neighbours' dogs attacked and hurt him. £450, a Sunday overnight drip, hundreds of pills and four weeks later, he is now as good as new, no thanks to me.

Today I poisoned my horse. With rat poison.

She was crashing around the stable, dripping all over with sweat, lip curling, rolling on her sides, scraping her front hooves on the concrete, gasping.

In a way I am relieved that I can still feel at all, and so hard. I was beginning to think that I had become a bit emotionless, but clearly it's all still latent. I don't know how actors can portray that amount of sheer grief unless they have felt it themselves, and it's taken me til I'm 54.

I rang the vet four times: "Hurry hurry hurry hurry" I sobbed. I got the picnic stool out and sat near adorable Vegas, gasping "I'm so sorry," to her, over and over and over again and stroking her sweat-drenched neck.

Gradually she quietened. I wondered whether she would shortly lie down and die.

After an hour I heard Vivian's car finally arriving, and she came in and took Vegas' heartbeat and listened to her gut.

"Clinically she's perfectly OK," she said cheerfully.

Vegas had barged through a blocked door into a small section of the barn which had two small trays of rat poison on the ground, and had clearly panicked as she couldn't turn around to get out again. She must have eventually backed out in fright.

On close inspection we found it difficult to believe Vegas had actually eaten any of the poison - it didn't look disturbed - and Vivian said that the behaviour I described wouldn't have been caused by rat poison. By now Vegas had started eating her hay. Vivian said she thought the incident had been colic induced by the stress of getting stuck into the small barn section, and gave Vegas a jab to calm her stomach.

She seems to be fine now. Just like Twiglet turned out.

So there we are. What a morning. I feel very odd. And not very proud of myself. Beware of your Mama, my pets.

Laugh Conquers All

02/07/2014

So with three internet dating sites on the go, everything's going a bit mad. Possibly bad and dangerous to know as well. I'm having a bit of trouble keeping up, but I think I'm still on top of things, just. And anyway - after this sudden peak, I am fairly sure all will suddenly disappear and there will be nothing left, within days. But at the moment things are quite exciting!

The other night a chap of 41 who lived locally, and was so utterly drop dead gorgeous that he gave me butterflies, contacted me. I got back to him, and he turned out to be Sikh from Leicestershire who had used a picture of a male model instead of himself, and completed an entirely fictitious profile, including describing himself as 'white/Caucasian'. Well what is the point of that? Just wasting everybody's time. All the same - I felt a bit spooked actually.

A day later an equally delicious young man of 34, Italian this time, contacted me, and looking at the pictures, he really is from Plymouth. But - now what? He's not brilliant at English and I can't imagine what we would talk about, or how he would make me laugh. I think he must be some kind of gigolo, but that is my suspicious mind.

Several of them write so utterly beautifully that you think they must speak like that too. And then they don't. Quite a lot of them look defeated and sad, even though they all say, "I love life. I am just looking for a lady to share it with," in their profiles. And we're not 'ladies' - we're people. Or 'someone' would actually be fine. They nearly all seem to be terribly keen on honesty. I bet if honesty really hit them in the face (in the form of me, say) they'd run a mile. All the beaches that allow dogs must be packed out by lonely hearts enjoying what they 'love best'. 'I'm just a normal guy' doesn't do much to sell anyone to someone like me, 'who enjoys the good things in life like eating out, going to the cinema and theatre, as well as cosy nights in by the fire' drone on the cliché-packed profiles.

So far everybody I've come across on the internet seems to have some kind of major drawback. Usually they are too old (I thought 60 should be my top limit - that's pretty old), too small, too fat, too bald, too glass half empty, or too boring. Annoyingly, I am also becoming increasingly convinced that it will only work for me with a private school person. Not that I'm particularly snobbish, but because ours is a little world of its own, where everybody has an automatic understanding of each other. So that cuts out a mere 95% of the human race.

What does unite everybody that I have met is that they all, bar one or two, appear to be extremely nice, decent, well-intentioned people. Just like anyone that you might meet on the street really. Which they are, if you think about it!

And my guess is that if they really made me smile, giggle and laugh with uncontrollable mirth, any other concerns might well go straight out of the window.

So if it's inevitable that you must be flawed in some way if you're internet dating, what's my problem, you may well ask. Well it's obvious isn't it? I am surrounded by sheep.

Beastly Boys

03/07/2014

Dear Faye was crying her eyes out and shaking with sobs, when I picked her up from school.

We seem to be having an emotional week, her and me.

A boy in the year above, with whom she has been at various schools since she was two, called her 'fat, with a low voice' in front of the little chap she love(s/d) most, and some of her other friends.

Nobody stuck up for her, and when she walked past they all went quiet and stared at her.

Aged twelve she has learned something that I didn't learn until I was 50. That few people put their necks on the line for you, whether they like you or not, in the presence of someone powerful.

I was more devastated by this discovery, than by almost anything else, when my marriage broke down. Faye will be much better prepared for the world.

Faye weighs the most in her year group. She is taller than the little squit who was being unkind to her. And his voice hasn't broken yet.

We went to look in the mirror together, and I explained the concept of body dysmorphia. "We are about the same fat, or not fat, aren't we?" I said to her, as we gazed at our joint reflections, "only you're without the tummy."

We're both statuesque, strong, robust people. Like Princess Diana might have been if she'd taken proper advantage of all those royal banquets.

My father was the President of the Boats at Cambridge. Faye and I would make good rowers, like her two stunning, willowy, 6' cousins who both rowed at Women's Henley last weekend. Faye agreed.

"Let's sing 'Feed the Birds'," I then suggested. She did so loudly, while I accompanied her on the piano, with as much exuberance as Liberace, but fewer sequins (and more mistakes).

"Sing that low G," I shouted at her over the din. She couldn't quite reach down to it. Her voice is not low enough. Just lower than the boy in question's.

The next day she was due to perform 'Let It Go', from the animated film 'Frozen', on her flute, in front of all those friends at the School Summer Concert. "You are truly going to Let It Go tonight," I informed her. "Are you allowed to wear mascara?"

"No," she replied.

"OK, put some on," I ordered. We tried on her old and new school skirt and jumper, and opted for the old one which is a little tighter, and she rolled up the kilt an inch or two. "And get yourself some new white socks from the school shop!" I shouted after her, as she got out of the car, ready to face down her unsupportive peers.

Ex and Granny drove 4 ½ hrs and 2 hrs each way respectively, just to hear Faye's four minutes of fame.

The school dealt with the bullying incident first thing, reported back to me, and by evening, my dazzling dearly beloved daughter was up on that stage, with the widest smile lighting up her pretty face from ear to ear. She even closed her eyes dreamily, as she performed the very last crescendo of Let It Go, and we all went home for supper kindly cooked by Ex before he left for London, reaching his home five hours later, at two in the morning.

Nice Philanderers?

03/07/2014

It must, by definition, be impossible to have an affair with a nice person.

Because if they were nice (if it ever got that far) they would say, "Yes I feel so much love for you too, but you must, must, must go back to your spouse - have counselling; do everything you can to keep the family together; do not betray your partner nor your children. As I must not betray mine. It would destroy them all. No, I just must not, cannot, even allow myself kiss you. It would be wrong of me. Go now, go, and we need never speak of this again."

Having an affair means that you must both behave dishonourably and dishonestly.

Viz (whatever that means, but Robinson Crusoe said it a lot) your new love is flawed right from the beginning. And as a result, although obviously some affairs work out OK for everybody involved in the end, for most it would seem that the 'happy ever after' is terribly unlikely.

Personally, in my new romantic adventuring, I tend to go for 'dumpees' rather than 'dumpers'. Dumpees seem to have a more steady neddy, sanguine approach to life; making the most of what is, and putting up with things, rather than nothing ever seeming quite good enough, and jumping ship.

TripAdvisor's Gone Mad!

06/07/2014

Sometimes I look at Wydemeet's reviews on TripAdvisor, and I feel like crying.

One after the other after the other. They are so touching. Every time some new guests arrive I get butterflies and think to myself, "They are going to be disappointed; they are going to be disappointed. I can never live up to what it says on TripAdvisor."

So far, well. Phew! Everyone seems very happy. More than happy. Astonishingly happy! I am soooo chuffed! But still constantly nervous too.

Anyhow, I've just had this brainwave. All the internet dating sites seem so rubbish that perhaps TripAdvisor might present another public 'portal', if that's the correct 'now' word. So I just thought I would put in a little mention of my search for Mr Right on it. How cheeky is that?! I bet they censor it. Anyway - we'll see - I've just done it this minute!

But, in the meantime, much more seriously and significantly, my lovely, lovely, lovely guests' enthusiasm has meant that, despite only being open for less than a year, and now only having two bedrooms available, so by definition having limited numbers of guests who could have written anything, we have risen to the grand position of Number 8 out of 183 Dartmoor B&Bs, and we're still rising!! There isn't any real reason why we couldn't hit the Number 2 slot! We will never beat the Apple Tree in

Tavistock though. They've got over 200 rave reviews, whereas we've only got 37. The only negative comment they've ever had is that the car parking is a bit tight.

My latest wheeze is to make a hair appointment with the lady who runs it (according to my hairdresser she is also a hairdresser, as well as a B&B Proprietor), and have a chinwag with her and pick her brains about how she does it so well, while she gives me a trim. Apparently she's only in her thirties. Respect! How Does She Do It?!

Bridget, Jeremy and Me

16/07/2014

People that I like tend not to like Bridget Jones, Jeremy Clarkson, Britain's Got Talent, or people who drive Range Rovers. Or the Daily Mail.

I am currently in the middle of 'Mad About The Boy', with "Is It Really Too Much To Ask?" lying by my side, missing my Range Rover, and looking forward to tonight's 'Battle of the Bands" - this beach resort's version of BGT, and I am inspired! I can write like BJ and JC! (I think..)

There are only two differences between me and Bridget Jones.

One is that she's a Mother Who Tries Too Hard, while I favour the Benign Neglect approach.

Two is that she's made up, whereas I exist.

There are also two differences between me and Jeremy Clarkson.

I sometimes worry that I might have upset someone.

And I am not a bloke.

Bridget Jones is not believable because she claims to be a Sloane but says 'toilet', and also, in the book a 29 year old hunky decent bloke falls for her via twitter without even a photograph. The chances of that are one in seventy-five trillion, as Clarkson might say.

Bridget Jones' books are structured over a blog-type thought occurring every minute or two. Clarkson's all resound with, 'And there's the thing' every three pages, when he instructs us all on how easily he could achieve world peace. Well I think I can probably copy both of them and publish a bestseller.

The problem is that if I do, the people I like won't like me.

Single Mum On Holiday

16/07/2014

"Might I join you?"

"No, we're having a family birthday party."

So I wander along to another table, with two couples sitting at it, and, again, nervously, ask whether I might be able to take a seat there.

I swore never to attempt another sailing/beach resort holiday alone with my children, and here I am again, £4500 later, going through the whole hideous experience all over again.

This time it's a Nielson holiday, rather than Sunsail.

At Nielson, unlike Sunsail, they have a 'Social Table' which is the biggest one, so it's usually occupied by the largest, happiest family groupings of all. I would be fine all alone in a villa miles from anyone, but being surrounded by literally 100 functional happy families I find very difficult.

Networking is my thing, so I regularly invade various groups of people every mealtime, but this time round so far none of them has proved very interesting. Except for Jake, the professional weightlifter turned tooth implanter, with tinted hair, aged 51 but who looks ten years younger.

He is here with his two sons and is not interested in talking to anybody because he spends his working days making small talk to people who, with their mouths full of his implements, can't reply.

There is increasing unrest in camp, shortly to become full rebellion I suspect, because it is advertised, amongst other things, as a sailing holiday, but no one has as yet been out in a boat. The quiet bay appears to have turned into a surfing beach with onshore winds and huge waves, so the black flag's up and we're not allowed to.

Both children have turned feral and disappeared. So I have met my main objective which is for them to thrive socially in their kids clubs. But it looks as though they're not going to learn to sail.

And nor is it looking hopeful that I'm going to bump into a wealthy hearty six foot hunk of rich single posh Dad.

Mad About The Ratings

16/07/2014

Units of revolting expensive Turkish Wine: 502: fags: 111; Baklava Calorie Count: 15,432; Minutes spent with children: 0; interesting conversations: 0; number of times giggled: 0; passes from Turkish waiters: 0; passes from English Dads: 0; minutes spent sailing: 0; lengths swum: 20 (it's an Olympic sized pool); wardrobe malfunctions: 1: (my swimming costume is a small size 12); clouds:0.

I love Bridget Jones.

A Whole New Me

17/07/2014

Will (15) has changed his name and has added a year to his age.

It's taken a couple of days, but he is already back to normal form, with his wraparound shades, baseball cap on back to front, and a trail of children wandering along behind him like the Pied Piper, only now they are aged 16-18, and some of them are over 6' tall. I woke him up for water-skiing this morning and commented "Revered Son, you appear to have a large smear of mascara on your cheek." He grinned proudly. At lunchtime he was sitting next to a slim blonde young goddess draped in diaphanous pink chiffon. His friends reassure me that he is what I would refer to as a lothario, not what they would refer to as a man-slag.

Meanwhile my new identity is pariah. I am struggling with this as I am used to being centre of attention.

I am so interesting that a screenplay has been written about part of my life, and that's just some of it! But here everybody seems to see through me as though I am made of air.

This week I find myself walking around grinning to nobody in particular, and making pleasant small talk to every tom, dick and pillock, but they're all doctors and surgeons. Someone mentions the word NHS, if it is a word, at which point (Clarkson rant) they turn their backs on me in unison and have a competition as to who can squawk the loudest about how they're now working 210 times as hard as what they signed up to do, their pay has been cut by 7,000% and their pensions have turned into 2 1/2p a year. As they buy another bottle of Turkish chardonnay for three million Turkish lire, and disappear off for an 'opi gel manipedicure', a 'Brush With Heaven' and back wax.

And I help myself to what's left of their wine.

What On Earth Is Happening To My B&B?

18/07/2014

TripAdvisor Ranking: 8 (going down); New Bookings: 0; Minutes spent worrying about this: 5.1/2; dates: 2

Oh dear. Here I am, basking in the Turkish sun, and I've just had a worry about what's going on at home.

Just before Will, Faye and I set off on our mad trip here, a couple of days ago (I'd arranged a flight from Exeter to Manchester, followed by another to Dalman, forgetting that Will has an understandable fear of flying, ending with a four hour coach transfer to here which is God knows where) - a couple of B&Bers turned up.

We had tea and cake together, and they then set off, with no research, on the 1 1/2 hr each way hike across the moor to Princetown, wearing flip-flops, returning almost immediately in some distress as the female half of said couple had been bitten by a horsefly.

Faye provided her with antihistamine and then they went off somewhere in their car.

Meanwhile lovely Sally arrived. I found her through the Parish Magazine and I thought that she was so nice that all my guests would love her too. So I invited her to look after the house, dog, horses and guests, in no particular order, for the week while we were away.

As we departed for our week's holiday in Marvin I had this terrible premonition that our new guests might have driven away in disgust, never to return! Thank goodness it was clearly me who had scared them off if so, rather than sweet Sally during her first hour of duties.

But back to today in Turkey..

1.32pm: Had lunch with widowed plastic surgeon from Harrogate (burns not faces)

7.24pm: Right now, I still have no idea whether my B&B couple ever came back.

7.25pm: Anticipating this evening's Event which is to be:

8.30pm: Turkish chef's Special Barbequed Goat Dinner, with widowed plastic surgeon from Harrogate, and ex-professional weightlifter/teeth implanter from Leicester.

Must wash hair and get out best spray-on black wraparound ancient t-shirt dress, and agonising matching patent sky high killer heels.

Just had a thought. Neither man is very tall.

Gee That's Better

18/07/2014

Number of people to stand me up: 1; Wine Units: 227; Fags: 0; Barbequed Goat calories: 3,456; Balaclava calories: 0; minutes spent in riveting conversation: 240; number of giggles: 10; number of rows with Resort Owner: 1; number of passes by Turkish waiters: 0

Wow! What a night! Just what I have been hoping for!

Heads were turning knowingly over breakfast this morning, even though we had come down at different times. This is how it went:

8.50pm: I am wandering around the bbq dining area but can't tell who anybody is because I refuse to wear glasses or contacts. But plastic surgeon should be quite easy to spot because he is the only gentleman of mixed race in the resort. Non. How disappointing. No one. I scour the bar area and finally alight on the silhouette of tooth implanter. He looks like he is out of the movies.

9.00pm: We agree we have been stood up by plastic surgeon and enjoy our goat. He comments with surprise: "You're funny". I don't suppose he has ever been forced to dine with a Size 14, six foot in her heels, 54-year-old FunnyMummy before. I giggle. A lot. How refreshing!

9.31pm: Acoustioke Night in the bar

10.23pm: Plastic Surgeon turns up. He had waited for us, given up and gone to another beach bar for supper with the flotilla-mob.

10.36pm: Ginger Bloke with Looks-Like-Me-Wife turns up. He's in the IT sector of the SAS or something, and tells us all how they managed to prove Shipman guilty, how Shipman continued to kill even from the confines of prison, and why it's not good nor funny that Will's best friend is able to hack into the school software system and change all the exam grades. Ginger Bloke is one of the most interesting people I have come across for a very long time.

1.00am: We all depart happily to our separate beds, except presumably, Ginger Bloke and his Looks-Like-Me-Wife.

Racing for Girls

20/07/2014

Lumps on head: 3: purple splodges on knees: 5; cuts on knees: 1; broken toes: 1 (maybe); muscles aching: all I have, plus more that I didn't know that I had; missing tarty toe rings: 1; minutes spent with children: 0;

passes from anybody, even girls: 0.

"Please would you give me a boat for girls," I pout coyly, my pretty sarong fluttering gaily in the gale, my bejewelled flip-flops sparkling.

If I can't win through good sailing, I can win using tactics. The eight most macho men of the resort, kitted out in black body armour, knuckle dusters and knee pads, and I, are choosing our Lasers (very fast and tippy sailing dinghies) for the Big Race.

At last we are sailing, and it's the most cut-throat event of the week - The Regatta.

Sure enough, I manage to take possession of the smallest girlie-Laser with the titchiest sail, which puts me in a class of my own, literally, tactics sorted; while the blokey blokes have to look macho so opt for bigger, faster, more gnarly (challenging) versions.

So I have already won the Laser 247 Class without setting foot in a boat, as I'm the only one in it.

The red flag goes up indicating conditions are too dangerous for amateurs in single hulled dinghies.

Off 25 amateurs in single hulled dinghies charge, all attempting to start at the same time between two rather close-together buoys, and no brakes between us. "Starboard!!" I scream, and the nicest, most dashing young Dad of the resort smashes into me hard. "I thought you were meant to be good at sailing!" I hurl at him, struggling hard not to fall overboard. It's dinghy dodgems!

Two crashes and quite a lot of swimming later; I finally stagger in to shore - triumphant and exhausted. Sailing is so nice when it stops. For the past hour I appear to have been using my head to physically move the boom backwards and forwards, smashing my knees on the bottom of the boat, and all the ropes or sheets or whatever they're called are tangled up, trailing out over the stern (back).

I came 8th out of all 25 sailors in the handicapped race in the end, being the only Lady-in-a-Laser and beaten only by Look-Alike-Wife, racing an easier boat, among the few female participants. Reeeeeesult!

Thank God that's sailing out of the way for at least another year.

Relax Hard

20/07/2014

I am the most beautiful person in Plymouth.

But the ugliest in all of Turkey.

I've been surrounded for the last week by a large group of young marrieds who've left me feeling old, unfit in both senses, very single, and generally past it (although still young and stunning when compared with the aquarobics class at my Plymouth-based Unhealth Club).

And I think they may be on the warpath. Quake in your boots, Nielson's! Your customers appear to be displeased that you have plonked the most glorious 5* £billion palatial hotel, meant for sailing, on what on the face of it, seems to be a surfers' beach.

The company's strapline is 'Relax Hard' and that's just what most of their guests do. These people rise at dawn for water skiing (normally cancelled because of the conditions).Then it's mountain biking. Then tennis. Then weightlifting. Then fitness classes including my three perennial hates: Zumba, Aquarobics and Pilates. Followed by Swimming, and Sailing (generally cancelled). And then back to the first three. There is not an ounce of fat between them all. Except for Michael, the surgeon, who is so enormous that he has bosoms, and snores loudly on his sunbed. And me of course.

At the end of the week there's a competition for 'The Most Perfect Family'. Teeth implanter and I pretended to vomit into our raki, but I was actually very jealous when my charming, bald friend (yet another surgeon, who I met when he was sitting down, and when he got up he turned out to be 5'4"), his lovely daughter and delightful wife deservedly took the honour.

I cannot imagine a more determined, intelligent, powerful force of people if this lot get the bit between their teeth. Even if most of them aren't very interesting.

They should be rounded up to sort out Putin and prevent World War 3, once they've dealt with Nielson's.

In the meantime, my diet starts the day the children begin their Autumn term.

I Hate Manchester

21/07/2014

"Are you expecting some kind of ménage-a-trois or something?" I shouted, and I'm afraid to say I hurled the door key across the reception desk at the smug, dour, two young scousers sitting behind it.

It was 3.30am Turkey time. The first taxi at Manchester Airport had refused to take us to our hotel because 'they didn't know where it was'. The second taxi kept driving for miles whilst I repeated 'Altrincham Road' over and over again, and dropped us at what turned out to be the wrong hotel in the opposite direction of where we were trying to go. It took ages for another taxi to come and £30 later we arrived at the Britannia Airport Inn, just down the road from the airport, as I had originally planned, complete with indoor swimming pool.

Avoid! Avoid! Avoid!

The upshot of all that is it's now 3.30am, and we are exhausted and fraught, rather than rested and calm, as I ask for the keys of the pre-booked triple room. There's already been two cock-ups with sorting out this hotel, because the bookers originally booked me into the Gatwick Airport Inn. Luckily I noticed on the booking form. I also noticed that they had only charged me £20 for the booking, instead of £117, which I kindly pointed out. They then, unkindly, didn't stick to their £20 quote (which I would have done, as I aim to offer a platinum service).

Anyway - here we are now. The two young men surreptitiously glance at each other.

We open the bedroom door and they've given us one large bed with three sets of pillows on it. Will is an enormous hairy 15 yr old, and Faye scratches her eczema all night and kicks you in the head. This is a no-go, and very much not what I asked for.

So, half an hour later, the young men sort us into three rooms, but mine hasn't been cleaned. Even I can't sleep in a stranger's sheets or use their towels.

So finally we are settled, as dawn begins to break. My alarm clock is packed in Faye's suitcase on the other side of the hotel. But I can't order an alarm call because the phone doesn't work, and looks as though hasn't for months.

In the morning the tv remote doesn't work.

At breakfast they have run out of mugs, bread (bread??!!) and bowls, my fruit salad is so old it's gone fizzy, and breakfast time still has supposedly another hour to go. Meanwhile I hear that my neighbours' hair-dryer has caught fire. Then I see a rat outside, running along the window-sill - oh no it's not, it's a MINK??!!

So I pop along for my recuperating swim and of course, there's no water in the pool.

You couldn't make it up. And I haven't.

What's Normal?

21/07/2014

We went to Hurlingham-On-Sea, otherwise known as Polzeath Beach, today.

I didn't look better or worse than anyone else there. Phew.

Ping! Kerplunk!

30/07/2014

My attractive glow dissolved into rivers of sweat, running down my face, my back, and under my arms. My heart started beating really fast and my tummy clenched.

Three tons of horse behind me, Will oblivious under his headphones in the passenger seat, and I couldn't steer. Was I imagining things? We had to round another small corner and the car felt funny again. Help! I put on the hazard warning lights and slowed to a crawl up the 1:2 hill, as the engine started going twang, kerplunk, ping; and, after what felt like an eternity, and using all the strength in my arms, I just managed to manoeuvre us all into the new service station opposite Exeter Racecourse.

Calling the AA was top priority, but my card was lost after my last call-out to them just a week ago, and my phone's battery was dying. Eventually I got through, and they said they'd be out in two hours but could not take responsibility for the horses. It was 4.55pm and all the car rental people would be going home in five minutes time. Unbelievably there was no phone number listed for the first Exeter 4x4 leasing place I managed to track down. But White Horse Motors, at 5.02pm, answered my call, and delivered the most enormous brand new Isuzu truck to me within 20 minutes. Meanwhile the AA arrived with its rescue van to take away my old Nissan. "The problem is just a couple of snapped cables" they said. "It'll cost £45 plus the cost of the cables plus VAT, ready by Tuesday."

At this point there were two rescue trucks, the AA van, the Isuzu, the Nissan and the trailer all grouped together in the carpark. I was beginning to feel quite important! And a bit poor, as White Horse were charging me £325 for their rental car.

Will, two horses, trailer and I were on our way again, on what should have been a relatively short journey to the livery near my Mum's. But now a giant juggernaut was taking up the entire tunnel in front of us. We dealt with that, only to meet an oversized tractor pulling a massive trailer of hay in a tiny lane later. I was so exhausted I made the tractor driver get into my Isuzu and reverse it complete with trailer, back down the lane.

We finally arrived at the horse livery just outside Beaminster, where I kept my first horse 22 years ago. A journey which should have taken two hours, had taken six.

But we had made it.

My second holiday of the month was about to begin!

Why Oh Why Oh Why Oh Why?

27/07/2014

Someone is reading this blog! In fact two people are! Thank you for your comments which prove it! I've no idea who you are, but I'm chuffed to bits!

I am cross and frustrated today. This is because it would appear that it is impossible to update my website and blog on an i-pad. Why?

So now I find myself on my Mums four year old Ancient Acer laptop in her kitchen, because I've rented out Wydemeet and have nowhere else to go, so I'm staying for nothing with her, and have no access to my normal computer.

Yesterday I rang up my webhost people in America, at midnight, and yelled "Your country managed to put men on the moon 42 years ago (or was it? and did they actually - the photo was all wrong) so why can't you make your stupid system work on the most popular and common tablet (or whatever it's called) of all in the whole world?!" The bloke replied 'Have a nice day' and hung up on me.

I have written to Manchester City Council about their taxi operators, and they have written back predictably saying that without reference numbers they can't do anything. Rubbish. They can tell their drivers to learn English, learn their way around Manchester without the use of satnav, and to smile.

I have written to Nielson who have predictably come back charmingly, saying they'll look into the matter over the next 28 days.

I have written to the Manchester Airport Inn who predictably have not replied. I have also written them a review on TripAdvisor which is so rude that the TripAdvisor computer came back to me saying, "please press this button if you really meant to mention bedbugs in your review." So I pressed the button.

I currently have court cases pending regarding Bill (my Shogun, more of that to come), BT, and a plumber from five years ago who is of no fixed abode.

My Angry of Wydemeet filing drawer is full to bursting, and I am finding being so permanently cross is very tiring and doesn't produce a flattering facial wrinkle formation.

What I don't understand is what normal people do when they find themselves being treated as idiots, as happens to me so often. Do they just let it go, so that the perpetrators go on to rip off more innocent, gentle, busy people who aren't in a position to stand up to them?

You tell me.

With best regards (and immense gratitude to my two readers)

Bridget Clarkson

Renting Your House Out Is Hard Work

31/07/2014

The first time I rented out Wydemeet, it took Sashka, Kathy and me nearly two months of preparation, stress and worry, thinking through what needed to be done, tidying up the garden, the field, mending things, painting things, deep cleaning; sorting out and emptying all drawers; throwing things away etc.

We were treading on each other's toes, with one person turning radiators off and another turning them back on again; one person putting things away and another getting them out again; all my precious beyond their sell-by-date pots being thrown away and me picking them back out of the bin; Kathy providing me with a pair of curtains to hide my extensive plonk cellar from prying eyes; Kathy hiding what's laughingly called my jewellery so that I couldn't find it; Sashka worrying about children going into the horses' field in case either party got hurt; me writing out extensive notes on how to work the Aga, the heating, the water, and what to do when everything goes wrong; Tesco crate after Tesco crate of the family's belongings all cleared out to be stored away in safety...

Well.

Last Monday I sat down for my usual coffee and fag with Sashka and her wonky knee (it's just her and me now, as Kathy has moved), and said, "They're coming on Saturday. Please could you do everything so that I don't have to panic about it. I've just remembered we're meeting friends in Polzeath today; we're shopping and swimming tomorrow; I've got an internet lunch date on Wednesday; and lunch with Mum and my brother in Exeter on Thursday."

"That's fine," she said, and hobbled off to make up the first two of five bedrooms.

Wydemeet, being on Permanent Alert for guests, is in a totally different state of overall repair now, compared with how it was 18 months ago. This is one of the many upsides about running a B&B business. But there are limits.

11.00pm Wednesday: Faye, who leaves for an outward bound weekend in Wales the next morning, says, "I am so tired I feel dizzy, I can't do any more."

"No worries, I reply, I'll finish clearing up your Hell-hole room tomorrow."

6pm Thursday: Guests call to say can they come a day early. "That's fine," I say - I offer a platinum service. Put down the phone and immediately call Sashka.

"Help! Help! They're coming a day early! What are we (you) going to do, wonky knee and all??"

"That's fine," says Sashka, "I'll rope in my daughter and niece to help."

11.00pm Thursday: Mary says to herself, "I am so tired I feel dizzy, I can't do any more," and lies back on Faye's unmade bed.

11.00am Friday: Mary comes in from mowing so hot she can't see through the sweat streaming down her face, bringing with it stinging mascara and sun cream sloshing into her eyes. To Sashka, who arrived at 7am and has just finished the strimming: "Sashka, I am so tired I feel dizzy, I can't do any more."

"That's fine," says Sashka; "Get out of my hair and go to your Mum's."

So here I am. Having done virtually nothing at all to prepare my home for a week of visitors; and yet, if they have read the blurb properly and genuinely enjoy remoteness, mostly thanks to Sashka they should be having a jolly nice time. Well I hope they are. I don't even know whether they're leaving a day early, or have just got themselves an extra day simply through asking!

I'm sitting typing away, looking out through the rain and pine trees at the most exquisite part of West Dorset. My horses are happily munching away at their livery in Mapperton - one of the most beautiful spots on earth, with high, deep, steep valleys of pasture, woodland, and winding river, long gallops and views across a patchwork of undulating fields over to the sea. I have just enjoyed one of the best rides of my life with Mum's delightful next door neighbour riding Mad Vegas; and the old banger Nissan made it from Exeter to the livery and back to Mum's house, now that I've had to return the rental Isuzu - a miracle in itself.

I haven't spent eight solid days with my mother since I was at school, but the only spat we have had so far was when she tried to make me eat some week-old ham when there was a perfectly good quiche in the freezer.

This is truly one of the most enjoyable and relaxing holidays I have ever had.

And every minute that I sit here twiddling my thumbs - the money is rolling in!

I think I had better just pinch myself!

Hymns and Pimms

31/07/2014

"The thing about Granny's house is that you think nothing bad can happen to you there," says Will.

I've done six days of holidaying at Granny's now, and I'm beginning to worry that I don't seem to have enough to worry about. I'm also struggling to manage nine hours sleep, when I'm used to seven.

It's the sort of house where you can go upstairs in your boots, and all the mirrors are speckly because Granny isn't really interested in appearances. Her face is a patchwork quilt, and her bony knuckles are of fascination to RS. I dare say I shall look similar soon. At least I will be shorter than I am now - Granny has shrunk by about six inches so far.

But her home is calm and feels safe. Even all the in-laws, and ex-in-laws, find they completely relax here.

Granny has been in a bit of a state for the past week because she is partially responsible for the annual Hymns and Pimms Evening tonight at the local church - where I got married 20 years ago, so I know that it seats precisely 70, as we personally measured each pew with our bums. I read recently, or heard it on Jeremy Vine, that a chemical is released that makes you more anxious and cautious as you get older. Well that chemical has been released in Granny and I hope they have found an antidote for it by the time it's my turn.

Anyway - there must have been 70 people there, as the church was full. Granny read a lesson, and I felt a lump in my throat - as I would have if it had been 12 year old Faye, rather than 84 year old Granny. She had been up to the church earlier to practise, and it showed. My Dad, who used to train young Etonians to read in Eton College Chapel, would have been equally proud of her immaculate and dignified performance, watching us all from his cloud in Heaven.

I was a bit unprepared that the hymns part of the evening turned out to include prayers as well - the less involved with praying I get, the odder it all seems. And I felt that I could have played the organ in a slightly more rousing fashion - although I have always found 'Jerusalem' a bit tricky.

And then, being Mum's daughter and on parade, despite having just got off a horse, I had to help, which has never been my strong point. I found myself handing round delicious smelling mini smoked salmon vol-au-vents, which, of course, I wasn't able to enjoy myself because my hands were full.

Well the thing is, it was really fun! And I just loved meeting Mum's local community. They are charming do-ers, mostly of my kind of age, and I am quite envious of her. One of them even personally knew two of the couples I've watched recently being featured on Four In a Bed!

But the coup d'état was meeting a beautiful talented 16 yr old girl who sang a solo of the first verse of "I Vow to Thee My Country" even better than Sue Bo, who will be at school with Faye, and who has already come across Will at some awful festival or other.

Post Hymns and Pimms, she and he were in touch with each other via Facebook even more quickly than I could manage via texting him about this encounter, and Will will be cycling over to her house from here on his return from partying in SW6 tomorrow. So church is still bringing young people together, just as back in the days of Thomas Hardy.

It's Going To Be A Best Seller!

Trip Advisor Ranking: 5; Number Of People Reading This Diary: 6!!!!!

How exciting is that?!

I'm Scared Stiff

08/08/2014

I am so nervous that I haven't been able to sleep properly for the past few nights.

I have entered Faye vs me in a horsey competition to take place in the middle of a forecast hurricane, on top of one of the highest hills in Dartmoor, this Sunday.

I've booked Sally to make breakfast for our six guests, while Faye and I rise before light to hitch up the trailer, prepare our horses, and arrive at the venue for not long after eight in the morning.

The list of other entrants has now arrived, and, as I expected, the rest of the people in our class are mostly aged nine, like Faye's friend, Willow, on her pony Twizzle who is very hairy and slightly smaller than a Great Dane Dog. Of 16 competitors, only three, apart from me, have undisclosed ages (although I did tell the organisers my age, so I wouldn't mind at all if they'd printed it.) I think there should be a cup for the oldest combination of horse and rider, as well as one for 'Best Under Ten'. In fact I think I will donate one for next year's competition.

There are three stages to the 'One Day Event'. We have to learn by heart, and perform a dressage test, which means walking, trotting and cantering around in circles. Faye has never done one of these before. Then we have to jump some painted poles, which fall down if you touch them. And finally we have to canter a mile or two around a cross country course jumping brown fences, which don't budge however hard you hit them. In Faye's and my class, the jumps come up to your knees.

Both of our horses are big, scopey, talented and experienced professionals for grown-ups, used to jumping huge, solid, wide jumps 3'6" high from the gallop, and to doing all sorts of incredibly complicated gymnastics in dressage. So both of them can easily manage what we are asking them to do on Sunday, with their eyes shut, asleep.

But the big question is, will they?

Big Bertha

10/08/2014

"Snoop Dog was fantastic," reported 15 year old Will on his mobile this morning, "but the hurricane has blown down all the floodlights, and the campsite is such chaos it looks quite funny. The campervans are OK though."

He had saved up £180 from somewhere to join every other teenager in the south west, from the local butcher's apprentice, to good girls from safe schools, to posh cool kids from avant garde schools like my son and his friends, to descend on the Boardmasters Festival at Watergate Bay, Newquay. And now the second day of festivities was to be abandoned, thanks to Hurricane Bertha.

The most interesting thing about this Festival, in my opinion, is what happens regarding sexndrugsnrocknroll. There had been considerable emailed correspondence prior to the festival, amongst the Mums of the four boys that I was delivering there, all of us working towards a united approach on alcohol consumption.

Views varied from "We will impose a complete ban on any alcohol and trust them to keep to it," to "We will allow them a couple of bottles of lager and after that they will be left to their own devices as to how they are going to source anything else."

I was responsible for collecting the boys from the railway station, bringing them home to Wydemeet for the night, and then driving them on to the festival. I had reassured the Mums that the only supplies they could have access to would be provided by the sheep outside my gate, or stolen from my Cellar of Plonk.

The Festival organisers, we understood, had imposed a complete ban on spirits, and a maximum of 12 cans of lager per adult, and no alcohol for Under 18s. Meanwhile the social media were alive with ruses for smuggling in booze; and that ghastly NOS stuff (laughing gas) - that Mums take during childbirth, and it jolly well didn't make me laugh.

Have you seen those pictures of pretty teenage girls in their LBD's breathing in and out of coloured balloons to enjoy a brief, legal, and apparently relatively safe and inexpensive high? They look absurd. The suppliers describe and sell the equipment as being useful for whipping cream. Eh?

Anyway, apparently the way to smuggle NOS into these festivals is to stuff the canisters, which you've bought for £7.50 off eBay, up the hollow metal legs of your picnic chair. Bottles of booze are incorporated into a carved out loaf of sliced bread, or the drink is decanted into a punctured coke can re-sealed with a glue gun. My feeling is that these adolescents are more excited about how to outwit the security men than in the taste of alcohol, or breathing in nitrous oxide.

On the way to the Festival I had to buy some croissants from Morrison's, some sausages from the butchers, and collect the laundry for my B&B. "You can all buy your lunch while I collect the croissants," I trilled merrily to my young passengers.

I reached the till with my purchases. Oooops. What had I just done? I'd proactively delivered the fearsome four into what to all intents and purposes was an offy! "You see those four boys over there?" I hissed to the till assistant. "Well they're all 15."

Hah - Got them!

She pressed a flashing light and pointed to her badge which stated that anyone appearing under 25 would be asked for ID. "I would have stopped them anyway," she reassured me. So all they came out with were some sandwiches and a packet of crisps. Phew.

Meanwhile yesterday, after cooking breakfast for six B&Bers, clearing it all up, and then preparing rooms for six more - missing the local fete as a result - Faye and I finally reached Widecombe to walk the show-jumping and cross country courses at about 6pm, while young Maggie plaited up the horses back home for £15, ready for today's One Day Event. I was so tired I could hardly stand up. How Sashka does it day after day I have no idea.

The show jumps came up to our ankles, but the cross country course was quite a different story. Several of the jumps were too large for me to step over. Terrifying!

Finally, as we got back to the carpark, having walked two miles up and down vertigous hills, a cry went up. "It's been cancelled!"

Thank God, in a way. Breakfast for six again this morning and I am a walking zombie. I think three rooms, or six guests, is too many if you are operating a B&B on your own, are over 50, and trying to do anything else as well. I have no regrets regarding my decision to restrict myself to two rooms in future.

Three rooms and it's no longer fun.

Readership Breakdown

10/08/2014

I think you, my loyal readers, number about eight now.

The thing about you of particular interest to me, speaking as a marketing person, is your demographic profile.

About six months ago, after a year of searching, I think I finally began to find 'my voice' in this blogging lark. I am a sort of Bridget Clarkson hybrid - part Labrador, part Rottweiler.

And the end purpose of all this now (quite apart from helping with SEO-ing my website) is hopefully to one day turn my blog into a book aimed at women emerging financially impoverished, and emotionally wobbly, from recent relationship breakdowns, to encourage them that not all need be doom and gloom.

But I am speaking to a void. OK Richard - you're not a void - simply not the audience I was targeting or expecting!

My sense is that about 70% of my readers are dry, clever, witty men. LOVELY!

About 10% are my friends who live abroad and want to stay in touch.

About 10% are my lovely B&B guests.

And finally there is the Mum of my son's friend from school. Eeek! I am absolutely chuffed to bits by your support, but will have to be careful! Will is not happy to be the subject of his Mum's blog...

My Thought For Today

14/08/2014

Have you ever seen a fat cleaner?

Well if you have, they're not very good.

Because proper housework, in my opinion, provides as much of a workout as rowing. That's rowing with oars rather than with voices. I have just finished preparing Dartmeet, and I am absolutely shattered. That's only one room! Last Saturday I did two rooms and I still haven't recovered properly. I got wrist strain from wiping the bathroom tiles, and it hasn't gone away.

Tax Credits Are Stupid (reprise)

14/08/2014

"£5,472.27 is due from you now."

That's what an innocent-looking letter I received out of the blue the other day from HM Revenue and Customs said inside it. I mean who has over £5,000 at their disposal to give to any old Tom Dick or Hannibal that asks for it, there and then?

I was so cross I decided to buy a car.

You may remember that back in the mists of time I was having a rant at the stupid tax credit system that gives well off people money for no reason? Well now they're asking for mine back. Fair enough in principle, but annoying because it's an illogical demand.

My issue with their system was that they are happy to give you £100s a month no matter how much you are receiving in maintenance from your Ex. If it's on offer, it is almost impossible to resist taking it. Even though your Ex might be a millionaire paying you £10,000s a month (mine isn't), you can top this up with even more £1,000s in child tax credits from the government, as your maintenance payments are not taxable income.

In my case, an uncle has died and left me some money; but it's all being used to pay off inheritance duties, so I don't actually see it - yet, at any rate. So in principle I don't receive any of that money to live off, and therefore still need help from the government. In practice, perfectly obviously it has always been ridiculous for me to be eligible for government assistance in the first place.

So I'm not saying "Poor Me". I'm simply saying "The tax credit system is really stupid and annoying, badly run, illogical, lacking in common sense, and scandalously wasteful." No wonder our country's so in hock.

Golden Monster

14/08/2014

I know everything about tow vehicles. For a start, that's what they're called. I learned all about them on Tuesday, and bought one this morning.

Some of the perceived pros and cons of different makes and models are, of course, personal; and some depend on where you live and the job you want doing.

First and foremost, after my recent experiences with the Nissan Terrano, I was after something reliable, in which I could feel safe pulling my two horses in their trailer up the hill past The Forest Inn. This has a One in Two gradient, is one car wide, and has a blind corner.

And I wanted a diesel automatic. It must cost less than £6000 and should have fewer than 100,000 miles on the clock.

As a result of these criteria, my search on eBay, Auto trader, Exchange & Mart, Pre-Loved, Gumtree, and something called 'Motors' narrowed right down to just a few cars in the country.

I believe Land Rover Defenders, Discoveries and Range Rovers tow better than anything - they're rated up to 3.5 tons, 'braked'. But I don't want any of them, because according to the on-line chat forums they're always breaking down.

I LOVE Toyota Land Cruisers.

Shoguns are man enough.

And then there's something called a Kia Sorrento, which the horsey ladies on the Horse & Hound website swear by.

By now I was down to about 25 vehicles in the whole of the UK.

So off I set yesterday to try out a Sorrento in St Austell, an Isuzu Rodeo (more comfortable, better turning circle, more reliable than the Nissan Navarro and Toyota Hilux I read) in Plymouth, a Land Cruiser in Exeter, and another Sorrento in Tiverton.

The first Sorrento felt like a big powerful box on wheels. "If you want a truly awful car that is a cheap means of towing 3.5 tons, this is the one for you," read the blurb. I quite liked it, but it got stuck in low gear 4 wheel drive.

The Isuzu (how do you pronounce that?) D-Max was golden. GOLDEN??!! Imagine me turning up in this F-off truck as big as a football field, at the Pony Club! I mean it's bling gone mad! Nevertheless, I got in it and it felt like a new car. 2006 reg with 69,000 miles on the clock, VAT included, used by one lady owner (the salesman's auntie) to tow her horses occasionally. A bit different from a truck used daily in the mud by a farm labourer wearing his hobnailed boots. Its size and power would mean that it wouldn't even feel a heavy trailer attached to the back, and stinky tack could go in the separate covered boot.

I was also very taken by the bloke selling it. He was a proper professional salesman - young and nice-looking in his beach shorts and flip-flops, chatting away like we were old friends about his family (his brother won the Grand National on Seagram) sounding oddly like a cross between Ricky Gervais and that tall west country cohort of his in 'Extra's'.

I am a complete sucker for professional sales techniques, and was particularly impressed by the clearly genuine pride he takes in his vehicles, pointing out everything that he felt wasn't 100%, such as a couple of scratches, a bald tyre, a lock, and valeting, all of which were to be sorted out the following day.

Then I went to see the Land Cruiser in Exeter. 1999 reg. It had rusty windscreen wipers, two tyres in need of pumping up, and looked old, sad and forlorn, even though it only had 99,000 miles on the clock. The seller didn't bother to return my five phone calls and wasn't there when I arrived.

The owners of the second Sorrento still haven't returned any of my phone calls, but in the description it says that the low 4x4 gear light stays on.

I reminded myself that the garage selling on my beautiful Range Rover insisted I paid for £3000 worth of work before they were prepared to display it on their forecourt. So I thought, "No, I am buying something in perfect working order from a garage which has given the car a full service and provides a three month guarantee." And went home.

Well you may remember my worry that I like people who don't like people who drive Range Rovers?

I've bought the Golden Monster. What on earth are they going to think about that?

Home Run?

17/08/2014

Yesterday I bought eight slabs of home-made tiffin tea cake for £5 from the local Bring & Buy sale - all they had, in fact.

I've packed it in cling film and put it in the freezer. Tomorrow I will buy some 'cookie jars' - if that's what you have to call glass containers for biscuits these days - and display my teacake in our Hexworthy and Dartmeet Rooms. I hope people don't eat it too fast, or that could get expensive.

I've done this because the B&B at the top of TripAdvisor's Leader Board of Dartmoor National Park's 183 B&Bs features a lovely close-up pic of a jar of bits of teacake, with a brown hand-written label attached on a ribbon, saying 'home-made chocolate biscuits'. And all its reviews refer to these delicious titbits. So I am going to copy them (only mine appears to be a bit on the soggy side). Otherwise on the face of it, there doesn't appear to be anything particularly special or outstanding about Dartmoor's new Number 1, which has somehow taken the place of the Apple Tree.

So my suspicion is that its owners are utterly delightful, and that they must offer an immaculate service, with delicious breakfasts with home-made compotes changed every day. And these nice owners, just like me, have presumably got wise as to how TripAdvisor works, and are using it to promote themselves for free. Good on them!

Meanwhile Wydemeet has been stuck in the Number 4 slot for weeks!

If you'd told me a year ago that we would reach Number 4 in just twelve months I would never have believed you. But now I know how TripAdvisor's system works - ie the computer checks out who's received the largest number of 5-blob reviews most recently - I am beginning to dream of the unimaginable possibility that Wydemeet might become Number 1 shortly!!!!!!!!

Wouldn't that just be completely amazing?!

So huge, huge, huge and enormous thanks to all of you who have helped us get this far. I am SO grateful! Your reviews really mean the world to me! I still can't quite believe the wonderful lovely gorgeous things you say.

Well. So wedding bells for me aren't looking in the least bit imminent. I was so hoping to end all this with "and then they got married and lived happily ever after." Perhaps 'TripAdvisor's Number One' might prove a fitting end to 'Surviving Solo'?

Coca-Cola

27/08/2014

TripAdvisor is like Coca-Cola, the sensible South African woman at the other end of the phone told me.

I had rung the TripAdvisor helpline to ask how to award myself a five-star rating; and to qualify for the 'romantic', 'family friendly', 'luxury' etc categories that line the top of their page.

The nice lady and I were chatting about how they measure the blob rankings, and she was explaining that it is down to a secret coding which nobody is privy to, just like the recipe for Coca Cola.

Meanwhile, to get myself a five star rating, I have to contact Expedia, she told me. And to get categorised, you need to have lots of the appropriate words quoted in your reviews. TripAdvisor's computers look for these key words, so the more reviews you have, the more likely you are to get categorised.

I contacted Expedia regarding the star ratings, and five days later they got back to me, and advised me to ask TripAdvisor about it.

Meanwhile, Wydemeet continues to languish in the Number Four slot, and I'm not sure what else I can do, other than entreating an entire family of four to write individual reviews for me (providing they enjoy their stay, obviously) and see if that gives us the boost we need! Or should I simply give in, acknowledging that there must be something in the Coca-Cola mix that we're never going to overcome, and we'll never achieve that Number 1 slot.

I've Fallen in Love!

18/08/2014

I could hear the throbbing through the bathroom window, and looking out, there was the helicopter approaching. This was my latest internet date dropping by for a coffee, circling the property, checking out the white tea-towel Sashka had put in the top of the horses' field to act as a landing strip.

We have had several visitations from friends in helicopters over the years. And every time, they never fail to cause the adrenalin to pump. Those little machines are just so loud, and their propellers go round so very fast; I find the whole thing hugely exciting!

The trouble was that I was still in the bath. Our definitions of what constitutes 'mid-morning' clearly being a bit awry. So strapping, tall, blonde Sashka had to go out to meet him. I bet he thought she was me!

He had described himself as being 68, but in fact, when I checked him out on Google afterwards, he turns out to be 73.

After we'd all waved goodbye I drove off in Ken, the Terrano, to swap him for the Golden Monster.

Well. I've fallen in love. I just LOVE this bling new car. It's unmissable. Unusual. Rather in your face. But steady, safe, reliable, practical, and does the job. Just like me.

I have never had a car so new. It's got a little gadget called 'Parrot' in it, which I dare say will turn out to be very useful when my children show me what it does; and I have worked out how to plug my phone in so I can listen to my own songs. Loudly.

And I can take this wonderful truck back to the garage for servicing at cost, while they provide me with a courtesy car.

It's so comfortable, and such a pleasure to drive, that now I'm doing the sums to work out whether it makes sense to give away Marvin the Magic Focus, and use the Golden Monster as my runabout instead. But all the tables on Google are in litres/kilometre so I can't work out the diesel mileage.

Dead

05/09/2014

"Just look at this brilliant thing!" I gushed.

The key in the lock went "click click click" and then nothing.

This was to have been my third outing in the Golden Monster. The children and I were on our way to Cornwall for the evening, to meet Judith and her new Encounters boyfriend, for a swim at their hotel, on the very beautiful, relatively ignored, Rame Peninsula, just across the river from Plymouth.

Tomorrow was Pony Club Camp Day, and Bank Holiday Monday. A two hour drive away, pulling both horses in their trailer, - the reason why I bought the Golden Monster in the first place.

We all quickly decamped into Marvin the Focus and off we set.

The next morning my two lovely guests, together with Geoffrey, who does all my mending, pored over the Golden Monster in the pouring rain, attempting to jump-start him from my B&Bers' brand new hire-car-Discovery, but to no avail.

So it was that the AA visited me for the tenth time in two years. I think I have probably reached the limit of my allowance of visits. The nice man started the truck OK from his powerful batteries, and then we had to leave him running with a brick holding down his accelerator, while I finished serving breakfast, found someone prepared to replace a 3 litre diesel battery on a Bank Holiday; as well as a farrier, because Mad Vegas had chosen this day of all days to lose a shoe.

Halfords! I love them! £126 and three hours later we were packing up the car; a farrier had been found who had driven over to us all the way from Torquay - what a jolly Bank Holiday he had had! - and I set off with the two horses and Faye to join fifty other children aged 10 - 18 for a week's camp in the Somerset rain.

I'm sure this was just a one-off blip on the part of Golden Monster.

Busy Bee

05/09/2014

Some of you loyal readers have been commenting that I've gone a bit quiet lately.

"Cat got your tongue?" one of you sweetly enquired the other day.

Well I've been busy. It was August.

On a couple of occasions I found myself serving seven people seven different things for breakfast, all at the same time. This made me sweat.

And won't be too attractive on telly, if Four in a Bed comes here replete with their full complement of B&B guests and I have to do that again, whilst being filmed, too!

Looking after this many people comprises a proper job. Full time. It is more than just a laugh. I have been working and earning like a professional, and there isn't time or energy left for silly fripperies like entertaining myself and you lot with pointless babblings on the net.

Especially when you've got a sprained wrist from a surfeit of house-work. That meant I couldn't exercise my horses, work efficiently, type efficiently, or even indulge in playing myself melancholic Chopin Nocturnes on my piano at the end of each evening. In fact the vague nagging pain made me feel a bit sick.

On top of which it rained every single day for the whole month.

My Turkish tan has entirely disappeared, leaving white wrinkles in its place, and I'm fast losing any fitness I had too.

So I've booked a flight to Barcelona. It was only £81 return! I think another holiday will be just the thing.

House of Love

05/09/2014

I had to meet Malcolm's new girlfriend last week.

He found her through Guardian Soulmates. She lives in Totnes. She'll be a crystal-polisher, then. She'll have straggly, unwashed, unbrushed, long thin hair with grey roots, wear floppy brown clothes all made from natural fibres, and on her feet will be hideously expensive, individually handmade, leather, Cornish pasty shoes. She'll exude the smell of musk, joss-sticks and what my son refers to as 'weed'. She'll be a Vegan Liberal Socialist (although if you ask me, there's nothing liberal about these people's attitudes to Daily Mail readers. Or people who were educated at Eton for that matter.)

Sigh. Better quickly mow the lawn between storms. And be late.

I roar up outside the quiet country pub in my huge bling truck, and quickly replace my bright pink wellies with more sober and tasteful sparkly blue flip-flops.

I walk in, there they are, and ping! She has something about her. I really like her. Immediately. Before she has even said anything. One of those unusual special people who exude an aura of calm, smiling, gently humorous, modest self-assurance. She's also got more hair than me, and is thinner, and trendier too, even though she is two years older. She's wearing undone little gym shoes with no laces.

She is so funny. She really makes me laugh. She and Malcolm feel to me like grown-ups indulging a kid, and I am allowed to be loud and to show off, and to be enjoyed. She is great. She is going to come riding with me soon. I am so glad that he is in such a safe pair of hands.

Ex also has a new girlfriend, predictably ten years younger than him, and apparently looking a bit like me only smaller. Faye gets on well with her daughter, and both my children like her. I had thought Ex would choose well when he eventually found someone whom he was happy to introduce us to. I have invited Ex to ask her to stay, but I don't suppose he'll be doing that in a hurry.

Just about all my guests are couples who seem very at one with each other. They either both completely get what I am on about, and love Wydemeet for its remoteness, beauty, comfort, peace, and amazing surrounding wilderness. Or they're both wondering where the wardrobes are and why there are bats in the trees. We've had an engagement and two pairs of honeymooners staying, in our first year alone!

Which leaves me. On my own. My love-life becomes ever more rubbish. I forgot to cancel Encounters, so I am still a subscriber to that, but Guardian Soulmates has recently run out. Just as well - the past three 'likes' I received came from bald men of varying strange religious persuasions. I emailed them back saying "I read the Daily Mail so I don't think you would like me."

Last night I sent a message to a hunk from Oxford who claimed to like all the arts, both highbrow and lowbrow.

I said, "What - even X-Factor?"

He replied with: "I haven't been lobotomised!"

I thought that was rather good so I came back with: "Pity, I love X-Factor. Clever you to be able to spell lobotomised."

Anyhow - this morning I discover that he has 'blocked' me!! I have never been blocked before. So I can't get back to him to explain that I am extremely civilised and erudite, despite my penchant for all things Cheryl Cole (or Fernandez or whatever she calls herself now). As well as Simon Cowell. He is a living legend.

My take on it is this. If you imagine you are at Exeter College with 2000 people of the same age and in the same kind of world as yours, and it's still tricky to find a suitable boyfriend or girlfriend, then it's no wonder that on-line dating can prove a bit slow, when there's only a handful of like-minded single, available people of the same generation living within a 200 mile radius of yourself. Your other choice, of course, is sheep. But they're nearly all ewes.

"So give it a chance!" my logical side says to my impatient one.

And I reply to myself, "Bring on Four In a Bed!

Wasting Time

05/09/2014

I have written five blogs today.

I've also had three mugs of coffee, and finished up two small slices of old chocolate cake designed to look home-made by the lady in Tavistock market, but actually she cooks them in bulk using margarine instead of butter.

But I've had no fags, Mr Lancashire Hot Pot. My most critical and loyal blog-follower.

And I'm not on a diet either. Big decision. I have agreed with myself - what's the point really? I would rather go out with someone fat, than starve myself for someone who at present doesn't even exist. Some people like me the way I am, anyway.

And all of this is despite my post-summer holidays ''to do' list being three pages long.

Because I am putting off 'It'.

'It' being the court's forms for my two litigious cases - one against the Okehampton garage who claim to have mended Bill the Shogun when they haven't - after all these months there's still a flashing little yellow light where there shouldn't be; and the other against BT. Both cases are scheduled to come up in court in November.

The whole process involves Small Print. Being Meticulous. Making yourself Cross. Urrgghh. Here goes.

And by the way. Who said this was an Indian summer? They're lying.

What It's All About

07/09/2014

Some time ago Ex and I reached a kind of truce.

It was based on the principle that if everything we do is in the best interests of the children, then there is no room left for argument. So we don't. Argue that is. Provided the subjects of Her, and Money, are avoided at all times.

I would like to imagine that this arrangement might work for many estranged parents, although I know it doesn't for those of my friends who made the unfortunate mistake of marrying complete nutters.

So as you've probably realised already, Wydemeet B&B exists primarily to fund the children's school fees.

These had already been covered once, but got swallowed up in the divorce, so I've had to save up for my half all over again. Bummer. Except that I've found that I like doing the B&B. And just as luckily, the children enjoy their schools. And the B&B too.

Never mind that 15 year Will occasionally can't have a shower because it's all been cleaned and made ready for guests. And sometimes he has to share his bedroom with his Dad, and not play his music too loud. And/or sleep in the shed.

He has discovered, rather to his surprise, that the people who come to stay tend to be rather nice, and he quite enjoys carrying up bags and making cups of tea and chatting to them. Most of the time though, our guests are asleep when he's awake, and awake when he's asleep.

Ex 'gets it' and does his bit too, without complaint. A set of guests once commented, "Gee I hear a polar explorer once lived here!"

I replied "Yes, he's serving your breakfast tomorrow!"

Today has been a bit of a red letter day on the children front, more particularly for Faye.

First, we had the hunter trial at the Pony Club.

Faye completed a confident fast clear round on my horse, Perfect Panda, and didn't cry once!

Meanwhile our new 'problem horse' Vegas WON!!! Out of a field of 31! Hah hah. That will show everybody who's so horrid about her. She should be called Marmite.

Later in the afternoon, bolstered by an hour's Disney Channel, Faye played Leonard Cohen's 'Hallelujah' on her flute, and hallelujah indeed! We now have Faye's potential music scholarship piece in the bag.

We're both going to bed very tired and very happy.

Uncle Tom Cobley and All

10/09/2014

One of the purposes of this blog is to help make sure Wydemeet's website remains high up and prominent in the Google Search Engines.

But I think that in order to do that, the blog is meant to feature on the front page, and to provide useful information, not this sort of drivel. No matter. We're high up enough already.

Meanwhile I thoroughly enjoy sitting here going on and on and on all about myself. Nobody is forced to read this stuff.

So, in order to do things properly, I should be including helpful info such as "On the second Tuesday of every September it's Widecombe Fair! Come and stay at our wonderful B&B from which to visit this Special Event!" (Never mind that to get there takes 45 minutes round the one way system.)

Well I forgot to include this useful tad of info in advance, so if you wanted to visit the Fair I'm afraid you're too late. It happened yesterday. You'll have to go next year instead.

At least this year Uncle Tom Cobley's mare was a mare and not a gelding. I think the last old grey 'mare' was so old that it died. This one belongs to my mate Venetia up the road, and was in her first year of standing around the large, noisy country fair, watching Morris dancers, and horses in fancy dress, from 8.30am til 5.30pm. She was very well behaved.

Anyhow, the point of this story is that Mad Vegas of the Rolling Eye, the Cross Country Champion, won A SOLID SILVER CUP for 'Best Local Hunter'!!

And my nervous little Faye, having begged "Can Louise (Sashka's daughter) ride her?" (to which I said, "No") came second in the Best Rider class! And, again, no tears either! Things are really looking up!

It would have been a perfect day, if only Twiglet hadn't bitten Norman's Racing Spaniel during the terrier race. Norman's dog had been winning up until that point. I've a feeling he's not ever going to speak to me again.

I Can Breathe Again!

11/09/2014

Yesterday I drove past Her house (I have to drive past it almost daily), hoping to see a 'For Sale' sign.

How incredible that in five years, what She has done has never been discussed between us, or even acknowledged, let alone apologised for, despite our being thrown together several times a week, and now it never will be, as the rumour is that She's off to London. Hurray!!

The new school merger has resulted in Faye finding herself being taught Latin by her favourite teacher in a class of her four best mates.

There have been other, less constructive changes at the school, such as the children being made to learn a song called "I love broccoli", in preparation for Harvest Festival. Give me 'Fight the Good Fight' any day. But by and large, I have never seen the school's remaining original teachers wearing wider grins, or cracking worse jokes!

Last Friday at a new school bonding drinks party, I ensured that I made the acquaintance of the new headmaster's wife, and then the overall new headmaster himself, who found himself stuck with me for 40 minutes. Where were all the other pushy parents I panicked, making more and more of a fool of myself, staring at his rugby player chest, remembering crying onto his predecessor's one on several occasions.

Eventually I made my excuses, seeking out the new head of the junior school, only for him to run away from me as he did last time I tried that. Not sure what it is about me. But I think that day I scuppered any chances Faye might have had of becoming Head Girl of her newly formed school. Sorry old thing. Pretend you don't know me.

Life Enhancer

15/09/2014

My goddaughter has just taken the best picture of me that I think I have ever seen! So what choice was there? I've re-subscribed to Encounters. After all, it's only £32 for a month, and could change my life for ever.

I thought you might be a bit curious as to how I've described myself on my 'Profile Page', so I am going to let you see.

WHY SHOULD PEOPLE GET TO KNOW YOU?

I'm good-looking, confident, clever, charismatic, sorted, solvent, sexy, posh, educated, easy-going, funny, cheerful, warm, , empathetic, decent and loyal, modest and humble.

WHAT ARE YOU LOOKING FOR?

You see the bigger picture. Clichés are not really your thing.

You are highly articulate, know what you want and like, and are so comfortable in your own skin that you don't care very much what other people think.

You are very strong and confident, with a terrific sense of humour and a ready, warm smile.

If you are a trifle egocentric, I don't care - you are entitled to be. I will respect you and support you, and together we can achieve the impossible if we feel like it - hand in hand. Or just eat scallops pronounced scollops somewhere nice - I hesitate to say 'in front of the fire'.

People will love us as a couple because we are friendly, funny, exciting and dynamic. I will enjoy that, but you won't be particularly bothered one way or the other.

etc

What do you think? I am hoping now to be inundated with messages. I'll let you know how it goes!

Name-ist

23/09/2014

I think you can tell a lot from people's names.

Most of the people on Encounters unsurprisingly have perfectly normal names. They send me delightful, charming, erudite messages and couldn't be nicer, better looking, more intelligent, or more charming. In fact of the many blind dates I have met, there's only one that I haven't liked. And no nutters at all, yet, anyway, as far as I can tell.

I've been dying to fall for all of them, but in my heart of hearts, I know straight away that it's not going to work if their name's not right.

I have a problem with names starting with 'K', and shortened names, for instance. These people almost always originate from a different tribe to my tiny niche one, and try as I might, always, always, always it seems that there's simply not enough common ground between us to make for a long term relationship.

They won't 'get' or enjoy my world. In fact they will be stultified with boredom. And at a complete loss as to why I spend such a ridiculous amount of money on school fees, thus ensuring that my children will never fit into the real world.

The other morning, my friends and I chatted for five hours about schools. When I visited the used-coffee room and surreptitiously checked my watch, it said 1.40pm, so I asked Diana what the real time was, and she said that really was the time.

It was my 55th birthday and we were enjoying coffee and birthday brownie-cake complete with those candles that you can't blow out. In the end we had to dunk the candles in the teapot before they set light to the hotel.

So I'm afraid I now seem to be name-ist, as well as height-ist, thin-ist (I don't want someone to fall over if I run over to hug them, because they are so titchy), fat-ist, and age-ist.

All of which cuts down my chances of finding true love to almost zero.

The other thing that reduces my success rate is that my potential suitors appear to really object to being lied to!!!

Well you know me. I am as honest as the day is long – eg at the North Pole on June 21st.

Until it comes to internet dating profiles. I put down that I am 49, so that I appear in other people's searches under 'Women aged 40 - 50'. I also said that I never smoke, whereas you know perfectly well - I like nothing better than sitting musing over problems accompanied by a very occasional supportive Silk Cut. Although I'm sure I would stop if someone really wanted me to (or if there weren't any problems). Unlike my Cava habit.

Finally I ticked the boxes for: I have no sense of humour, I wear bifocals, my favourite colour is brown, my favourite clothes are my Granny's cast-offs, and I sport a beard. I thought it was par for the course to make things up on these profiles, but it appears that I am upsetting people when they discover that I haven't got facial hair (not that much anyway, yet) after all.

But at the end of the day, all I really want is a bloke with a great big huge smile. Is that so much to ask?

It's a Hard Life

28/09/2014

So. £80 or so has bought me a return ticket to Gerona, and three days of doing nothing under a murky sun at one of the houses belonging to my Norwegian best friend (they call it BF now don't they?) Lindsey. This one is her primary residence. It's on a totally unspoilt part of the Mediterranean coast in Northern Spain.

And staying with her has turned out to be cheaper than being at home! I had thought. Until I discovered that Bournemouth Airport had charged me £105 for the use of their carpark!!

Whatever – it was a much needed break after the madness that is August in the B&B world.

"Please, Mary, if I drive the car up to the gate, won't you even come and visit the nudist beach just down the road? It's really beautiful and no walking involved..." Lindsey had pleaded with me. But I wouldn't budge. She thought I was mad. But actually I was just totally, utterly exhausted.

On my arrival, Lindsey had announced matter-of-factly that a Hollywood Superstar would be joining us for dinner. "I will have a shy-on," I fussed.

It turned out that the icon of glamour, now residing in this unknown corner of Spain, used to regularly stay down the road from Wydemeet. In a shack which makes Wydemeet look positively urban! It's called ' Little Sherberton' and is located at the end of a muddy track which goes through the rocks that comprise Neighbours' farm track, and beyond, across a boggy field. This mega-soap-superstar-household name used to be next door but one to me! How odd is that? She funded its new roof back in 1997, and she was even more famous then! I don't think even Neighbours had a clue who she was, as she drove backwards and forwards between civilisation and her hovel, through their cows!

After posting my new pic and re-subscribing to Encounters, all went mad, and those three blissful days in Spain were spent replying to 1000s of messages, or lying on a sunbed chatting to Lindsey, gazing at the view across the harbour out to sea.

Back to Wydemeet, two hours turnaround time to unpack, check emails, say a quick 'hello' to our new B&B guests, and off for a 7pm dressage lesson for Faye, horse in tow, an hour away. Bed at midnight again.

Lindsey I miss you! Can I come back?!

No Dogs is Good!

28/09/2014

Guess what. Someone has found this blog useful!! A first!

Whitelady House is a stunningly beautiful house near Lydford Gorge. It sleeps 12 people, and is run by my friend Kay, who has extremely high standards, and she has never received fewer than the full five blobs on TripAdvisor. Don't go there just because I have mentioned it. I want you here! Wydemeet may not be immaculate, but it is right in the middle of the moor!

Well Kay invited me to meet her friends the other evening at the Trout and Tipple, so they could pick my brains about running a B&B.

I started talking to this couple, but found there was nothing much left to say, because they had read this blog and I've put everything I know into it. They said it was helpful. Hurrah!

I have had one or two further thoughts recently, though.

One is that I have discovered my new 'No Dogs' policy doesn't keep people away. Quite the opposite! It attracts them! Other People's Dogs are a nightmare! Worse than Other People's Children! They bark throughout the night. They whine during breakfast. They have to be taken out at 6am, the tramping around disturbing everybody else who's trying to sleep. They smell, and pant in your face. They poo in the garden. And completely distract their owners who can't relax in somebody else's house even worse than if they'd arrived with a two year old toddler! Who wants to stay in a B&B stuffed with horrible stinky, hairy, muddy, Other People's Dogs? Yuck! So the answer is - borrow ours! Hello Twiglet!

Something else that has recently come up, is that not only is Wydemeet probably the best centre in Dartmoor for walkers, but also for fishing! Apparently you can spend a day happily trout-fishing the Swincombe, which is 100 metres from our door, for just a tenner, while your wife relaxes in the hot tub, reads a book, or chats to me. And I'm told that all the best seatrout and salmon pools, such as 'Queenies', are within a walking radius of Wydemeet. No need to get in the car.

No wonder the original owners chose this spot in which to build this fishing lodge! And I never knew any of that!

Yet only two fishermen have ever come to stay here, to take advantage of this extraordinary facility. Where are you all? I even have one of ghillie Brian's last home-made 'green flies' for you to try!

Another small point of interest came up recently, when some guests badly wanted to stay for only one night, despite our minimum two night policy. I suggested an extra 50% charge, which they were happy with, and so was I!

And what should I do about single people staying? Normally I don't deduct anything from their bills, but try my very hardest to ensure that everything possible is provided, and they can use the house as if it was their own home. I will even go out specially to do any extra shopping that they might need. Not a trivial matter from this location!

I guess I might have my arm bent if circumstances decreed.

I so love it that in running a business like this you are entirely free to make your own decisions and be as flexible as you like, completely spontaneously, responsible to no one. Every guest who stays is quite unlike any other - each has his or her own totally new agenda and requirements. Life as a B&B proprietor is certainly never dull!

What It's All About

29/09/2014

I had one of those moments the other day.

When you remember what it's all about, and why you bother.

I had been out for an organised evening ride on the western part of the moor near Tavistock, everyone was heading for home, and the time had come for Panda and me to turn around and return, alone, to our trailer.

Perfect Panda, who hadn't been out with other horses for months, was fed up that she had been made to go so slowly, for such a long ride.

As we turned, she leaped into a fast gallop, flying across heather, gorse, ditches, bogs and rocks, the sun sinking slowly behind us, and the colours of the moor gradually mutating from greyish into dark greens, yellows, oranges and deep reds.   I remembered how to go with the flow and not fall off, as we careered as one at 30mph, to the battered old trailer, loaded, and finally arrived at the oasis which is our beautiful home, uniquely located right in the middle of the moor, bathed in moonlight.

Sex Wax

29/09/2014

The entire house had begun to reek of coconut. It was becoming truly disgusting!

So I called up Will and said, "The entire house is beginning to reek of coconut. Why?" Will likes the smell of coconut - he thinks it smells of cool surfing, and I believe a lot of his Lynx products are flavoured with it. In my day, boys of his age used to have those little green bottles of Brut instead. I always kept my 17 yr old boyfriend's spotty neckerchief nearby to sniff, as it was drenched in the stuff, and to my nose the smell of Brut remains highly evocative and smells lovely! Old Spice isn't bad either!

Meanwhile, as far as I'm concerned, coconut smells of 15 year old son, and I don't want it wafting around the parts of our home that guests occupy.

Will advised me, "There's a small piece of cardboard hanging from the lamp in my bedroom at the top of the house. It's called 'Sex Wax' and you can move it to the Bothy if you like."

Well I did just that, and the awful aroma disappeared from our house straight away.

I daren't open the door of the Bothy again though, I might faint! At least it will no longer stink of tobacco and joss sticks. But I am now worried that this 'Sex Wax' thing's smell is going to start permeating around the garden and everyone will think they're on a beach!

Eating Ponies

07/10/2014

There's been a lot of discussion in the media recently about tucking into sandwiches made from cuddly wuddly Dartmoor foalies.

I think it was my mate, Charlotte Faulkner (her real name), who first went public on the subject. Charlotte founded The Dartmoor Hill Pony Association nearly twenty years ago, and no one could care more passionately about Dartmoor's ponies than she does. With endless loyal support from her extended family, she has devoted the latter part of her life to their cause.

I know quite a lot about marketing meat because I used to work for the British Turkey Federation, so I'm particularly interested in all of this.

In our promotional materials we would never use pictures of cuddly wuddly live turkeys. We had to completely divorce the idea of the cling filmed slab of cream fillet in the supermarket from anything that had ever been alive. I eventually stopped sending press releases to The Independent (the least independent newspaper of them all if you ask me - worse than the Daily Mail. At least nobody reads it except journalists) because they would simply use my info as a catalyst to call up their friends at 'Chickens Lib' (yes it does exist), and give poor old Bernie Matthews another roasting.

I have even turned down opportunities to appear on the Today programme, because I know they're just after a slanging match between the Turkey people and the veggies, which is never going to sell more turkey sausages.

So I was a bit horrified to see on our local BBC Spotlight programme a large slithery piece of red pony fillet being swirled around in a bowl of what looked like dark red blood, but I think was actually wine, interspersed with shots of merry foals gambling on the moor and licking tourists' ice creams.

However, on the Jeremy Vine Programme it was a relief to hear about 95% listeners talking sense.

The only two against grilled Dartmoor pony cutlets were both clearly barmy wimmin. They sounded quite mad before they'd even reached their bit about pony-eating.

Charlotte is clear about the real problem of not having enough ponies on the moor, which has been somewhat overlooked in most of the coverage. Ponies keep the moor in good order. They eat scrub - gorse, bracken etc - that even the sheep won't touch. With numbers of ponies down from 30,000 to 3,000 or something, the speckled warbler is apparently thriving - good for it, but being understocked, the moor itself is becoming ever less accessible for walkers, riders, cyclists, farmers etc, the heather is disappearing, and at the bottom line - it's less beautiful than it was when we first moved here in 1995.

The Dartmoor commoners continue to maintain some ponies. But a lot of the foals get shot, and fed to the hunt hounds, or their carcasses torn to bits by zoo animals. Why can't they be nicely packaged up for human consumption?

Unlike the millions of hot housed chickens and turkeys we consume, Dartmoor foals have a jolly, free life til it comes to the crunch.

Oxygen

08/10/2014

Today is Goosey Fair - an historical event put on annually by the attractive Devonian market town of Tavistock.

The first time I went I was rather hoping for a goose sandwich - I rather like goose. Makes a change from Dartmoor Pony, or turkey for that matter.

Well, there was not a goose in sight, I searched and searched. Instead I came away with five watches, all of whose batteries expired five months later, and a pair of slippers in Size 8.

The staff and Mums at Faye's school dread Goosey Fair, which is held on the first Wednesday of October every year. I'm the only I know who looks forward to its buzz and naffness.

Of greatest interest to me is the almost universal inverse relationship between precocious child and scary ride. Faye's best friend Jocelyn is a slight, gentle, very polite, obedient and intellectual creature, meanwhile determination and courage do not feature at the top of the leader board for Faye, when it comes to the hockey pitch or the cross country course.

And yet. These two, aged 10, insisted on queueing up for the scariest rides available at the fair. The tallest, fastest, highest, loudest one is called 'Oxygen'. Dorothy, (Jocelyn's mother) and I both felt sick as we stared up at our two little girls whizzing around backwards and forwards and upside down, 200 metres above us, laughing their heads off.

Their Alpha peers waited next to us at the foot of the horrifying, thumping, crane-like edifice, gazing up in wonder, a newfound respect emerging for our sweet daughters. Then they quietly slid off to their own favourite ride - one where you sit in a giant teacup and, very slowly, go round in circles.

So I'm off there again in a minute. I wonder whether the fairground people have managed to build something even wilder than Oxygen? Our two girls are beginning to find it rather tame, now they have reached the great age of 12!

The End?

14/10/2014

Google Analytics sent me an unsolicited email yesterday. It had some very interesting statistics in it (I think). They're rather complicated to understand, so I don't know if they're good or bad.

The email informed me that last month, out of 657 visitors to my website, 243 'exited' direct from this diary page. It's clearly not very good then. What an insult! Except presumably those 243 visitors must have read a bit of my incoherent pointless ramblings, before exiting in disgust. Unless most of these visits were from me, checking that no further boring comments had been posted underneath my pros, requiring instant deletion.

So I still don't know exactly how many individual readers we're getting, because I can't work out which button to press to find out. But my guess is that it's now quite a lot more than 13, though still none from my target audience of bewildered, bemused, broke people freshly dumped from a relationship they thought was going well.

The trouble is, riding along on my horse this morning, I couldn't think of anything new to say. Now we've done a year or more, the same old Goosey Fair, Dickensian Christmas etc are going to keep returning, round and round. But I have some news:

WE'VE GOT OUR FIRST RETURNS!!!!!!!!!!!!!

So after a little over a year's operation, our first returning visitors have re-booked for a weekend in November. They are one of our favourite couples. They were incredibly nice about it when we knocked their drying gilet, worth £120, onto the Aga and it melted. And together we finalised the names and content of our speciality breakfast of Eggs Florentine and Royale.

Well the whole thing is a birthday surprise, so I'm not saying anything more, but it represents a turning point. Some of our guests voting with their feet - in through the door, rather than out of it. How wonderful!

Just as well, because it would appear that I really have over-honed down on the marketing, so business is a bit slow and I'm going to go overdrawn soon, unless some miracle happens. I'm back in touch with the agents, so they can start taking all my money again. This is such a flexible business - you can turn it up and down, on or off, like the knobs on a radio!

Meanwhile Encounters has gone ballistic again. It is beyond me how the 'top twenty most popular people' cope, because I must be a long way off that, but I am being courted by several people 15 years my junior and can't really keep up! And highly erudite and flattering they are too! I am going to become a worse show-off than ever at this rate!

Relationship-wise, there won't be anything concrete to report for months, because it's not your business yet, so wedding bells are still not going to be the ending to this book, if it ever becomes one.

And finally, in the summer, Faye will start weekly boarding. What shall I do all day? Well that might just become the start of a new way of life and a whole new book perhaps!

So give me a sec, and I shall start looking into publishing this thing, and going mega-public. How exciting this is going to be! Can't wait!

Another Country

21/10/2014

Miles driven: 650; time spent driving: a couple of weeks; coffees consumed: 25; fags consumed: 25; taxis paid for because late for school pick-up for Beloved Daughter: 1; new boyfriends attained: 0.

MPG: 40!!! Result!!!

"We are from the same world, but inhabit very different countries."

I don't normally write personal stuff about any of you on this site, because I don't want people to stop communicating with me in case I go public on them.   But honestly, this bloke has made me so cross that this time I am.

Like a total moron, having corresponded with him for hour after hour, week after week, writing all sorts of hilarious stuff especially for him that could easily have entertained all of you, my numerous, lovely, loyal readers who support me through thick and thin asking nothing in return, I drive six hours each way to see him, and two days later I get dumped by text without even a "but you are pretty", or "thank you for coming all this way"!! I ask you! AND I had stopped off en-route for a quick spot of TK Maxx therapy, in Slough where I was born so don't be rude about it, but why on earth my mother couldn't have chosen Royal Windsor like she did for my siblings I will never know, and I have to admit to it on at least one form a month ... anyway, where was I?

So first I was hurt. Then I was a bit affronted. But all the time I knew he had a point, which I think he expressed in a rather perceptive and concise way, as opposed to a pretentious one. Which do you think it is? I have actually started using it myself, as a quick, easily understandable and not too rude way to fob off the 98% of inappropriate people who contact me via Encounters.

During our meeting, I had quietly admired his nicely ironed striped shirt, his shiny cufflinks, orange socks and light tan brogues. I thought they matched my Golden Monster rather well. And he was considerably taller and heavier than I am. I just love that.

So. Sigh. The thing is I belong everywhere and nowhere. I don't have a country. Anyone who isn't posh thinks I am. And anyone who's genuinely posh knows I'm not. And there's no-man's land in-between. So I think this annoying bloke has hit it on the head in a sentence.

My 'country' currently comprises a great deal of chat about private schools, swimming, riding, doing lunches, school run, watching children's matches and events; oh yes! And running a successful B&B business!

How do I provide time to make a man feel special in and amongst all of that?

Well – shortly the weekly-boarding-effect will kick in.

Or I may even have to give up Wydemeet and move. Or delegate more. Or become famous being interviewed all around the world about my amazing first book. Or move in with some other bloke.

Smells

27/10/2014

"Your house smells nice".

These were the first words that my friend's autistic son addressed to me, as he walked in through Wydemeet's back door.

Ahhh! Just one of the greatest compliments! Such a shame that it's not usually the sort of thing people say when they visit other people's homes.

I think different smells can be as mood-changing as different kinds of music, and I am verging on the neurotic about smells in this house.

"Dead mouse" is one that makes me freak out the most. Even worse than my son's Sex Wax.

Our best cloakroom, that all our guests come into the house through, has been smelling of dead mouse recently. What a way to greet them! The smell just wouldn't go away so I went mad on eBay, bidding for 24 bottles of pot pourri reviver, and three packets of rose, autumn mist, and lavender pot pourri's. I won the whole lot.

So I'm going to make quite sure that any smell of dead mouse is drowned out by dried bits of flower in future.

Living where we do, a mouse invasion is a constant threat, and they like to come in - between the inside and outside walls - when the temperatures are sub-zero. An immediate assault with poison is highly efficacious (God I'm sounding like 'The Scaffold' now). Apparently, having been poisoned, the wee mice go off somewhere to drink, and die by the water source and mummify in some strange way. Normally under our cloakroom floor it would seem.

I was also becoming extremely nervous about the smell of mildew finding its way into the main body of the house from my private new bathroom.

I favour carpets in bathrooms in this back of beyond location, to keep us all warm and cosy - which is fine until the overflow gets loose and starts leaking. My bathroom has a roll top bath, a silver-grey deep pile carpet (top of the range remnant from Trago), a silver and blue chandelier, and bright yellow blind. It is featured on this website and is much admired. I think bathrooms should smell as lovely as they look.

So I cut away the mouldy bit of carpet and slipped an ice cream container under the offending leaking pipe, only for the smell to get worse! After many, many days of this, shutting my door, persuading myself that I was making things up, I made myself have another search around for the offending source, and discovered that all this time the radiator has a leaky joint. Which also accounts for the fact that I am having to constantly prime the central heating.

And then I realised why the front cloakroom was smelling so horrid - a waste paper basket full of old McDonalds left-overs from the car, combined with a pile of horse rugs waiting to be washed in the utility room next door!

So I have spent weeks worrying over something that could have been put right in minutes. And now I've got to think of what to do with the 23 bottles of pot pourri reviver I have left ...

Rage Against The Answerphone

30/10/2014

I hate Radio 1. It goes tsch te te tsch te te tsch te te tsch irritatingly all the time in the background, while some youth with an unintelligible regional accent shouts above the racket using obscure teen language, interspersed with electronic noises with no tune and angry ghetto-speak rattled off more quickly than you can say 'supercalifragilisticexpialidocious' (correct spelling); impossible to sing along to, and entirely devoid of any sentimentality.

Yet Faye's Latin and English teachers, both as old as I am, enjoy it! They danced happily on the bar, to everything played during our school ski trip disco, whereas the only tune I recognised was 'Happy'. They have teenage children and told me that Radio 1 is good during the afternoons. But I can't miss Steve Wright.

I'm having a bit of an argument with the Golden Monster's radio at the moment. It doesn't seem to be very good at tuning in to anything.

So it happened that last night, at about 7pm, while I briefly gathered that Radio 4's Adam Archer appears still to be the only gay in the village, and I sadly missed Radio 2's Midweek Mosh, I found my ears being assaulted by someone ranting down a phone about her brother leaving butter and jam all over her table and floor. Then a Kiwi called 'Zane' shouted about how much he hates too much butter on his bread. Then someone else started yelling about how boring it is when people tell you about their dreams (couldn't agree more).

Next a little kiddie was screaming about how they're planning to make the school day even longer - "school, school, homework, dinner, bed"; followed by a teenage bloke furious at hysterical girls who wreck live recordings.

Now this is my kind of radio.

It turned out to be a show on Radio 1 where they encourage you to phone in and 'Rage' at their answerphone. All compered by a charming, clearly well-educated and civilised young man, with a very nice voice and gentle sense of humour, whose father is a teacher.

So I've got a plan. I'm going to ring that answerphone myself and 'rage' to it about how much I hate Radio 1 going tsch te te tsch te te tsch tee tsch and not playing any proper music with tunes.

Meanwhile, the smell of dead mouse in our smart cloakroom has intensified. It appears not to have been old McDonald's leftovers causing the stench after all. I now have the area surrounded by three potpourris, a vase of real live lilies, and a very expensive reed diffuser. But even this army of aromas is unequal to the battle. I fear some floorboards are going to have to come up.

Nine out of Ten Judges Prefer Me

06/11/2014

Dah-doing, dah-doing, dah-doing went my heart at 180 beats per second. Sorry. Minute.

I paid another little trip to the Ladies.

I have often been told that it doesn't show when I'm nervous.

I hoped it didn't show now.

I was outside Court Room No 2 waiting to be called in by the judge, sitting in the same small room as my adversaries.

"Odd," I thought. "I feel just like this when I'm stuck in the same room as my Nemesis, only I don't hate them as much as I hate Her. I just don't want to look at them and will pretend they don't exist."

My next thought was, "This must be what being on The Apprentice feels like."

The internal phone rang.

"Hadow vs Doodah. Lord Whateverhisnamewas will see you now."

We followed the receptionist lady into an intimidating room with My Lord sitting way above us behind a barrier on a sort of platform at one end, surrounded by microphones and other paraphernalia.

"You may sit down," the elderly gentleman from my sort of world commanded from his stage.

"Yes M'Lud" gushed my ex-garage-man, a short, fat, t-shirted version of Uriah Heep.

Well the outcome was always obvious. Two hours later his judgement was that the garage should keep Bill the knackered Mitsubishi, and return the £2500 I had paid them despite their not repairing him properly, plus £275 I had paid in court costs. Just as anyone could have predicted. The whole thing was a complete waste of everybody's time, money, and nervous energy. A pyrrhic victory. I did not in the least feel like jumping around grinning and punching the air, as they wrote me out my cheque. Instead I felt like hitting them. Stupid, thick, idiots.

What was most interesting to me about the whole experience, was how the garage man's bottle blonde girlfriend streamed lies - so many that I couldn't keep up and remember them all when it was finally my turn to be allowed to speak. Under no circumstances may you interrupt either the other party, nor the judge. And if you start writing things down you can't keep up with the rest of the c..p.

Amongst 1000 other things, she claimed that my "man friend" and I had both been aggressive towards her, that I had thrown the car keys at her, and run out of her office. In fact I had thought that my "man friend" - an internet date whom I'd met twice, who had very sweetly agreed to accompany me into the fray, and was keeping out of the way near the door - wasn't actually as supportive as I had expected he might be. Meanwhile I had left the keys in the car for the garage to check out what was still wrong with it, and drove off with my very kind and generous date, who has since turned into a good friend, for a delicious lunch at the Mill End Hotel outside Chagford, in his sports car.

I think, though, that she believed every word she was saying, while even the judge appeared to be raising his eyebrows slightly. He termed my encounters with the garage staff as "unsatisfactory" and it was fairly clear to me that he had a pretty good idea of what had actually transpired.

I wonder whether hours and hours and hours and hours and hours of court time are wasted like this.

I hold my hand up and put the problem down to education. The pair were just, simply, massively THICK, and I can't hate them for that. I know that I am privileged to have received a first rate education and am automatically at an advantage.

I have now won nine of the ten of my small and middle-sized claims. These include the cutlery company whose 'lifetime' silver plate went green after less than a year; two plumbers; BT (twice); a holiday company who neglected to supply an aeroplane home, a removals company who left behind half our belongings, and whose lorry we had to push up the hill in the snow; and an ex-friend for whom I bought a horse, who sold it without telling me and sniffed away the proceeds. Most of them were already bankrupt and knew just how to avoid the bailiffs, so I haven't necessarily received compensation, but I do feel that they have had some sort of comeuppance.

The case I lost was the burglar alarm company who charged double their estimate without checking first that I would be prepared to pay that much, so I didn't. They sued me, and I now have a credit rating problem because I was on holiday when the order arrived telling me to cough up.

So my question is, why am I the only person I have ever met who gets herself into these situations? I may be blonde (a real one!) but I won't put up with people treating me as one. Because my sense is, as I think I've said earlier, that they will treat other people like this, who are less able to look after themselves, such as my Mum. I absolutely do not enjoy the process. But I won't have them getting away with being so hopeless and/or so horrid. So there.

Hey ho. I can relax now. £2775 to put towards my child tax credits bill.

Hairdressers

10/11/2014

Continuing on this litigious theme -

I think you ought to be able to sue hairdressers. I blame my ex-hairdresser for my divorce.

Why would he want to make me look like a bloke?

In the Spring of 2008 he cut off all my hair without being asked to, and then told me that I would look like all the eventers I admire most - like Zara Phillips, Mary King etc. Well if he had asked me whether to cut off all of my hair I would have screamed NO! NEVER!!!

Throughout my childhood my mother used to take me to the local (very cheap) barber for haircuts, and/or cut my fringe herself, really short.

Being an athletically built strong, tall sort of girl, the result was that everybody thought I was a very plain boy, and despite my best efforts, I never managed to become a teacher's pet. Clearly I have never quite recovered. I still really love it if a teacher actually likes me!

Anyway, every time since, whenever I have tried having short hair, it has ten times out of ten been an A1 catastrophic disaster! Yet this plonker went and did it without asking, and charged me for the privilege.

Well guess what. Less than twelve months later I had no husband.

So I went to the head hairdresser at one of the biggest national chains, and asked him to sort me out.

"Whatever you do, don't give me layers, or I end up looking like Linda McCartney," I said. So what did he do? Gave me layers. Without telling me. So I never realised that he had. And what did I look like? Well I can tell you that every morning I looked shorn, as the few wispy bits he'd left at the ends disappeared altogether.

Fast forward a few years; Ex has gone off, and I've got no money, so I gave up the luxury of a master hairdresser and risked a cheap place in Tavistock instead. And guess what.

"We need to grow out these layers," she said. Well I'd wondered why my hair always looked so awful in the wind and in the mornings, and now I understood why.

And it's taken four years, FOUR YEARS!!! to grow out the stupid layers. That I'd forbidden the bloke to put in, in the first place! We finally achieved it last Wednesday. At last! Hurray! They say age is just a number. Well I think it's just a hairdresser. Thanks Charlotte! You are the first decent hairdresser I have come across in 54 years!

Last Post?

10/11/2014

Hmmm. I'm wondering whether business could be brisker? Is it just that it's November and it's raining again?

Or could it be something that I've done?

"You never want to see how laws and sausages are made," wrote one of my potential internet dates the other day.

Re-reading what I have written recently - well its hardly how you would normally advertise a B&B is it?! And I call myself a sales-person!

May I just reassure all potential guests that Wydemeet is the most utterly, wonderful, fantastic place to stay! 47 x the full five blobs in just one year, giving us TripAdvisor's top ranking for any B&B in central Dartmoor - well. Golly wow!

I am so massively proud of our home and the service that we offer. Our little team tries its absolute hardest to make sure that everything is immaculate at all times.

Meanwhile, attempting to provide light-hearted, quirky advice for anyone thinking of setting up a B&B, which is what this blog has been mostly about, and then putting it on the same website as marketing that B&B is actually, in retrospect, completely nuts.

So, potential guests, please bear with me, and be assured that everyone visiting Wydemeet has an incredibly memorable, enjoyable and relaxing stay - as far as I am aware anyway. So do come!

And, once we've discussed all the best nearby eating places, you've popped out to experience for yourself the magical wildness and beauty of our immediate vicinity, we've talked about what you'd most like to get out of your stay, and what you'd most like for breakfast, where and when; you'll be prepared and braced for whether you want to hear any more of this kind of drivel!

The second explanation for slow business is because of the inefficiency of the booking agency. I think I have rung them five times asking for them to reinstate me on their site. I have even advised them that I won't pay their latest invoice until they do so, and had no response as usual.

Well yesterday I discovered why their company appears to have gone a bit wonky. It was national news on the radio that they are being targeted by fraudsters claiming to be accommodation providers, taking deposits for bookings, and disappearing. Well. Fancy! But right now I need them! Please reinstate me! All is forgiven!

So this diary has been performing rather a lot of functions over the past year or so. Whilst it was primarily intended as a Self Help Guide for the bemused, broke and bewildered coming out of relationships, wondering what the future might hold, I'm not sure a single person like that reads it!

I have a feeling that not very many potential guests read it either.

However, it's certainly proved useful to give potential internet dates a clear picture of what they are letting themselves in for with me.

And various friends check in and out in order to update themselves on progress here.

But all of this has meant that I have to be pretty careful about what I go public on.

So now I've had a new idea.

I think the Search Engine Optimisation of this site is already pretty good, so it probably doesn't need a regular blog - and if I find out I am slipping down the rankings by not contributing any longer, I can update it with banal observations on the changing seasons of Dartmoor. All is going golden brown at the moment, by the way.

Meanwhile, I thought I might now change to a more secret, fewer holds barred diary which could be published at a later date, so hold on to your seats guys!

And in the meantime, thank you all, so much, and goodbye. I will miss you. It's been tremendous fun. I have enjoyed sharing the progress of my life and Wydemeet B&B with you so much.

With love to you all

Mary xx

And Finally....

Here is the thank you letter sent by my 'Returns' shortly after their stay (for those graphologists amongst you, you may be interested to know that the writing is of the highest possible form level, it shows a narrow stroke, it's written in black ink pen, on two pieces of thick A4).

November 2014

Dear Mary, Faye, Panda, Vegas & Twiglet

I just wanted to say an enormous thank you for helping to make Amanda's birthday weekend such an amazing experience. We both came down believing it would be impossible to top last year's experience, but we certainly did manage it. Despite the appearance of a B&B, the weekend felt like home from home and was like staying with friends – which we now consider you all are!

Thank you so much, and in particular for supper on the Saturday. It was lovely to be able to eat with you in the 'heart' of Wydemeet, especially after such an exciting day on the moor. A 'Cook' meal and wine is an unbeatable combination.

My biggest thanks go to Faye for looking after Amanda whilst out riding. Amanda might be a good horsewoman, but without your expert reassurance that galloping over such rough ground was OK, she'd certainly be worse for wear, and I'm sure would have popped off!

Have a wonderful Christmas and New Year and look forward to meeting up again, hopefully, in the depths of Dartmoor sometime next year.

With love…

∞

Unplugged!

∞

Me Back!

10/11/2014

So hello, hello, I'm back again! (don't worry, I'm not Gary Glitter)

How nice to be here! Back blogging again – but this time on a secret website, only available for viewing to you very few, very special friends who are privy to the secret code!

It's been nearly a year that I've had to watch out what I said!

Maybe it wasn't such a good idea outlining the pros and cons of setting up and running a B&B in front of my potential customers' noses! It was certainly a struggle, thinking how to phrase things so as to keep it interesting while not putting people off coming to stay!

So I've given up the struggle and gone private. And now I can put down what I really think, no holds barred!

And then when it's done, give it to a libel lawyer before hopefully putting it all into print. And possibly making a lot of people jolly cross. But hey ho! What the Hell?

So here we are again, and the reason I've gone private is this.

I am thinking seriously of selling Wydemeet.

And the main reason why I'm thinking of selling is because I am worried about my beloved Faye becoming socially marginalised, rather as I have felt over the past twenty years.

A secondary reason is that I appear to have set up this B&B business in order to have people paying to use rooms that I wouldn't otherwise need, and can't afford. Basically the house is too big for just Faye and me, so we won't need B&Bers if we move to something smaller.

You have heard me moaning about being a Pariah before.

Well it all came to a head last Friday, Hallowe'en. Faye had a disastrous day at the Pony Club Show Jumping Competition, getting eliminated for three refusals at the second jump, having waited five hours for her turn to go. Driving back she was desperate to go to the Pony Club Hallowe'en Party - thirty miles in the opposite direction, for which we would arrive 1 1/2hrs late, exhausted.

"I have only been able to have three Hallowe'ens in my whole life, because of where we live!" she cried.

We hadn't yet come across anyone else planning to attend the party, because the three 13 year old girls who live within a three mile radius of our house were already having a party of their own; the girls at the show-jumping competition already had something going on; as did Faye's normal group of friends from the Pony Club who mostly live 15 miles west of us, within a couple of miles of each other, they all go to the same school, and all have matey Dads as well as matey Mums.

So when we finally reached the Hallowe'en party we were dismayed to find just five people there, knocking around in the cavernous village hall. Faye bravely went in, while I sat in the local hotel until the dot of 9pm, when I whizzed back to collect her, and found her looking distinctly disconsolate by the entrance. No friends, and the boy whom she thought liked her, having walked straight past as if she wasn't there.

We returned home to find Will almost comatose with post-party exhaustion, and therefore not in a very charming mood.

"Why do we live here anyway?" he queried. "Why can't we live near Granny in the middle of Dorset where all our friends are? What's the point of driving all the way out here all the time?"

Well. Maybe he's right. I have been hanging on to Wydemeet in order to give the children stability and continuity. So if they now don't want to live here, I guess it's time to go.

Wydemeet is the most utterly wonderful family home. You provide your own nucleus within the local community - which has varied from idyllic to dysfunctional and back again over the past twenty years. You have a natural 'fit' with the other families. You don't feel weird throwing large parties for everybody in the hamlet. You give, and are invited to Sunday lunches and dinner parties with other families from the posh school, who are dotted in a circle, of which you are at the centre, all around the edge of the moor. But as a single Mum the entire structure collapses and you and the children are left bereft.

On Saturday nobody was interested in X-Factor except me, and both children complained that I made supper late and it was horrible leftovers as usual.

Worst of all, on Sunday I smacked my nose so hard on Vegas The Mad Mare's neck that I think I have broken it. Anyway, I went all funny and giddy and morose, and cried when nobody was looking, between making everyone 'Breanner' - a cross between breakfast, lunch, tea and dinner, before Will went back to school. I could hardly stand up, but got reprimanded for providing turkey breast. Apparently they only like chicken. Agh!

And now I look as though I have been the victim of physical domestic abuse. A huge dark blue swollen bruise has appeared nowhere near the source of the pain - slipping halfway down my cheek to join the wrinkles. Thanks a bunch, gravity. And no amount of Clarins Honeycomb Foundation (Medium) can hide it. Everyone keeps commenting. Grrrrr.

So. There we have it. An unusually horrid, thought-provoking weekend.

We've got to move.

Shattered Dreams

10/11/2014

"It's not the location, it's the social life, isn't it," commented Ex.

It's so annoying he buggered off with my ex-friend, Her - five or more years ago now. I always felt we were much better matched than most married couples. And now everything else has fallen over like dominoes.

I had pulled into a lay-bye to fully appraise Ex of my moving plans, in order not to get arrested, and I didn't hold back - letting him know that I thought a lot of the decision to move was because it has proved untenable, or un-sensible, or simply stupid, attempting to remain in the middle of nowhere all on my own, when it had been so do-able as a family unit.

Our shared dream had been to create a home for our two children for life. So that when they were asked where they came from, they would always straight away say, "Dartmoor." The family home would always be here, and they would know that they could drop into the local pub anytime and bump into old mates they'd known since they were born.

Accordingly we sent them to the local babies' group, two local toddlers' groups, local pre-school, and local primary school. I would often take them to pre-school myself, rather than leaving it to the nanny, and I put myself on its committee. Initially nobody even turned around when we entered the hall it was held in, and no one ever started a conversation with 'blow-in' me. My children were regularly left out of the others' social activities, and I had never felt so invisible. Over the years, though, gradually the locals grew to understand that we weren't about to move back to London, and the committee proved to be one of the most effective groups of people I have ever worked with; and the most fun!

Disappointingly, our immediate neighbours, despite having children the same gender and almost the same age as ours, never embraced us as family friends. Tears used to drip, plop, from my eyes onto the concrete as I mucked out the horses, feeling their lack of interest almost palpably flooding down towards me in waves across the river towards us. I dare write this, because they would never dream of picking up a book by boring old me!

I just couldn't think of anything I could do to change things. I felt that the next door Mum and I should have been living in each other's houses, sipping endless cups of coffee together like sisters, we had so much in common - but it was not to be.

When Ex went off, it seemed very few people gave much thought as to what it might be like for me, being a fifty year old Mum left alone in a large house in the middle of nowhere with two young children and no money. The other Mums continued driving past my gate to visit

Neighbour, but seldom, if ever, dropped in to check that I was managing OK on my own.

Over the years things have improved, but Hallowe'en was an indication that our social situation is precarious. I have invested two decades of my life into living here, in the middle of Dartmoor. It was a very happy place to be as a nuclear family. But face it, Mary. Being here alone is just not really working. I am too busy, and have too many friends elsewhere to feel lonely. But I feel marginalised by the happy families. I've struggled and railed against it. And now I give up. My dream is well and truly over. I have failed.

So I think we should move towards Faye's new school in Tiverton. Where we can both get properly, instead of marginally, involved with the horsey set, through the school, the pony club, and the hunt. I will join the David Lloyd Health Club where I am already friendly with several members, and the men are hunky; and should all else fail, I could even get involved with my old university again - Exeter. The wheel turning full circle, 50 years on!

Oh - and maybe I could join a rock'n'roll club! How exciting it all might turn out to be!

Wood!

09/11/2014

Oh you are so patient!

Can you really bear having to hear the whole background "why I'm having to move" rigmarole? You are not the only ones to suffer.

Firstly, I ran the whole thing past Malcolm's new girlfriend, when we were out riding together the other day. She thinks it's an excellent idea to move. I hope she likes me and isn't simply being kind, listening quietly to a relative stranger going on and on and on.

Then I called my sister. I always do what she says without question. "Before you go on," she says, "I think it's a great idea." Well that was fairly straightforward and rather quick. Bloody Hell. I'm going ahead. Yikes!!!!!!!!!!

So now I've got to sell this house and buy another.

How?

Well marketing is my thing, so I thought I'd have a go at doing it myself! I wonder whether I will manage to?

My belief is that everything sells through Google now. Ads in the paper and those expensive property brochures could be a waste of money these days. Meanwhile, with my B&B marketing experience, I ought to be able to get Wydemeet to come up first for anyone googling: "Houses for Sale Dartmoor". And if I fail, well, it won't really have cost anything. I would really, really get a buzz from getting myself up higher, or better SEO'd than the professional estate agents! Watch this space! We will see!

So I'm going to make a website selling Wydemeet, very like my B&B one. And I can tell you now, I won't be including this blog on its diary page!!

The one problem is that outside my gate is a sea of wood reaching to the sky! All hill farmers have to diversify in some way or other if they are to survive. And in my neighbours' case, they have invested in a sawmill. The trouble is, their farm is on the other side of a narrow bridge. So literally hundreds of tree trunks have been dumped outside my gate where they stay, year after year, and every year the piles get higher, deeper and longer until my home feels as though it is drowning behind them.

I don't like making trouble, but if someone is going to fall in love with Wydemeet, something will have to be done about those logs. I am going to have to have a meeting with the neighbours to discuss it. Oo-er.

Meanwhile I have been looking at what I might buy. A clapped out house to improve, in a smallholding outside Exeter - with easy access to both children's schools, my Mum, old friends, new friends, Dartmoor, the sea, equestrian centres, the health club, the university, cinemas, shops, garages and a Rock'n'Roll club. They exist on Zoopla. Now I must go and find one ...

How exciting!

Selling On Line

23/11/2014

This website-making thing.

It's taken ages and ages and ages and ages and ages. And it's given me a headache.

But now it's done!

You will find Wydemeet for sale under "www.house-for-sale-dartmoor.com".

I've had quite a lot of fun doing this, actually, copying my friend's house-selling brochure, combined with my own brand of humour/observations. Have a look and see if I succeed in producing a wry grin from you!

For the immediate future, I am giving AdWords another go. So if you google something such as 'properties for sale dartmoor' up I will pop as an ad. Try it! But please don't click on it as that will cost me 40p and eat into my daily budget of £3 max.

So far 73 people have clicked the ad, which has set me back £29.78. I expect they're all estate agents checking out what's on offer, as nobody has contacted me about my unique Dartmoor offering as yet.

The ad goes: Dartmoor House for Sale. www.house-for-sale-dartmoor.com. Freehold, Remote, Walkers Dream. Hexworthy. 5+ Beds. Guide: £995,000

I have spent several hours dreaming up words and phrases which will ensure that it pops up a lot, for people looking for property on Dartmoor. The AdWords analysis advises me that the most effective phrases they've tried are 'houses for sale dartmoor' (11); 'for sale dartmoor' (12) and 'houses for sale in dartmoor' (10). So it's hardly rocket science and I really enjoy trying to second guess what people are going to go for.

I have already reduced the price - from £1 million 'offers', down to £995,000 'guide price', because I thought it sounded better. I can't see any other properties being sold privately. As bad as the law courts. Everybody pays so-called experts to do these things that they could manage perfectly well themselves. Maybe there's a reason why nobody else appears to be doing what I'm up to, which I will discover after three months of no enquiries, and I'll go grovelling cap in hand to Knight Frank or whoever.

I keep checking whether the google 'spiders' have done their work so that Wydemeet pops up on its own, without the assistance of AdWords, but no joy as yet. I think it takes about three weeks until your website finds itself a place on the net.

I have also contacted Zoopla, who haven't replied. I think they're probably only interested in representing proper estate agents, but I will call them again tomorrow and find out.

And I've been in touch with the property search people my sister recently used to find her mansion next door to Downton Abbey. These people are completely in touch with what is going on property-wise in their area so, for a commission, are able to offer properties to people before they come onto the open market. So we'll see if they're prepared to work alongside someone like me, who isn't represented by an agent. They wouldn't charge me anything for selling my house, so that would be a mega-bonus! Fingers crossed! Watch this space!

Girlfriends Everywhere!

23/11/2014

My life is weird.

Last Friday I had dinner with Malcolm, his new girlfriend, and another friend of mine.

And the next day Will brought his new girlfriend home for the weekend, and Ex brought his new girlfriend and her children over for tea on both the Saturday and the Sunday.

God, all this Love. What about me? I couldn't be working harder at finding it (more about that later, now we've gone private!) But I'm getting absolutely bloody nowhere still!

Anyhow. I received lots of advice on Friday. One smidgeon was - on no account to start upsetting my neighbours. Apparently there is now a clause in property contracts about neighbourly relations, so to make them cross would be really stupid. Any anyway, argued my friends; the sort of people who would make a fuss about the wood are the sort of people who would never buy my property in a million years.

So instead I have emailed my neighbours advising them that they are the first to know of my plans, and please could they possibly keep the wood and mess to a minimum, and be nice to anyone making enquiries. (And please would they buy Wydemeet so I don't have to work any harder to sell it) was the undercurrent of my missive, but perhaps they don't have £1 million handy right now.

Meanwhile I had a lot of fun with Ex and his new little family. They are delightful. Two little girls who get on so very well with Faye that the three have just the most lovely time together, and I wanted them with me as much as possible, succeeding in encouraging them to stay and use the hot tub, rather than going off to the public swimming pool, while their Mum, Ex and I chatted together over a cup of tea. Or was it. Ex had made it for me and I couldn't tell whether it was tea or coffee. And then I realised.

"I think you put coffee in it, and then forgot and added a teabag," I suggested.

"Would I do that?" he replied

"YES!!!!!" his girlfriend and I responded in unison.

I think she and I are going to have some fun!

Blocked?!!

23/11/2014

I have been 'blocked' again, by the only bloke on Encounters who currently looks as though he might be suitable for me! How dare he?! How very dare he?! So rooooooooood! I haven't even blocked my troll Peter who has been genuinely rude, as well as boring which is an even more heinous crime!

So I am racking my brains as to why this bloke, who calls himself 'ruth69er' or something, would do such a terrible thing. I liked the look of him a lot because he has a broad grin in every pic, doesn't use clichés, and comes from the same sort of background as mine. Well there's clearly something about me that he doesn't like at all. I suspect it's my great age.

I discovered this shocker as I was idly glancing at my iPad during a break from X-Factor - its third outing this weekend. X-Factor's first airing is at 8pm on Saturdays. Then there's a second showing on ITV+1. And if you've forgotten to record it and still missed it, your third chance to catch it comes at 3pm on Sundays, shortly before the results get announced in the evening. Followed by "I'm a Celebrity".

Call me a Reality TV addict. I won't mind.

Anyway, I have just popped up to my office to continue putting this blog-book together, and up has popped another Lonely Heart. This one says he's 6'3" tall and promises to provide the 'strength, excitement and charisma', to my 'loving, thought and care'. He is even prepared for the new woman in his life to be 'high maintenance'! Probably into S&M or something. No doubt we will find out. But he's put a zing back into my step after that rotten rejection!

Oh dear. The reply has pinged back. He's called Brian. The last two respondents prior to him were called Clive and Ron. At the risk of upsetting some of you readers, I'm afraid I just can't entertain the thought of potentially spending the rest of my life with a man with a name like that. Is someone at Encounters having some sort of a joke with me?

I Hate Christmas Cards

24/11/2014

Mid-life crisis isn't just men going off with their secretaries - or their wives' friends - or whatever.

I've noticed other recent changes too.

For example, a lot of my mates seem to be moving house - I suppose before becoming too incapacitated to create a new and final community for themselves for their dotage.

I've just come away from a hurried two hour coffee break with Jilted Juliette who, like me, is also finally giving up on the family home – eventually of her own volition, after five years of seeing children through day school, threatened eviction, and wondering what is going to happen next.

All this moving is most annoying, as it means I've got to make endless changes to my Christmas card list. Why can't everyone stay in the same place??!

At the moment there are 418 people on my list (not that they've all remained friends, or are even necessarily still alive). I have everyone listed on Microsoft Excel, and to my shame, every year I print off address labels for Christmas cards - in italic comic sans to make them look as much like real hand-writing as possible.

But even still, I find the palaver of producing, writing and sending out Christmas cards takes days, and is ultimately a time-wasting, expensive, pointless exercise. And receiving them is just as bad. Either you prop them up and they all fall over in the wind whenever anyone opens a door. Or, if you're like us, you stick them up on a piece of ribbon, so that after you've lived in your house for twenty years, you've got twenty drawing-pin holes at the top of the wall in patches around your fireplace and door frames. And then, being paranoid, when Christmas is done you count them, to discover that you've been sent far fewer than you sent out; and then you throw them all away in huge black sacks.

Every year I try to get a relevant personal Christmassy picture of some sort printed, so that the card brings with it a sort of intrinsic message, meaning I don't have to bother with individual written ones. But this year, again, it hasn't snowed, so I haven't got any snowy pictures to use, and I don't know what to do instead - meanwhile time is marching on.

Not only are people of my generation moving house, but also they seem to be having reunions with friends from decades ago, as we have a little more time to ourselves, and enough money to get ourselves around a bit.

For instance, for the first time in what seems like a couple of decades, I am now free to play, every Thursday night, while Faye boards at her prep school. So it is fun dreaming up treats for myself as how best to use this special window of opportunity.

Last Thursday I went to London for supper. With my sister and three old friends, all neighbours from my childhood, all daughters of Eton housemasters. In the olden days, 45 years ago, ("Were you a Victorian, Mummy?" asked Faye, not so long ago) we were able to run or cycle around to each other's houses, crash through the front door and shout up the stairs for our mates.

We had tea together every day having walked home from school in a group. The destination of choice depended on where you could guarantee to be served cake and chocolate biscuits, and watch 'Bewitched', ideally on a colour telly (not at our house, sadly).

We threw each other's Sindy's and Tiny Tears's out of the window onto the tail-coated boys below, and took our dogs for endless walks. Nobody knows every inch of the playing fields of Eton better than I do.

Since I last saw these three girls, I have been married for nearly twenty years, and subsequently divorced. None of them ever even met my husband, although they would have been invited to the wedding. Meanwhile they are all approaching their thirtieth wedding anniversaries!

But otherwise not a lot has changed. One was involved with the first production of Spitting Image, one was a high-flying banker who married another banker and gave up work in order to look after her boys properly. I thought she was her immaculate elegant mother when she opened her front door - she was about the same age as her Mum was when I last saw her! The third, whom all the Etonians were helplessly, hopelessly in love with, remains the sweet, beautiful creature that she was when she was twelve.

And all this, just a week after my oldest, best friend of all, another housemaster's daughter who lived literally next door to us for ten years, came from Kent to stay for a night, to reminisce, and to ride my mad horse Vegas.

So it would seem we are come full circle. The upside of being 50-something. Just a few more wrinkles.

In a couple of Thursday's time I am to receive the ultimate treat! I am joining a Blind Date from Encounters at the Races in Taunton, and then being taken out to dinner by him. He must be a gambling man! I hope he's got the odds right and is not disappointed by me!

Eighth Most Expensive Thing on eBay?

25/11/2014

Oh dear. Give me an unexpected hour to spare, and I do something stupid.

Mad Vegas has lost a shoe so I can't ride today. It's foul weather out there anyway - cold, grey and rainy. Typical Dartmoor November.

So instead I'm sitting here and I've put Wydemeet on eBay. I wonder what will happen. It's the eighth most expensive thing on the site. The most expensive is a house in Knightsbridge, on at £4,500,000. We come just under a beautiful looking place in Cornwall which has its own riverside quay.

eBay charged £35 to list Wydemeet, so it would be good if it sold this way. Although rather surprising!

My next wizard wheeze is to phone up The Week and suggest they list it as 'Property of the Week'. They can only say 'non'.

How Rich Are the Booking Agents?

25/11/2014

I have bitten the bullet and re-signed up with a booking agent.

Business over the winter months has become too slow, just using my own steam - even though we remain Number 4 on TripAdvisor, and Top of the Pops if you google 'Luxury B&B Dartmoor" - above all the proper official companies and agents and everything!

But over the winter it would seem I still need to depend upon the services of the professionals.

So I rang them. And rang them. And rang them. And rang them. I left message after message after message. And would they sign me up again? Would they cocoa.

Meanwhile I had lots of lazy lie-ins. But was beginning to get frustrated. And a bit poor.

I think that they can afford to behave like this because they are absolutely raking it in while all they have to do is sit on their bums.

If you think about it, say they've got half a million properties on their books.

And they take 15% + VAT on all bookings, even if just one booking lasts a year! They are BY FAR my biggest expense! That's why I hate them so much!

Say somebody booked for 7 nights, my second biggest expense would probably be the laundry, if I bothered to change the sheets and replaced the towels once mid-week, which would cost £26. But my mates at the laundrette work jolly hard for their living! Meanwhile I would be paying out around £140 in agency fees and tax to the agents! And that would just be for one room!

If you do the maths, if the booking agent has half a million properties with, say, five bedrooms occupied every night, at an average of, say, £100 a night, well how much does that come to? It's gone off the scale on my Neanderthal calculator which is just showing me an 'e'. I'll do it a different way. £50 million!!!! For operating a website and an accounts department from an office! Have I made a mistake somewhere? And a lot of their staff can't even speak English properly! And I don't think they ever actually set foot in most of the properties on their books.

I find the whole thing absolutely extraordinary. Fascinating. Appalling. And rather worthy of respect!

100 Potential Husbands

25/11/2014

Say I have met 100 potential husbands through this internet dating lark.

Of them, 97 want a relationship with me, but I don't want one with them; and the only three that I like aren't interested in me. It's a long haul of a roller-coaster and isn't good for my sleep patterns, nor Cava consumption. But I haven't given up yet.

And at the moment I am on a rather exciting 'up'!

There's my scouser who's asked me to the races. In his picture he looks identikit to Malcolm on a particularly good day. Which is where any similarity ends. Malcolm comes from one of the grandest families in the land, and is very politically correct. Meanwhile my scouser only drives Range Rovers and wrote 'bugger the planet' to me in his first email.

Having said that, he claims to do more than anyone to save it, because his business is fitting new homes with insulation, and is the biggest company of its kind in the country. So Big Respect to him. We chatted for an hour or so. He runs lots of businesses, believes in delegation, and so has time to play. Interesting. I do so like a self-made entrepreneur. But I have never succeeded in having a proper relationship with anyone even solvent in my entire life, so is there some catch to all this?

Will the private school thing matter? His children are at private school near where he is based - bloody miles away - in Worcester.

Then there's RunRabbitRun. He's not very smiley in his pics, but is very good looking, so I think it might be something to do with his teeth. He comes from E Sussex and has just sold his 30 acre smallholding after 20 years, so is in the same place life-story-wise as me. His son and daughter both had horses, so he knows one end from the other. His son's at Bournemouth Uni and he's coming to visit me very soon - he loves walking on Dartmoor.

Jago is very tall and good-looking, quite fun, and quite earnest. I think he's going to be disappointed by how not sweet I am. But he has been warned! I'm having dinner with him on Thursday, after having had lunch with Peter - my good looking charming date with the sports car, with whom nothing is ever quite going to happen. We are friends.

Finally there's TreeHugger, who isn't quite what he seems. Not a Gruaniad type at all, but in charge of felling a quarter of a million trees in one afternoon somewhere near Basingstoke. He is really, really, really funny. Tall. Aged 58. He and I both have high hopes. But every first phone conversation can prove a real killer. Eeek! Watch this space!

As you are gathering, I am travelling further afield these days, in search of love. Now that I am approaching Stage 3 of my life, moving, giving up the B&B etc, I will find it much easier to get away, and will have more time on my hands for you know what. Hopefully. I hope the men concerned believe me when I say I can travel, and that they are finding the whole thing as difficult as I am. That perfect person just around the corner appears to be most elusive.

And then finally, finally, I am meeting Little John from Taunton again, for the second time, during Faye's flute lesson tomorrow. He is only 5'7" so I wear high heels to make him feel worse. Actually that's not the real reason. It's to make me look better. I met him through Guardian Soulmates when they had a special offer on. He doesn't read it either - prefers the Telegraph.

Anyhow - the AA says it's 6 minutes and 40 seconds from Faye's lesson to the very nice hotel where we meet. Little John buys me one Spritzer for £9.30 and a packet of crisps. That leaves us with exactly 45 minutes and 40 seconds in which to drink and to chat. He is really delightful, very charming, and full of flattery. I can't get enough of that. Like a tyre with a puncture that needs constant inflating. The short chaps are nearly always the most jolly.

So all most exciting, but be prepared to be deflated, like my tyre analogy. We are all beginning to get used to this internet dating bollocks never working, aren't we.

Success on eBay

03/12/2014

Well it took 24 hours.

I received an enquiry from an eBay customer about my house. Oh ye of little faith.

It turned out to be from a land agent-type selling company who said they would put it on their books and market it, and put it on Zoopla. And this wouldn't cost me anything as it is their buyers who pay their fees. Whoop di doo! What's to lose?!

So now I'm on Zoopla even though they only list estate agents' properties!

That's the good bit.

The bad bit is that I've only got 19 days and 22 hrs left on eBay, and while 507 people have 'viewed' Wydemeet, I've had no other bites.

Meanwhile, the Google 'spiders' haven't worked their magic yet, so if you put 'house for sale dartmoor' in the search engine, Wydemeet doesn't appear. Instead you can buy 'wreck of the week' which is a Duchy ruin which was for sale a couple of years ago.

So I will have to continue paying for AdWords - a bill of £59 for 164 'clicks' so far, but no enquiries, boo hoo.

Talking to friends about my decision to sell, 95% think it's a good idea for me to do so.

"You've given it five years, and you haven't been pushed out, you've taken this decision on your own terms upon finding out that living on your own in a large property in the middle of nowhere isn't really for you. Do it," advised Malcolm.

"Don't do it! Will will soon realise that a Dartmoor address is the coolest place to live in the world!" exclaimed one friend who has lived in Dartmoor all her life, has a solid marital relationship, and isn't concerned what others think or do, but is entirely self-reliant. Her own house is even nicer than Wydemeet!

But Will never goes out of the gate, and Faye only goes onto the moor on four legs. And Yours Truly only ever ventures out of the garden to collect the bins.

With my current selling system I am free to change my mind at any stage, but perhaps the final straw came yesterday.

Vegas With The Mad Rolling Eye had lost a shoe after a 30 mile ride across the wildest, bleakest, boggiest part of South West Dartmoor on Saturday, and my dear farrier bust a gut to get it put back on last Monday, so that I could go out yesterday. Riding the creature is scary enough; loading her into the trailer on her own is even worse.

I summoned up my courage and called ' Neighbours' to see if they might pop down and help. They called back to say that they were too busy.

So that is really the reason that I am going.

Come on and do your work, Zoopla!

Tick Them Off

03/12/2014

Every time I meet a date appears to mean that I can now tick him off my list. They just don't cut it in the flesh. Unfortunately.

So Jago arrives in his mini cooper. He climbs out and he's nice and tall but oh no! He's wearing a white polo neck jumper! Bye!

Less than a week later a convertible Porsche glides up the drive. Werrhay, result!!

In his blurb he says he is 5'11" so I am in my stiletto's. I should have realised that if he was really 5'11" he would have put himself down as 6'.

I stride out to greet him and his eyes are in line with my chest. He is a runner, lightly built, wiry. I come from rowing stock. I am big boned - like Diana used to be. I probably weigh two stone more than him.

And he has booked into Prince Hall Hotel for two nights! Oh no!

The only ones left are now TreeHugger; and Kodak the Brummy/Scouser. I can't really tell which one I'm going to like more.

TreeHugger is a clever chap from Winchester. He's never been married nor got any children 'that he knows of'. But he says 'heck' as opposed to 'fuck', so I suspect ours isn't a match made in Heaven. I'll find out on Saturday anyway.

Kodak, on the other hand, gets me.

I asked him what he meant by referring to me as a 'proper bird' and he said: "Forthright, unique, articulate, fun, interesting. Many things but mostly wanting to be a woman, not wanting to be 'better than a man'. By laughing with us, not sneering at us (men)."

Well, that had me walking on air for a day, but since I emailed him to ask him how much he weighs, he's gone quiet...

Ground to a Halt

03/12/2014

I was getting a bit annoyed by a potential B&Ber who appeared incapable of booking herself in online through my website for the first two nights of 2015, who kept bothering me with unnecessary emails and phone calls.

Eventually, in exasperation, I went into my Booking Online page myself, put her dates in, and discovered that the system was, for some reason, telling all prospective customers that all rooms were completely booked, forever!! No wonder business has ground to a total halt!

I whisked off a furious email to their Customer Relations and then rang them up.

As I ranted they checked my details and told me that I had neglected to put in any prices for any rooms beyond the end of November 2014.

Ooops.

The customer services lady was extremely patient, and very professional, as I grovelled, and metaphorically washed her feet with my hair.

How stupid can I be.

So I am welcoming the couple who were so determined to come and stay at Wydemeet that they took the trouble to call me, with enormous gratitude, and hope their stay might even exceed their wildest expectations!

I Hate (other people's) Dogs (reprise)

03/12/2014

I think your own children and pets are always nicer than other people's.

I am pleased with my new 'no dogs' B&B policy, even though I have just discovered that I have paid AdWords £5.86 for the keyword or phrase 'dog friendly accommodation'. I must put that right straight away!

If I like my internet dates, and they're not an embarrassment, I tend to allow them to take me to my mate Fi's utterly wonderful Prince Hall Hotel, up the road. This is one of the perks of being a single girl/old woman. Until embarking on this dating lark I was beginning to despair of ever being taken anywhere nice ever again for my whole life!

Anyway, the other day, after exquisite amuse bouches, sea bass and raspberry parfait, my date and I withdrew to the bar area where there was a cute little ball of fluffy 14 week old border collie pup.

Its owners politely asked if it was OK if they let it off its lead. Bleeding, and with a hole in my expensive sheer stomach-pulling-in tights, half an hour later, I regretted our acquiescence.

Somehow, with dogs everywhere you look, the hotel doesn't smell, there are no hairs, no mud, and no barking. I don't know how she does it. But I am certainly not going to try.

And I still believe that there will be an overall greater demand for my B&B as a result of my 'no dogs', rather than 'masses of dogs' decree. We will see. At the moment there is absolutely no demand at all for Wydemeet, so perhaps I have got this wrong! But it means that Faye and I are having a rest, and I am getting rather fat.

I've just received an email from Four In A Bed saying they definitely want to use Wydemeet if they get commissioned for another series. I am quite pleased about this, although I am quaking in my Size 9s if I'm going to have to cook loads of different breakfasts at once, depending on the programme's format at the time.

I feel that between us all, me and my little team have now got most things working quite nicely, and looking quite good. My latest eBay purchases were two pretty little teapots to go in the two best bedrooms - rather than expecting my honoured guests to make tea from a teabag in a mug.

And if my competitors still manage to find a 'curly' between the mattress and the mattress cover, well, tough shit.

Skin

04/12/2014

'Will might have something useful for staying warm while riding in this hurricane,' I thought to myself, and pottered up the attic stairs to raid his drawers.

Sure enough - I pulled out a black and yellow slimy sort of garment made of plastic and put it on.

It slurped up my body so I could hardly move. I had to sort of peel it on, and its sleeves came right down, half way down my hands.

I thought it must be something that they wear these days under their wetsuits.

But Faye advises me that it's called a 'skin' and accounts for the black bits you see on rugby players sticking out below their shorts.

It smells.

But. I say. We went out on another of the wildest, bleakest, highest parts of the moor, somewhere beyond the Avon Dam towards something called Red Lake. No fun. And seriously cold. But I could tell that this garment was 100% windproof, while everybody else was chilled to the bone.

I think I must research a 'skin' made for a woman's shape, that fits, and doesn't smell. It was really, really good. I am so modern.

Broken

12/12/2014

I've got a broken nose, two broken arms and a broken foot. All because of that stupid mad mare called Vegas. First it bonked me on the nose with its neck; then I knackered my arms grooming it, and then it jumped on top of my foot, which is now very fat with a purple imprint of a hoof across the top of it. If it doesn't stop hurting I might finally have to go to a doctor, but I can't imagine what they would do about it.

So in the meantime I have been flat out with hacking, dressage comps, swimming, lunching, Christmas cards, ensuring Faye wins her scholarship, forcing her to perform every night in every production the school puts on at the end of term for practice, selling my house, selling my B&B, selling my holiday rental (all to no avail currently thank God), and meeting internet dates.

And here I am popping out the other end!

I met TreeHugger last week, in the carpark at Keyhaven, outside Lymington, and commented how odd it felt to be back 30 years later, after sailing here with an old boyfriend. Well, TreeHugger knew this boyfriend's brother, so we went to visit them. Found their house, left a note, and proceeded on our very merry way in the sunshine catching the ferry to Hurst Castle, a lovely walk back along the sand bank, and lunch outside, *outside,* in December!!! on the roof terrace of a wonderful cafe in New Mitford or somewhere, a little further along the coast. TreeHugger thinks I'm like Downton's Dowager Countess, using something called Aphorisms all the time, which means that I make weighty remarks based on zero evidence. Well that sounds about right.

Yesterday I hobbled out of the carpark at Taunton Races to meet my Scouser solar panel supplier. He's an ex-racehorse-owner. We have had a very large number of laughs in our correspondence. He sounds like the mirror image of me, even if he did leave state school aged 14 and live in Asia for a long time. And was married to the girl in the Special K ad. He only sleeps 5 hours a night and is very full on. I finally retired at the end of the day's racing exhausted by his company!

It is a bit less effort with someone of your own ilk, so I'm driving all the way to Winchester tomorrow, to meet TreeHugger for the second time. His messages make me laugh and laugh. He likes experimenting with 'Vibrant Purple' and 'Earthy Orange' in his emails, and we appear to have rather a lot of friends/acquaintances in common. OMG. What will he have heard about me from them?!

And then – assuming Peter doesn't work out for me, I'm hoping he might be right for my mate Judith. I've put her together with him – he's my favourite date who came with me to the Horrid Garage. I'm hoping they will end up skiing happily together in Zermatt shortly.

So, today I'm thinking there's a lot of fun to be had with this internet dating bollocks, as well as the head-messing of it.

Hiccups

15/12/2014

Ooops.

I really do seem to have gone too far with pruning down my internet marketing costs.

Having said a temporary goodbye to the booking agents; a permanent goodbye to lovely Sawdays, and totally ballsed up the booking system on my own site, I've had no punters for weeks now, and no more are due til January 2nd!

Phew! Or I would have gone mad, or collapsed with exhaustion, or had a stroke or something. Lucky I don't completely rely on my B&B business for my livelihood. But nevertheless, I'm feeling a bit poor! And massively insulted by my unpopularity!

Also not a single enquiry about my house for sale on eBay. Nor via the land agent people who have it on Zoopla.

Except. For.

A rather cross email from some bloke who has somehow stumbled across my public blog and seen a copyrighted picture of his being used on the B&B and land agents' sales websites.

Uh oh. I really hate upsetting people, when everything is supposed to be so jolly. I've emailed him in a hopefully pacifying manner, and am currently wondering which pic he's referring to! I've used loads after googling 'Swincombe Images' - I hoped they were all so low res that they were fair game. I've already been fined once by Image Bank; I wonder what's going to happen this time!

And another little online social event. A previous owner of Wydemeet has contacted me, very sweetly offering me two pics of the house to buy. We are having lovely reminiscences - her son (now 45) is delighted and relieved to know that what they called the 'chalet', and we call the 'Bothy', has reverted back to its original use: as teenage boys den, complete with its lava lamps.

Well. So I am having grudgingly to come to the conclusion, that perhaps I am not such an oh so brilliant marketeer after all. Mind you - my blurb on the dating sites appears to be having the right effect! I'm inundated again!

Getting to Sleep

18/12/18/2014

As I was nodding off, my head about to crash onto my desk, I thought I heard him say, "I could talk you to sleep.."

WHAT???!!!!!!!!!!!!!!!!!

This was the so-called charm offensive of some internet date calling me from Plymouth, whose 'username' I would give you if I could work out who he was.

I had answered the phone with: "Is this NoButYesButNoButYesButYesButNo?". Well the answer was no.

I had thought he was somebody else going under the username of "NoButYes". Some time ago, this one had blocked me when he had read in my blog that I once had a cigarette a decade ago - his no-compromise area.

But it wasn't NoButYes calling, and naturally enough the anonymous bloke at the end of the phone was a bit perplexed by my question. So he started going on about something else, and he really was talking me to sleep. No wonder he's still single!

Meanwhile Guardian Soulmates has sprung to life with two extremely erudite and articulate fans materialising within two minutes of one another, so I sent them the same reply, saying that I like the Daily Mail, X-Factor and Jeremy Clarkson. I am now massively frustrated that neither has got back to me as a result.

In the meantime, TreeHugger has become a very good friend - everyone will like him wherever he goes because he is clever, funny, and self-deprecating. He's also tall and very fit, eg he cycled 2012 miles around the UK in 2012 for charity. But it's not going to happen. He is properly hearty, whereas I will only use a portaloo if there are horses involved, and even then I will be grumbling all the way there and all the way back. And he punches me on the arm with enthusiasm, whereas I am supposed to be oozing mysterious sexuality, not being somebody's blokey mate.

So, meanwhile, you are allowed to think that I have become addicted to this internet dating lark and gone a bit mad. I would agree with you.

Encounters runs out tomorrow, and I only signed up to Guardian Soulmates because it was 50% off this week, meaning that just £16 could change my life forever!

I really, really, really would like to share my life with someone. But who that someone is going to be is proving most elusive!

It Should Have Been Andrea!

18/12/2014

I am desolate.

I have been gunning for Andrea of the big voice, short legs, beard and jolly Christmas jumpers, all the way.

And if not him, then for Fleur, who did a faultless rendition of Bruno Mars' current Number 1 hit.

But Ben won X-Factor. Boo hoo! Too many pre-adolescent girls voting for white van man, just because he's tall, sweet, genuine, and modest. But I'm very much afraid he'll soon be forgotten, hopefully unlike Andrea and Fleur. One Direction, Rhydian and Sue Bo don't seem to have done too badly, and none of them won.

And then there was The Apprentice. The lovely Irish girl went, because it turns out that her low calorie, filling, delicious, upmarket ready meals, using an ingredient so far unknown to man, actually already exist.

Well as far as I'm concerned, there can never be enough low calorie delicious upmarket ready meals. So I'm sure there's room for more. But Lord S's business team was in agreement on this one. What a pity.

I'm afraid to say that Reality TV is what I like best. So I am delighted to inform you that Channel 4 rang yesterday to let me know that (surprise surprise not) 'Four in a Bed' has been commissioned for yet another series, and they were just checking that I am still available.

My B&B - the truth!

19/12/2014

"God I don't care about the B&B!" I exclaimed to TreeHugger, when he suggested that I might get upset if somebody criticised some aspect of my fledgling business on Four In a Bed.

"I will just do absolutely anything for my normal guests to make sure they really love their time here - like drive three sides of a square to collect them if they overdo it on a walk, or collect something they need from the chemist ten miles away, or make the tea or coffee hotter or colder or however weirdly they want it, graciously with a smile - or let them cook stuff in the kitchen, or play the piano badly all day.. but if they find a 'curly' between the mattress and the mattress cover well, that's just life."

But this momentary lull, actually weeks now, of no guests, has proved most relaxing. If things go wrong in the house these days - well who really cares?

In the current hurricane, the new motor on the gate has proved so robust that the gate has ripped down the granite wall that it's attached to, and the motor is still humming. The 5 bar gate is at a wonky angle, struggling limply away, up and down, for odd periods of time, like a dying animal, in the torrential downpour. Lovely farmer down the road says he'll fix it for me. Thank God for that. And meanwhile I needn't freak about how guests are going to get in and out.

Last week I had no water for four days. That was because my wonderful new plumber, Gary, had mended the tap in Dartmeet that didn't work, and fixed the leaking radiator that caused a smell of mildew, but hadn't realised that if you turn the water off, you have to press a small button on the side of a box in the tack room to turn it back on again.

He has come back and found the button, so we've got water at last, he's mended the central heating in the sunroom, and taken up the floor in the cloakroom to unearth what's causing the smell there. No - not a leaking waste pipe from the loo. A total mouse warren! Nest after cosy nest made up in the lagging surrounding the central heating pipes under the floor! So it's the smell of their poo and wee and dead bodies that keeps wafting up through the floor boards! Right under Twiglet's bed!! What to do? I have no idea. We have put down lots of rat poison, so presumably shortly the smell will get even worse as the entire colony quietly perishes under our stockinged feet.

During the summer we had two much more serious incidents going on that I couldn't write about on a blog on a website advertising Wydemeet as a B&B.

Last Spring I turned on the tap in Hexworthy and the bath filled with black bits. "Just a rotten washer," I was cheerfully advised by my plumber. A few months later and the same thing happened in Bellever. But Bellever's is a new tap. Not a very good one, but it's new.

Shortly after that a man insisted on coming from the council to check my water supply. I already have it checked once a year by a lady who arrives in the kitchen with lots of gear. I was so rude to him that Will made me apologise and offer him a biscuit. After the visit he sent me a thirty page document repeating everything that I had already told him. There didn't appear to be anything major to worry about, so I breathed a sigh of relief.

Some weeks after that, I was cleaning my teeth and I thought the water smelt funny. I summoned over my children, and then my plumber, they all sniffed, and nobody agreed. But nevertheless I started putting out bottled water in my guests' rooms.

Fast forward, I was washing my face in Bellever's basin, looked in the mirror, and it was covered in small black furry bits.

"EEEEEEEEEEEEK!" I summoned a plumber urgently from Ashburton. He said he couldn't do anything about it.

Finally I tracked down Gary. He turned on the tap and out came bits of tiny bone and feathery stuff. "Aaggh! I've got people coming to stay on Friday! Please, please, please check those water tanks that I have been asking and asking various people to cover for me, for the last year and a half!"

So up went Gary into the roof, in pitch darkness, took a breath, and plunged his hand down deep into the nearest water tank. Bingo! Quick grab, a splosh and a plop of something into the washing up bowl he'd taken up with him. Half a dead bat. I've drunk the other half.

We flushed out the system as best we could, and I bought two water tank lids off eBay...

A month later the water-checking Lady was back with her specialist equipment. I had butterflies for the next few days until her report arrived. CLEAR! Phew!!!!!!

But that's not all! Your life is shortened by the stress of being a B&B Proprietor.

It's a lovely hot sunny day, after a long gorgeous warm spell, and I have my record of seven guests staying, as well as Ex and the children. Very full house.

Ugh. What's that smell wafting about, as I'm trying to sunbathe in the garden? Cow? No - it smells more like human. Poo. "Pleeeeeeeese don't try sunbathing or using the hot tub right now!" I am silently begging my guests in my head. I ring the number I've been given in case of crises with the cesspit, which had been emptied relatively recently. It was originally built to deal with a village, when the house was used as an Adventure Centre. It is a huge double green concrete and plastic thing, which you can only get to by chopping your way through a forest of bamboo - the only plant that thrives up here.

Well, £350 later, the bloke told me that there must be another pit somewhere, which should drain into the plastic thing, and sure enough, a bit more bamboo hacking later, and he has found a mire of black stinky sludge. An overflowing cesspit that hasn't been emptied for twenty years!

Thank God my guests went riding instead of sunbathing, and we could deal with it quietly while they were out.

They don't write about such things in B&B guides. So I've written about it for you here instead.

Oh, and did I tell you about the night when I was coming upstairs at about midnight, to find Hexworthy door open and my guests jumping up and down on the bed in their pyjamas?

That time it was a bat flying round and round their room.

I got a double sheet and threw it over the stupid thing and we were sorted. But I think that was the one and only time that I received just four TripAdvisor blobs.

There must be a bat colony hanging from the eaves outside Hexworthy. Since then, I have advised guests to only open the bottom window during the summer.

How nice to have been able to share these secrets with you at last. I have felt terrible keeping this stuff to myself over all these months!

Lonely This Christmas

23/12/2014

I turned down three offers of £2500 to rent out my house over New Year. But got none for Christmas when it was free and empty. And then I discovered that my friend Helen, who is also a jilted wife and has a similar sort of place to mine, just outside Widecombe, turned down three offers of £2500 to rent out her house over Christmas, but would have been happy to vacate over New Year. We really must communicate more effectively.

My little family's Christmas was spent at my sister's new pile in Berkshire.

On Christmas Eve I limped in to Newbury's Mole Valley and Sainsbury, to buy last-minute stocking presents for the children, and then went on to A&E - the first moment in two weeks I've had to have my foot looked at, since Loony Vegas jumped on it about six weeks ago – around the same time as she broke my nose. Row upon row upon row of empty chairs, and lots of signs saying 'queue this way' above empty echoing corridors. There was only one other person in the whole building. Interesting how nobody's ill when there's important shopping to be done. I sat for hours watching a special Christmas edition of Shrek until finally they took an X-ray, declared my foot 'fine', and sent me home advising me to stock up on Ibuprofen.

Meanwhile, having cleared the ha-ha of mowing cuttings, unwittingly dumped there over several years by the polish couple from the cottage next door, my extended family shared a delicious 'Cook' lunch together, and then all relaxed in my sister's beautiful new drawing room, in front of the vast open fire, sipping coffee, listening to the Kings College Carol Service - an eight foot proper Christmas tree bedecked with real candles as well as electric lights, twinkling in the hallway behind them.

Because I was the only lone adult staying, I found myself sleeping on a mattress on the floor, and subsequently on one of the many sofa's, in order to avoid having to share a room with Faye and her night-long eczema scratching. Just think – if I had succeeded in finding myself a boyfriend, I would have qualified for a vast double bed in which we could have made mad passionate love all night. In total there were 14 extended family spread in various beds between eight bedrooms; leaving poor old me on the sofa in the telly room.

I came into the kitchen on the first morning to find two husbands making tea to take up to their much loved wives. So I made myself an instant coffee and went back to my lonely sleeping bag.

Then that evening my sister was thoughtful enough to put a few things into a little stocking for me. Everyone was very kind and sensitive towards my plight.

A well-to-do Berkshire village provides a stark contrast to a mid-Dartmoor dysfunctional hamlet. On a beautiful frosty sunny Christmas morning we joined many others in the walk to the village church (actually I drove in the Golden Monster because of my squashed foot), to find it completely packed, almost entirely with people we had been at school with, or our children were at school with. Every Dad was in a tweed jacket or suit and tie. And the organist's day-job is assistant Head of Music at a top public school, so he was really rather good! Unlike the alcoholic who plays in the village down the road from Wydemeet, where you have to concentrate hard to recognise what carol the dirge is meant to be this time.

I loved it all! Sometimes I would give my right arm to live somewhere where I am surrounded by people just like me!

Eat My Shit

02/01/2015

The lights on the plastic Christmas tree are flashing away as directed by their electric chip.

The fire is crackling in the grate.

And Faye and I are enjoying New Year's Eve in, alone together.

"I wish we'd been invited to a party," she sighs wistfully, laying her pretty blonde head on my lap.

Two years ago I discovered that my South Hams gang - my best friends around here, or so I had hitherto believed - were all celebrating together, even including Ex and my children, while Malcolm and I were left rotting on top of the moor in the Forest Grim with a crap band and six other people, having a few days earlier asked my South Hams mates to join us there, if they were short of something to do. In despair EP and I gave up on the jolly pub and joined Jools on the telly to see in the New Year. I cried later.

Well not this year.

"Perhaps we'll organise a party ourselves next time," I reply. "You can't expect people always to ask us out, if we never have parties of our own. Now. What would you like to eat most in the whole world for supper?"

"Packet macaroni cheese," is her all too predictable request. This will be the fourth night running.

Well I choose Lidl's frozen De Lux Prawn and Scallop Cassoulet, and we settle down in companionable silence in the cosy sitting room to watch Chatty Man chatting arrant nonsense on his sofa. Except out of the blue, 12 year old Faye suddenly asks if we can turn to an award-winning arty film on BBC 2 about black home-helps in Mississippi in the 50s. One of the servants had served her racist mistress human poo in her meat pie. Urgh. Anyway - how impressive of my daughter is that? Most encouraging.

Faye retires to bed when it's finished, to get enough sleep in order to manage riding the next day. Now left alone, I ponder on the forthcoming year. This time next year I might be relaxing in a new home with a new boyfriend, with a whole bunch of new mates from in and around Exeter, Faye's new school, and the healthy David Lloyd health club which has members who are better looking than me in it, and both my children will be boarding. It could be a whole new chapter. Or possibly nothing will have changed. Watch this space to find out!

And then I settle back very contentedly to see in 2015 with my old mate Jools again.

The only shame is the next day, when my tummy tells me that I didn't heat up the Cassoulet thoroughly enough.

New Year's Day Snog

03/01/2015

The joy of this 'secret' blog is that I can put stuff on here that I would never get away with on my B&B site.

So I am extremely proud and excited to be able to announce to you that I have just enjoyed my first full throttle snog for a year! By which I mean for 365 days - not since 2014.

It was with a chap four years my junior, sporting a full head of blond hair. I came across him on Guardian Soulmates, and he has the same username as my horse - Vegas.

His daughter will be going to Will's school in September, and his best friend is my best friend's sister, from when we were ten.

He came for tea, and Faye went behind his head and gave the thumbs up sign, and mouthed 'Yes!'

Blind dates cannot possibly stay here with me, B&B or no B&B, legal or not - I do hope I don't get sued on this one. So we put him up in my mate's glorious Prince Hall Hotel and I joined him for a Taste of the West Gold Award winning four course dinner there.

I was dead chuffed that he started trying to snog me in the bar, but I just couldn't have that - not in front of so many of my friends' daughters who work there - so I told him yes, but no, and finally extricated myself after a rather jolly time.

The next day he emailed to say that he wasn't the right 'b-f' for me, which is a very kind way of putting it. I think what he actually meant was that now free after a very long marriage, he didn't want to get tied down to family life with an old bag like me, when he could be having fun with all sorts of people, and finally settle with someone ten years my junior!

Hey ho. On to the next one!

Second New Year Romance?

08/01/2015

Guardian Soulmates gave 50% off, and then Encounters offered me a free week's subscription. How is a serial online dater like me going to resist either one? So of course I've taken up both and things have gone a bit potty again.

On Christmas Eve five of the friends I've made through online dating emailed to wish me Happy Christmas, which was massively touching.

And last week I met up with Blueberry Man at the Warren House Inn - the second highest pub in England - which is equidistant - 20 minutes each - between our homes.

I can usually tell who my blind date is the minute I walk in. They are sort of standing or sitting there, looking up anxiously every time the door opens, and a blast of delight, or, hopefully, at least relief, crosses their face as I enter, as I'm blonde and 5'9", often in heels, looking very un-rural, with big eyes and big teeth.

It turned out that Neil had been a client at my old PR consultancy in Cromwell Road in London, when he worked for a company selling biro's. So he knew my old boss, who once took me to the opera and asked me to be his mistress. He always asked the tall, posh, blonde execs to be his mistress. When I refused (in a flattered sort of way) he said, "I suppose you still believe in all that love nonsense." For Christmas he used to give his female employees lacy black stay-up stockings. His navy three-piece pin-stripe suits were all bespoke with very tight trousers. He had a handle-bar moustache and was the drummer who went 'boom' at the start of "Waddya Want To Make Those Eyes At Me For?" I was very fond of him and hope he's still alive.

Blueberry Man told me how the nation's food is almost entirely produced by around five companies - even the ones that sound sort of home-made that you find in supermarkets. Apparently the producer goes to one of these companies and tells them what is wanted, then they make it, package it, and distribute it in massive bulk. Small suppliers can only work with individual outlets and farm shops, he told me, as they simply can't begin to supply either the quantities, or the specialist expertise required in the manufacture of literally tons of product that the multiples require.

Our Dartmoor landlord was loudly crashing about from 10pm, I suspect unsubtly attempting to get us to go, even though the pub doesn't shut til 10.30pm. We were the only people there but ignored him and continued a fascinating chat through until closing time. Yet another good male friend made. But it's not love.

One Day Too Late

08/01/2015

Did you realise that a scholarship to a private school can commonly be worth around £35,000?

£35,000!!!!!!!!!!!!!!!!!!!!!! That's more than lots of people earn in a year! Or roughly 25% of full boarding school fees over five years.

Well I wish my parents had put me in for a scholarship. I might even have got one! I was brainy back when I was twelve.

Anyway.

So I think it is completely mad, if your child stands the slightest chance of winning a scholarship, not to have a crack at it. I mean how much effort would you put in if you were pitching for a £35,000 deal at work, say?

So of course poor Faye has been subjugated to months and months of abuse, since this came to my attention, back in June last year.

I have put her in for an 'All Rounder' which means she has to play two pieces of music on two instruments (or sing), recite a two minute 'monologue', perform music and drama with other contenders for twenty minutes each, take some special papers in English, maths and critical thought, and be interviewed by the head of music, the head of drama, and the head of school.

So at the beginning of last term we changed music teachers, and every week I drive seventy miles each way for flute lessons, and last week we also did a 150 mile round trip in the opposite direction, during the holidays, for an extra singing lesson.

We, and when I say 'we' I mean 'we' - it has been like pushing water uphill - have prepared pieces on three instruments - two classical flute pieces, two musical theatre songs, and "Say Something I'm Giving Up On You", which she's done entirely on her own, singing mournfully and passionately as she accompanies herself on the piano. And her English teacher has written a special monologue for her. It's Curley's wife from John Steinbeck's 'Of Mice and Men', moaning on about what a miserable life she leads, which Faye loves.

She has already practised her interviewing technique when she applied for the head girl post at her current school, and in the forthcoming interviews she'll have to demonstrate all round massive enthusiasm and a wish to be a good role model in the new school. So let's pray for a good mood!

"What will you give me if I get it?" she queried the other day.

"Nothing - all the money I have gets spent on you two anyway. There'll just be more for treats." Rewarding children for doing well in exams, or bribing them not to smoke, is about as pointless as giving out surprise tiny bonuses at work, in my opinion. You're either going to do your best at the job, or you're not. But hey ho. Nobody agrees with me.

Well anyway, if she doesn't get the scholarship, the exercise has provided a focus, and her musical ability has already improved beyond all recognition, so - there we are. And anyway, she's actually beginning to almost enjoy the process, and she really loves her new music teachers.

I emailed the school yesterday to double-check whether they would like her to board overnight during the two-day auditioning process, and guess what they said. That I haven't sent in the application form and I have missed the deadline by a day.

I just about started shivering and was very close to tears. The form, I discovered, has been lurking at the bottom of my pending tray since November.

"It's OK though," said Tania in admissions.

So now there's a white envelope in tomorrow's post, with a completed form inside, and a massive first class stamp! Sometimes I could shoot myself.

Going For A Million Quid

08/01/2015

"Guys, saw the house featured for sale online and wondered what your current position is? To establish a little credibility and indicate that I'm not a "tyre kicker," I sold my business back in 2012 for a lot of money and could complete a deal very quickly, with no need for external funding or any downward chain. Modesty prevents me from saying much more, but you can check my credentials online, if you haven't nodded off already!

"On the back of that, price isn't the biggest driver here, but property style and position absolutely is and from what I've seen, your place has the latter two in spades. So, do please let me know if you're still looking for a buyer and even if not, my compliments on your guest house website, it really made me chuckle (in a good way!)"

Well guess who's chuckling now!

I've looked him up and he sold his business back in 2012 for £283 million. And on top of that it's clear that he is a very nice, solid, family man, who likes horses.

How weird is my life.

He's coming to see Wydemeet tomorrow, and will also be discussing publishing my blog/book.

Ha ha! How rich am I going to be this time tomorrow night? Don't hold your breath, but what a roller coaster eh?

Life-Changing Day

11/01/2015

I slept OK.

Rather well actually.

I've put myself back in my original bedroom, Hexworthy, the posh one which faces South East and South West so it gets all the best light until mid-afternoon which is when I get up for preference, and last night for once I almost slept solidly through the entire night. Surprising in the circumstances. I think it's the highly efficient black-out blinds which help. And probably all the interrupted nights of the past year are a hormonal thing.

Because anyway. Today is a massive day. It could prove life-changing on two fronts.

Firstly I am meeting my multi-millionaire who anticipates spending two hours with me, looking at whether he will buy the house, and if he'll publish my blog.

And tonight I am meeting a blind date who ticks every box! Having come across him through Encounters, it turns out that he is part of my childhood Dorset social circle!

I texted a great mate of mine, whose views I have immense respect for, saying "Potential blind date with whatever-his-name-is. Good or bad idea?"

And she texted back:

"I think he's lovely. Colourful - both in attire and communication, and amusing." Blimey! What else could you ask for? And he's 6'4" as well. I have spoken to him and he has an enormously attractive, friendly voice.

For once, I am nervous!

Sashka gets the house and garden ready for the £1 million inspection while I faff around getting in her way making myself breakfast.

Bang on 11.30am, Twiglet is leaping 6' in the air by the stairs window, which means someone has arrived.

And here he is. Bald, as anticipated from Google, but tall and slim, and slightly aloof and scary.

I boast that, being the ultimate B&B, he can have any tea he likes, but when he asks for Darjeeling the best I can do is Assam teabags. After lots of kitchen chit-chat I finally say, "Well.. first impressions are everything. Would you still like to see around the house? Would that be a good use of your time?"

He says yes, so we inspect Wydemeet, and then go for a little walk to where you can see the nearest set of stepping stones. He has no cover for his bald head and is wearing black shiny leather shoes. There is a hurricane blowing based from somewhere in Scotland, and it is raining and wild. I shout over the wind that there are bridleways there, and there, and there, and there, gesturing frantically.

He leaves on time, and I feel a little frazzled. He is not warm and cosy but quite reserved, a stance which as ever has me prattling banal rubbish. He wants the house as an investment, let out most of the time at £3-4,500 per week. It will need a lot of renovation to command that. He says he'll do the sums and get back to me by the end of the weekend.

So now I'm off to meet my new husband.

As I walk in through the door, here he is. Um. Not sure what the problem is. Can't pin it down. We have friends in common right across to a pub called The Bull in Ticehurst, E Sussex. But I'm not feeling it. Lots of mutual interest to discuss. He suggests I have a starter but he won't. He selects a delicious Rioja from the wine-list. A perfectly pleasant evening, and then the big shocker. I am expected to go Dutch!!!!!!!!!! Well, dahling. It's been a long time since that happened to me. I have enjoyed all the nice, free meals I have been treated to over the past twelve months. Call me old fashioned.

Sorry. That's curtains.

So I actually prefer 'my gypsy'. I met him, with no expectations, yesterday for lunch at the Double Locks - a delightful pub on the bank of Exeter Canal. To reach it, you have to negotiate a very narrow bridge (a challenge in a Range Rover or the Golden Monster) and drive down a long tow-path. It's hidden away behind Marsh Barton Trading Estate, and you can find it by looking for two enormous light green square boxes which are a recycling plant - the bridge is just beyond.

When I was at Exeter University 35 years ago, the pub was tiny, and had a goat and a parrot tethered outside. Now, in high summer, it is a tourists' paradise, with marquee, adventure playground, bbq, lawns etc. On winter weekday lunchtimes, though, it is silent and empty.

My gypsy's not much taller than me. On the phone he sounded as though he smokes 60 a day and sniffs as though he's a cocaine addict, and didn't say anything very interesting. As I walk into the bar, he looks at me sidelong, and grins.

He has an earring, sideburns, rings on his fingers and bracelets. He attended Barnstaple grammar and has S1's (that's the old S'levels which only unusually clever people even take) in maths, further maths, and applied maths, and a degree in psychology. He's currently negotiating to buy up a couple of film studios. I like his attitude towards me. Immediately my wine glass is empty, he jumps up to refill it. And he insists on paying the bill.

When the time comes to say goodbye he hugs me hard and says he would very much like to see me again. But I am wriggling free because I am deeply late for the school run.

And now, having met up with a whole series of dysfunctional public school types, I'm beginning to wonder how much damage a private education can wreak.

Devils Spawn

12/01/2015

That's how my multi-millionaire refers to estate agents.

Well I liked the chap who came from Savills. He knew all my huntin/fishin/shootin mates from around here, and we had a good gossip. He also made some quite interesting observations about selling property.

Apparently Savills has more offices in London and around the world even than Knight Frank. He says I have a very small, but keen market, who will be London-based.

And that the first month of putting your house on the market is what really counts, so I must not put an unrealistically high price on it.

"Why do you think rich people are rich?" he said.

He showed me an example of a lovely looking place near Gidleigh Park - the poshest end of the moor - which he says has a history even sadder than mine. The owner was originally advised to price it at £1.2 million, and so the house languished. Savills have taken over and reduced it to £895,000, but in the meantime, the owner has probably lost some people who might otherwise have been interested in buying.

"So don't overdo things on Zoopla etc," he advised, "as they show how long the house has been on the market, and how many people have looked at, and rejected it, which is very off-putting to potential purchasers, and also gives them bargaining power."

He wants a 2% commission, not the 1% that I was expecting.

"But I have already written all the copy and done all the photos for you!" I protested.

He appears immovable.

So I'll see what Knight Frank has to say.

Life-Changed?

12/01/2015

Putting together your profile for this online dating lark forces you to reflect carefully on who you think you are, and what sort of a partner you are looking for.

I find that every time things go a bit wrong (ie every time I meet someone) I reappraise things again.

This time I have come back realising how much jolliness and a spontaneous, infectious grin matter to me.

I am also bored with feeling obliged to respond to messages from men who take no trouble to make themselves attractive, eg they send me a message saying 'Nice Profile'. Why would that make me want to respond to them?

I have been unsure what to say, if anything, to Dorset Man.

So I was relieved to receive an email today which went:

"Title: Marvellous to Meet You!

Message: But Virgo Meets Leo .."

Phew! (Although what was it about perfect me that didn't float his boat? And also, I am only half Virgo.)

I sent back a reply, copied and pasted from Google:

"Leo and Virgo

When Virgo and Leo join together in a love match, they may initially overlook common interests and feel they have nothing to gain from one another. This is a relationship that evolves over time. Leo is extroverted, dominant, and charismatic, and often has a short fuse. Virgo is studious and withdrawn, possessed of more versatility ...

Blah blah."

Spurred on by this disappointing encounter, combined with receiving a boring message accompanied by a photo of one of the most unattractive men I have ever seen in my life, I have just amended my profile. I've added:

"You will make me laugh so hard that I do the nose trick down my front.

My car/truck is gold.

You wouldn't dream of describing yourself as 'an ordinary guy looking for a lady'.

Because you are as unusual, upbeat, and charismatic as I am. Or preferably more so! You understand and genuinely enjoy women, you have a spontaneous, contagious grin, and a knowing twinkle in your eye.

Send me a message saying 'nice profile' and I will reply because I am innately polite. Send me something more interesting with an attractive pic, and who knows - sparks might fly!"

And then I receive an email from Millionaire-Man.

His figures do not add up.

How surprising is that?

Not at all. Wydemeet is all about living the dream. It's never going to work as a business investment. But his email is delightful and he's asked me to stay and get to know his family at their palace on a peninsula on the River Fal in Cornwall. I may well take him up. I would like to know more about him.

Also, I am not sure whether I have ever seen a 73' private room before - the size of his sitting room - except possibly at Buckingham Palace.

I am neither disappointed nor deterred by this decision. Bring on Stage 2. Now I will have to sell Wydemeet properly through the agents.

And summon up the courage to call Neighbour for an adult discussion about those logs.

Rock Bottom

17/01/2015

He has destroyed everything that we built up together over 15 years. Everything.

When we met I could have gone almost as far as I liked in the PR world. I had my own house in London which I swapped for Wydemeet, and I drove a bright red Golf GTi.

In getting rid of me, he has lost his profile, which was the key to his freedom in the workplace.

The business we built up together is finished, the family is over, our Devon-based social life at an end, £1/2 million savings earmarked for things that mattered gone, and the imminent loss of Wydemeet signifies the final end of all our joint dreams.

During our time together I was more-or-less sole breadwinner, child-carer and nest-maker, business advisor and publicist, and what is there left to show for it? I am down to my last £3,000. That will last a month.

Why did this happen? Because I was 'controlling'.

So now he has a nice, pretty, intelligent girlfriend eleven years my junior. Well she wouldn't have got him to the North Pole!

Meanwhile I am back well behind Square One, looking to downsize my home, my career over.

It's a fucker. Yes, of course I am angry and bitter.

And today I have flu. So I'm letting the inner turmoil out for once. That is the beauty of the private blog. I can delete this tomorrow, and nobody will know.

Chemicals

26/01/2015

"What does 'mellow' mean?" asks Faye. I have just told her I'm feeling it.

We are driving home from another 'Trec' competition, the one where you get butterflies from making your horse do the most potsie-pie things. You have to walk very fast, canter very slowly, stand still, and go over a large blue plastic bag. It is a particularly Good Thing for elderly ladies on carthorses.

Hah hah! I beat my twelve year old daughter! That was in the first competition. In the second competition, where, again, I have pitted Faye against people who represent the country in the sport, she beat me soundly, doing even better than one of the grown-up professionals! Foot perfect, fluid, like poetry – scoring straight tens over six obstacles.

And may I just add that the people at the top of the sport are superb equestrians on stunning, valuable, able mounts!

I found the whole thing just so proud-making, And also 'such fun', as Miranda's Mum might say.

But I think I'm still ill.

Valentine Nightmare

02/02/2015

This year will be the first Valentine's Day that I've received no card on, since I was 11.

My other problem is who to invite to Will's School Valentine's Ball.

I wouldn't miss it for the world, as Will is playing the tenor sax in the Dance Band.

But I've got no one to go with.

So my options are:

- take an internet dater. But it's Valentine's Night, and they will have to pay for themselves (£40), so they might get the wrong idea, and/or it doesn't seem fair if they've got no involvement with the school; and Will may not like seeing me prancing around in front of his peer group with some stranger with whom my relationship is unclear

- take my Mum (84) or Faye (12), but I would have to pay for them as well as myself, which is rather a lot

- find another Single Mum to come with me. Only a Mum involved with the school would be interested. I've found a really fun one, but she is still undecided.

So I've emailed the organisers who are the school's Music Department, explaining that I'm Billy No Mates, and might they put me somewhere out of the way in the background, and not too embarrassing, possibly on the music staff's table?

Which Estate Agent?

02/02/2015

Who would you choose?

They both seem almost exactly the same to me.

They both boast excellent reputations, are highly professional, extremely charming, and I suspect delightful to work with.

I have enjoyed long visits from each, and they both said the same sort of thing.

They both have lots of offices in London and abroad, with extensive contact lists of rich people.

One has been marginally more efficient and accurate in their eventual proposal document. And have slightly more offices. But the other valued Wydemeet slightly higher.

I did like it that one is apparently a private company, whereas the other has to please its shareholders, if I understood what they were saying correctly.

Each advised that I should go public on the house when its garden and the moor are looking good, and that the first month of selling is critical. Each said that it should be put on 'at a figure starting with 8' inviting offers above that, and to hope for a bidding war.

So the deal-breaker was when one offered me a 1.5% commission, compared with the other's 2%.

I was just about to sign the contract when I spoke to a Property Developer Internet Date, who advised me that he typically puts his properties on with both at the same time, for a 2% commission.

So I'm holding my horses, and finding out about that!

Wood You Credit It?

02/02/2015

"Is your husband there?" I asked my next door neighbour.

"No, he's out at the moment," she replied.

"Do you think he could call me, because we need to talk about all that wood," I said. "I can't sell my house when it's like that."

I put the phone down and collapsed into a chair, with a fag.

I've been putting off making that phone call for ten years.

"If I was Mary I would have him up in court," I have heard is the general local consensus, but I don't like making waves, and I certainly don't want to cause a neighbourly grudge. Those can cause ructions for generations around here!

And despite these generally-held sentiments, no one, to my knowledge, has ever dared publicly complain about how all this wood has been allowed to ruin one of the prettiest valleys on Dartmoor. People just mutter and moan into their scrumpy and look at the floor in a grim, gloomy, dour, Dartmoorish sort of a way, and regularly inquire of me "What do you think about all that wood stacked up outside your house?"

So it was that last week, at 2.30pm, in the pouring rain, me half dead with flu, Neighbour and I put on our macs and strolled along the lane next to the wood, discussing what it was all for, and what was to be done.

I was genuinely interested to find out all about this eyesore that has been piling up for the last fifteen years outside my gate, getting higher and higher and higher and higher and higher and higher.

"Do you think you could move that 'don't climb on the logs' garish sign 90 degrees so it's not the first thing potential buyers will see as they turn the corner, after their blissful moorland drive, as they approach my house?" I queried.

I learned that each 'bay' of tree trunks (there are about ten bays) weighs around 6-7 tons and is worth around £6-700, comprising around ten tree trunks, which can be removed and sawn up in about a day.

"Yes, it all makes about £30,000 a year," he said.

"WHAT?????? All that wood and effort? And it's just thirty grand?! That's what I do!" I exclaimed, waving at my home, shocked at the investment, effort and hideousness, generating such a small profit.

"In only two days a week," he continued.

We walked on.

I had been under the impression that some of the logs at the bottom of the pile had been sitting rotting for a decade, but it turns out they're all moved on fairly regularly.

Neighbour told me that he has several clients (two of whom it turns out I was at school with) whose estate foresters chop down a whole load of trees and then ring Neighbour up and tell him to come and collect them, before they're chopped up for firewood, or left to rot in situ. So he's not really in control of when the wood comes, or how much of it at a time.

But he volunteered for himself that there is now too much, and the 'bays' will gradually disappear.

So we moved on to the matter of the biggest log you've ever seen - grown from one of the first redwood seeds imported into this country - and a large pile of gravel sitting next to it right outside my gate, both of which have been there for years and years.

The huge log, about 150 years old, has been paid for by a sculptor, Neighbour told me - about £6-700 again - who is now going to be told it absolutely has to be collected. Meanwhile any excess gravel delivered by the council will in future be taken over the narrow bridge and up to Neighbour's farm/sawmill the day after it arrives.

The logs on the left-hand side of the lane were not supposed to have been left there, and have since been removed and won't be replaced; and the huge sea of tree trunks abutting my garden wall will gradually be reduced, he added.

"Please call me the day before anybody is due to look at your house, and I'll do some tidying up," Neighbour reassured me. "In the meantime, it won't be immediate, but you'll see that the majority of the logs will gradually disappear over the next few months."

And that's how we left it.

I am SO proud of myself. I felt we parted with really quite a lot of mutual respect. How mature can I be when it really, really matters?!

Both Barrels

02/02/2015

I was so angry I turned Radio 2 up really loud, and drove off at ninety miles an hour.

Two days earlier I had enjoyed the best 30 minute phone chat with this internet date, that I'd had with anyone for a year. He had a lovely voice and made me laugh - a lot, even though he kept calling me 'Darling'. I identified with a huge amount of what he said, and our mutual acquaintance turned out to be the rather glamorous divorced Mum of Will's best mate, whose home is in Gibraltar.

His username was 'CliftonMan' and he had been pursuing me quite energetically via Encounters, as initially I hadn't found him very inspiring and so hadn't responded with much enthusiasm. For example, he had 'messaged' me: 'Let me be your Prince Charming' which I thought was a bit weak. I hit back with 'What else?'

Anyhow. Best chat for a year! The best one since Mr Dumped-Me-By-Email.

But then it transpired that in two days' time he was off to Gibraltar and away for three weeks! But first, he was off to overnight in London with his children. The very idea of "is he or isn't he 'the one'?" filling my head for over three weeks, filled me with dread. So I had a wizard wheeze. I could meet him for a coffee at the Services on the A303 opposite Hazelgrove School, as I drove back to Mum's from visiting Will's school in East Dorset, and as he drove back to Clifton from London via the A303 and the A37. The AA said this route would be 32 miles longer for him than the normal route of taking the M4.

Would he Hell? He wouldn't even listen to my suggestion. He'd never heard of the A303(!) And then he accused me of being the sort of girl who is used to getting her own way. (OK I do, but usually nicely.)

Then he told me that I am 'in a hurry for love'. (OK I am, but in a pragmatic, un-needy sort of a way).

And then he referred to me as 'Sweetie-Mary'.

And he's very Anglo-Catholic, whatever that is, but it means he talks about God as if God were a person. "God has a very good sense of humour, he loves laughing," this man informed me. Oh yeah?

I stayed calm and friendly, until I received a message saying "YOU ARE QUITE LOVELY AND QUITE CONFUSED. I WISH YOU WELL" all in capitals for some reason. That was too much. It took me an hour and a half to compose my email to him.

"I'm a Virgo mate - we are NEVER confused!" I ranted, and told him that I hadn't been made quite so angry for a very long time.

Being not listened to, and patronised, are not really my things.

I ended the rant by saying how interested I would be to meet him on his return, to see if we could laugh it off, or to find out whether we absolutely hated each other.

I don't suppose he'll reply, because I actually made myself sound a bit mad.

Hey ho. Back to Dutch 'Gerard' from the New Forest, and the four Johns, two of whom I'm meeting this Wednesday, one for lunch and one for a drink later.

Clever Little Thing

06/02/2015

She got it!

After ALL that, Faye has won an All Rounder Scholarship to her first school of choice!

I was surprised by my reaction. Not by the tears smeared all over my face, but because I suddenly realised that now she would just simply have to believe that she is special and talented. It's no longer only Mummy saying so.

And secondly her awe-inspiring Highly Revered Elder Brother (who is also an All Rounder Scholar) can now relax in the knowledge that his younger sister is not, after all, going around making herself look uncool all the time, and he can stop worrying about it.

Two out of two little scholars now, eh? I am feeling the most smug and complacent Mum ever, considering I'm a rotten mother in most ways. I would keep away from me for the next couple of weeks, or you may find yourself wanting to be sick!

Action!

06/02/2015

Just as I was beginning to feel particularly poor, bookings have kicked in.

I've had two a day on some days!

Things are not entirely moribund after all!

Whether it all adds up to enough to cover fantastic, lovely Gary the Plumber's recent invoice is another story.

But I do genuinely find a real sense of achievement in working and earning.

Despite everything, though, once I've paid the school ski trip bill I will have zero left in my account.

I drafted a letter to Faye's new school wondering whether there may be any additional funds available from them, on top of the scholarship award, but then worked out what my income for the next year might be, not counting selling the family home nor cashing in my pension, and I thought they might laugh!

The small issue that I have overlooked, is that living the life of Lady Muck is expensive, as you've probably guessed, if you've stayed with me this far.

Hunting two horses, health club, holidays abroad, large house, 3 litre four wheel drive gold tank, private school for two children, Sashka doing all the horrid things...they'd split their sides!

So in order not to have to give up any of the above, I must continue to live off my wits, or start doing my own housework and cleaning my own tack. Ugh. My current plan is to keep working on this book idea, so here I am, back again!

At the moment we have our second 'Returns' staying, who run their own very successful six-bedroom B&B in Cornwall, opposite St Michael's Mount. They are already booked up for the whole of July. Meanwhile I don't have a single July booking for either of my two rooms.

So I told them that they must be undercharging. But we agreed that it would be really horrid to have a guest to stay who was unhappy and felt that they'd been ripped off. It's a very delicate balance.

Anyway - this couple brought their best friends with them, and they all had dinner around the kitchen table last night, and then sat in the cosy sitting room in front of the log fire for cheese and port. I found it very difficult to tear myself away from them - I really do have such lovely guests, and when they've come back for a second time they turn into friends.

This morning I was talking so much that I forgot to lay any forks, or the butter.

They didn't seem to mind, and told me that mine is the only B&B that they have ever returned to. They also gave me a bottle of Prosecco and some narcissi.

Cheers!

Bring on The Sale!

07/02/2015

We've dealt with the smell of dead mice in the cloakroom by ripping up the floorboards.

We've dealt with the smell of wee wee in the downstairs loo by washing the rug. Honestly. MEN!

We've hopefully dealt with the smell of mildew under the £3000 newish front door by kicking it hard, after locking it shut, hopefully preventing the rain from coming in under it in the future.

We've dealt with the smell of sewage in the garden by emptying out the second cess-pit.

We haven't dealt with the smell of mildew in the sitting room caused by damp coming in through the gap between the window casing and the granite walls.

Nor have we dealt with the smell of death emerging from the tack room, finding its way into the kitchen through the cupboards. At some stage I am going to have to clear the whole place out, to reveal a rat's rotting carcass covered in maggots. It's funny how, of all these smells, the smell of death stays with you.

Godfrey, who used to be Mr Fixit for a 12,000 ton frigate in the navy, after twelve hours at £15 per hour, has finally tracked down the problem with the fusing downstairs electric sockets. This turned out to be a 50 yr old fraying wire under the dining room floor.

Once he's sorted that, he'll have to deal, as usual, with re-priming the central heating because it still leaks from somewhere, despite our sorting out the radiator in Bellever bathroom.

Do you know what? I can't wait to sell this place! It's doing my head in!

Do other large Edwardian houses suffer from such things? I'm sure they probably all do. And are eminently deal-able-with, if you are a proper family, with a Dad around to keep an eye on things.

But in my case - bring on that tiny modern bungalow!

See What Sticks

07/02/2015

My method of getting what I want is to throw everything at it, and see what sticks.

My top priority, as you know, is to sort myself out into a couple again. Although I enjoy my own company very much indeed, I am definitely not happy on my own, long term.

To achieve this happy outcome I have:

- joined every website known to man or woman, favourited, messaged, tweaked profiles, photo's, met people, met more people, til I'm blue in the face, making bugger all progress, and now it's all ground to a halt

- arranged to promote myself via Four in a Bed, whenever they're ready

- put my family home on the market so that I can get closer to humanity and the David Lloyd Health Centre which is full of eye candy, rather than fat, white, shaven-headed, tattooed yobs

Desperate? Or pragmatic. You tell me.

And to sell my home I have sorted out:

- ebay

- my own website, to be found through SEO

- my own website, to be found via AdWords

- joint estate agency with the top two estate agents in the world, or at least in the UK

EBay is currently going rather well! The agent who picked up on my entry has put me on Zoopla for free, and has just asked me for information to pass on to an interested party, about local private schools. I sent them practically a book, as you can imagine! I haven't heard back after all that though. Boo hoo.

My own website to be found through SEO is less successful. It is called www.house-for-sale-dartmoor.com; and I put it up last November. Yet even nearly three months later, if you google 'house-for-sale-dartmoor' it still doesn't appear. My IT man has given me lots of tips as to how to improve things. Including attaching my new website to my B&B one. I'll have to think about that.

My own website to be found via AdWords has just produced a frantically exciting enquiry! It's cost me about £100 so far with people clicking on my ad, which takes them through to my website. A retired naval officer rang, who knows all my mates at the top of the navy, and whose wife keeps her Andalusian horse at my best friend Daisy's livery down the road. In fact I met her once, years ago.

Anyway, they are very interested in buying the house and running it as a B&B, and obviously they already know what it looks like, where it is, and all about Neighbour's wood. In fact they have been to a talk given by Neighbour so they know what he's like too! They can afford the asking price, they say, because they own 19 buy-to-let properties in Plymouth and are selling a further house in Henley. They're coming to see inside the house this Wednesday.

All too good to be true. So it probably won't happen. But an interesting bite nevertheless.

So my professional agents are on 'hold' until we know where we are with the above. We're not planning to go properly public until March/April/May anyway, when the moor and garden are looking at their best. The joint agency approach is going to cost me 2.66% + VAT in commission, which comes to a staggering £32,000 if we manage between us to sell the place for £1 million. But Savills and Knight Frank ought jointly to reach all the richest people in the world, so I do reckon it's worth a bit of a blast, and hopefully a whole load of Russian Oligarchs will start bidding against each other to reach some ridiculously stratospheric final figure.

III

07/02/2015

I brought out the drinks tray.

On it were Night Nurse, Day Nurse, Beechams All in One, Beechams Cough Tincture for Children, and Lemsip All Day. And two little plastic measuring cups.

I offered my guest to take his pick, then returned to the sunroom where Faye and I helped ourselves too. Flavour of the month proved to be Night Nurse. Annoying because you can't get it delivered by Tesco.

The phone rang the following morning, after I had dropped Faye off at school, interrupting my preparation of the most complicated breakfast four guests could possibly dream up.

"It's your daughter, she's ill. She's got a temperature of 38," gasped matron.

"I thought she would be. She was ill yesterday. Can she just stay there do you think? I've got a load of things to do this morning," I replied. These included joining some girlfriends for coffee, followed by swimming at the health club.

Sashka, overhearing, was appalled.

"It would be different if she'd broken a leg," I muttered, and carried on with my Egg Florentine with the muffin but without the hollandaise.

I blame the cross country run. This year Faye did well, only coming fifth last, using her inhaler every second step and crying most of the way round as usual; sobbing into my arms at the end. All totally predictable. She and I aren't built for long-distance running. Our bones are too heavy. If she had another year left at the school I think she might mysteriously suddenly have an extra flute lesson on Cross Country afternoon, as her un-sporty friend did this time.

So she was ill the next day, but we ignored that because it was the highlight of the year - Danny's Valentine Disco!

"Nobody's asked me to the disco," sighed Faye sadly.

"Has anyone else been asked?" I queried.

"Florence has been asked by six different people, but turned them all down," she said.

"Anyone else?"

"No."

In the event the funniest boy in the school did ask Faye, but when he asked her to dance she said no.

I think that was most unkind, and when she's recovered a bit, I will ask her to apologise to him. What he did was unbelievably brave in my opinion.

It turned out that staying vertical for the disco was worth it for Faye, as she was the only person there who knew the routine not only to the Time Warp, but also to Macaracca.

And her reward now, is to be able to sit in her pyjamas on the sofa in the sunroom glued to Disney Channel for twelve straight hours, two days running.

Meanwhile, with no riding, due to the icy weather and ill or busy Faye and me, the horses are getting fatter and fatter, and for once have retained all their shoes between farrier appointments. Also their hair has grown back where their saddle sores were. I'm just a bit nervous of quite how bouncy they're going to be, once all the snow and ice finally disappear.

What's Flu?

13/02/2015

I sit down on an upturned piece of granite, feeling a bit dizzy and sick.

"It's worth a million quid," I scold myself. Heaving my reluctant body to its legs again, I lug the frozen molehill heavily into the waiting wheelbarrow, and stomp about on the many dips and mounds left by the wild Dartmoor ponies the last time they escaped onto my so-called 'lawn' (what a joke) just a few days ago.

My own horses are nibbling placidly at the spindly bits of grass forcing their way up between the patches of frozen snow in the field, stables are swept, leaves gone off the back steps, and the fallen lumps of moss hiding the bothy's asbestos roof cleared. Now I must quickly give the interior of the house a major face-lift before my potential purchasers arrive.

I make up and light the log fire in the sitting room, make sure the rug in the hall is covering those Twiglet mud-stains, move one of the many pot pourri's in the cloakroom into the downstairs loo to cover up the smell of wee, squirt my secret stash of Woods of Windsor Mimosa Room Fragrance around in my bathroom, and pray that a fresh cafetiere of Douwe Egberts freshly ground will drown the smell of death now permeating its way into the kitchen.

Clip clop, clip clop, and here they are. I can't believe it - how could I have forgotten that they are riding over? Thank God I've cleaned up properly in the stables for once, instead of leaving poo everywhere like I normally do - I mean does a horse really care if there's a piece of plop here and there?

So. My first proper viewing. It's taken me two hours to get the place ready and I'm on my deathbed. "This is even more important than making the place look nice for my B&Bers," I keep up the mantra in my head, despite my temperature of five million degrees, and manage to maintain a facade of charm throughout their visit.

As they plod off, I help myself to some cold coffee dregs, sigh, and struggle up the stairs one at a time to my bed, and my waiting copy of 'Gone Girl', left open at page 132.

I'm not looking forward to going to all this trouble over and over again, assuming that in due course the estate agents arrange one viewing after another.

And, I wonder, what is the definition of flu? Forty years ago they said it was when you felt too ill to go out into a field to pick up a £50 note. Since inflation I guess it would now be a £1 million note. So I guess I haven't quite got proper flu yet.

Valentine's Day

16/02/2015

I got three!

Sort of.

On the eve of Feb 13th, a red rose arrived from TreeHugger. He sent it by Interflora. Actually no he didn't. He sent it as an attachment to an email, rather cleverly done in 3D. Anyway - so that was a start.

In the post, on the actual day, came an actual card! It came from Little John, I'm sure - the chap I meet on Wednesdays while Faye has her flute lesson. He feels pure, like a breath of fresh air, after the many disappointed, complicated divorcees I typically meet through the websites. He's just a bit short.

For instance, such a lot of internet dates tell me that their wives have a drink problem, so they had to leave them. What drove them to drink, I often wonder. Perhaps Ex describes me as a hopeless alcoholic with my daily £4.99 3/4 bottle of 11.5 per cent proof Tesco's Cava Brut?

And then on the morning of Feb 15th my mobile showed 'XX' - a Valentine text from another of the John's I'm in touch with.

Anyhow, so I'm feeling well chuffed.

After all that heart-searching about who should partner me to his School Valentine Ball, Will called to say he was ill. I've had to go and pick him up from school. Lucky I'm feeling better myself now.

Yikes! So what is my poor divorced Mum-friend, who was going to be my partner, supposed to do now? Bye bye £80!

Don't get divorced! Life is such a bummer for single people!

Muddy Matches

20/02/2015

"The online dating and social networking community for country-minded, or 'muddy', people. This site is for anyone who leads a muddy-boots lifestyle and wants to meet like-minded, country people, be it for friendship, shared interests or dating."

I've been languishing on the Muddy Matches site for years - nobody ever contacts me. The only message I've ever received was from my mate Mad-James who is also on it, who dropped by through the ether to say what-ho.

Then fellow jilted-wife Juliette emailed me to say the site was offering 'Free Messaging' during Valentine's Weekend.

So I 'signed in' and discovered that Muddy Matches has been telling its members that my subscription expired in February 2011. And the profile and pic are several years out of date. That explained quite a lot.

I updated my entry and spent Saturday sending out messages to anyone with two legs and a head.

The responses poured in. Well, dribbled.

Nonetheless, over the past few days I feel that I have been drowning in potential on-line dates. Only now, having spoken to a couple, do I feel that I am beginning to emerge, out the other side.

Larry from Launceston shoots a lot. He doesn't realise that we have been in touch before. Nor that he had a chat with my mate Judith from Cheltenham, via Encounters. He calls, and sounds like one of those dissatisfied disappointed types. That's him done.

Then I speak to one of my John's. It turns out that both he and Jeffrey Archer went to the wrong Wellington School - Somerset, not Berkshire. He sounds nervous of me. I can't be doing with that.

So now I'm left with Nick from Bude. He used to be an event rider. The thought of going hunting with a really good horseman fills me with excitement! He's coping with half-term at the moment, but we will meet next week.

Alistair runs a B&B just down the road from here, and is learning to play polo. His place has got rather poor reviews on TripAdvisor. "It needs a woman's touch," they carp. He's ideally after somebody who will give him babies, according to his profile, but I suspect he's missed the boat on that front. Certainly has with me. Anyhow, I shall return his call later today.

Another John, a back surgeon from Wales, wants to meet me next week, but he sounds rather a gloomy soul too.

And then there's..... Oh. My. God.

What's going on here then????

".... as one rocket scientist to another with no sense of humour at all I prefer you vastly to the many highly intelligent loggy firey sexy beach walkey cosy pubby make me laughey hags who have been invading me covered in debenhams jewellery... "

ChelseaChap is the first person for ages, on any site, who makes me titter.

He is currently holed up all alone in his family castle in Austria.

At last I am excited by this emailing dating lark - I'm even getting butterflies.

And then the bombshell.

He's famous! He's a living, breathing, proper, real film star!!!

Aagghhh!

There are pages and pages on him on Google - he even has a fan club!
And in 'images' he is so drop-dead-gorgeous-looking that I feel faint!

This is my come-uppance at last! I am no longer in control. He is
wealthier, better looking, more successful and cleverer than I am. I am no
longer in the driving seat! What do I do? I have never been in this
position before! His ex-wife is far more beautiful and miles posher than I
am (she is also first cousin to Malcolm, small world). I don't have any of
the right clothes and I am much too wrinkly and fat for premieres.
Heeeeeeeeeeeeeeeelp!!!

I am so glad that he and I have come across each other via the neutral,
agenda-less, taboo world that is Online Dating. I would have been scared
stiff of meeting this bloke at some dinner party or other.

He likes me! He responds with enthusiasm to my garbled messages! Eek!
I mustn't appear too keen. Can't reply again til this evening. Oh my, I am
all of a jitter!

Ex-Mother-In-Law

20/02/2015

How grown-up am I?

I've invited Ex's mum to stay.

And she is coming! Despite the fact that it's February! She would never
have done that before, so she must really want this too!

She and I used to have loads of fun together before everything went
wrong. We both liked doing the same things, like driving around
Dartmoor, spending the day at Bovey Castle Hotel, going to hunt meets

etc. And she was very good at wrapping stocking presents, and peeling, at Christmas time. I have missed her.

She arrived on a beautiful sunny afternoon in time to see Faye falling off during her jumping lesson.

Granny says she can't eat cheese, chocolate, alcohol or spices, so I find cooking for her very straightforward. School dinners. As I roasted the children, I mean chicken, I checked out the sitting room and there was Will playing Scrabble with her, in front of a roaring log fire. With her little dog curled up at their feet. I took a picture.

After a jolly dinner, including lots of puddings made from lemon, Main Item on the Agenda began. Boggle. I always win, no matter how much I drink or smoke during the games. I win by writing down the most, shortest words more quickly than anybody else - nothing particularly clever about it. Everyone was out to get me but it was fine. I won as usual.

How lovely, the next beautiful morning, for Granny to see both me and her elegant granddaughter at the hunt meet on our impressive hunters, amongst 94 other horses!

Fast forward, more Scrabble, more chicken, more lemon puddings, and more Boggle; in which Faye (12) beats Will (aged 16, and fifth top in his year at English), and Ex beats me!!!!!!!!!!!!!!!! Huh.

The Smell of Death

23/02/2015

Two frisbees - delete. A Grays tennis racquet, circa 1935 - delete. Metal detector - oops, I've just trodden on something; I appear to have broken it in half, but anyway - delete.

I am gradually making my way towards the back of the tack-room, throwing behind me all the rubbish that the charity shop might want but we don't. I'm beginning to feel a bit sick as gradually I work my way inch by inch, closer and closer to the maggot-infested source of the hideous smell which now permeates throughout the house, squashed and dead behind or under the final Tesco crate right at the back of the room.

Trying not to gag, I heave out the crate, and there is ....

Nothing.

All I can see, rather than the rotting corpse of a rat, badger, or possibly even a human head, are three holes leading down to some drains, in the floor. They're located just beneath the water tanks that are something to do with the borehole and its pump, which supplies us with water. There is the most unholy reek coming out of one of them. God knows what's at the bottom of it.

I stuff in a couple of old Tesco's bags, and replace the tape that used to cover it up.

The smell subsides.

My insides go back to where they are supposed to be.

The biggest winner in all of this? The charity shop.

Craig

24/02/2015

"Hullooooo .... my .. name's ... Craig," he says in an unusual voice.

"God it's you. That is really bad acting!" I retort.

"Is that ... er ... Wyde .. meet?" he continues.

"God, you sound just like David Walliams!" I exclaim.

"Is ..er ... that .. Mary...?" he goes on.

"Urmmm, I suppose I am, " I finally answer.

"I'm ..er ... calling about the piano," explains Craig.

Oh my God I am mortified. I have been expecting Famous Film Star to call and knew he would be up to something like this. Instead, Craig the piano man has inadvertently impersonated my film star impersonating him. Agghh! I bluster, and backtrack, and blush to my greying roots which he can't see.

"You are quite bonkers, I am smiling all over my face," he reassures me.

This morning he rings again.

"Hullooooo .... my .. name's ... Craig," he begins.

"Oh hello Craig, how are you this morning?" I reply.

"I .. er.. want to book a room for my .. er.. honeymoon," he says. "I'm marrying him next Saturday..."

"Oh God it's you - I thought it was Craig impersonating you impersonating him..." and so my much awaited first call with Famous Film Star commences.

I have been so completely absorbed in fantasizing about him that I have become entirely distracted, forgetting things, unable to plan things, unable to concentrate, driving too fast with the music on too loud. I am incredibly excited by all this - what on the face of it seems really to be like total fiction. I absolutely can't think about anything else. I have spent hours and hours giggling out loud to myself as I correspond with him via email, and no time at all on this blog, nor finalising putting together the book. It will all turn out to be a complete waste of time, I am sure, but goodness how wonderful to be utterly buzzing at last. Everybody else I have met is grey next to this man.

We chat for 40 minutes. We have talked about so much before, and there is so much more to cover. I can't get enough of him. But he is finishing writing a play due to go on in the West End in the summer, so he is a pretty busy person. We might get together next week though. Can I wait that long??

Bunch of Bananas

02/03/2015

I am totally consumed by my film star.

I can't think of anything else, and things are slipping - by which I mean *things*.

I was talking to a fellow Dartmoor B&Ber on Friday who only markets herself via AirBnB. She has a lovely house but no en-suites and her rooms are much cheaper than mine. She is pleased with AirBnB but it turns out that I have turned over more than £1500 in the first two months of 2015, while she has only just received her first guests of the year this week.

But am I looking after my guests properly, with my mind on other things?

This morning the Tesco's man arrived, carrying a bunch of bananas up the drive. I quite crossly told him that I had added to my original order, which was critical for the running of my B&B, and what was I to do now, since their stupid computer hadn't clocked all the breakfast staples that I had gone to such trouble to order last night? Whereas, thinking about it, I believe I forgot! That's £9 for a bunch of bananas, and no breakfast!

Two nights ago, as I was indulging in another episode of 'Four in a Bed' at about 11pm, minding my own business, one of my guests, fully dressed, tapped on the door of the sunroom.

"There seems to be some alarm going off," he said.

"I can't hear anything," I replied, but we braved the freezing cold outside, and there was indeed a quiet eee-awe sort of a whining noise. It wasn't our cars, and it wasn't Neighbours across the valley - it turned out to be the burglar alarm box, high up on the wall, right outside my guests' window! Aaagghhh!

We went back into the kitchen and I attempted to turn it off from the control box. But it continued to ignore my button-pressing.

There was a Newton Abbot telephone number on a card stuck on the wall below the control box panel, so I called it, and guess what? A miracle! Someone replied! And they still 'do' burglar alarms! And were prepared to come around and sort it out at midnight in the freezing cold, including climbing up a ladder in the pitch black, while I went back to Four In A Bed. And, when the man arrived - very soon after I put the phone down - he was wearing shorts!

I now await the bill with some trepidation.

Meanwhile I have just received a summons to court for parking a car without insurance on a public road. Well Bill wasn't parked on a public road when I last saw him. I left him on the forecourt of horrid-garage.

And anyway, who cares about any of that, because I'm meeting my film star in London for lunch this Thursday, and that's all that matters. So now I must make an appointment at the hairdressers, and buy some new clothes.

Depressed

08/03/2015

I am so depressed.

Nothing's interesting or fun. Nothing.

I haven't heard from him for 24 hours.

That means that he is acutely re-considering, frantically busy, doesn't want to put aside time for me on Thursday, and if I chase him up, regarding our lunchtime meeting, then I will end up driving all the way to London for an embarrassing, expensive meal in Chelsea, that he doesn't actually want, and he'll be trying to hurry it up to get back to all his projects, of which there are so many, and for which the work has been piling up since he has been away in his family castle.

All is grey and bleak.

I sent him a jolly email this morning, and he hasn't replied, and now I must go to bed.

And now it is morning, and still no word. My laptop is in the kitchen and every time I pass it, which is every five minutes, I press the refresh button, and all I get is yet another missive from some strange stalker on Encounters.

Lunchtime. OMG! Bingo! He writes: "Have you fallen off Dobbin?" Hurray! Phew! He clearly didn't get yesterday morning's message from me. I leave things a few hours, so as not to look too keen, and reply,

"So there I was worrying that you'd fallen under a bus."

Lunch is on! How exciting!

One Retailer vs Another

08/03/2015

I've got nothing to wear!

And it's all the fault of my favourite discount retailer.

Whenever I go there, I buy every black jumper and every pair of black trousers in stock that fit (I only ever wear black during the winter). I treat the shop as if it were a jumble sale, because everything is so cheap I don't bother to look at the price, and you're constantly fighting everybody else's elbows.

The mystery is, though, that if the garments really are top quality brands reduced by £100s, as they advertise, why do they seem to be such poor quality? Is it me?

When I get home, I wear the stuff, then put it in the washing machine on 'wool', and, whatever it is and however it started out, it looks like a rag at the end of the wash, and is many sizes smaller with no elasticity left; or alternatively it has shed hairs all over everything else.

So to meet my sophisticated, to-die-for-good-looking Famous Film Star, in SW10, which is far smarter than SW6, I raced off to my preferred fully priced retail outlet, and bought shop-branded black jumpers and black trousers which were considerably more expensive, but which I hope will last through the wash. I also bought some new flat boots in case he is really short. He says he is 5'11" on his profile, but I bet he'll turn out just like that last one – a wiry little runner-type of about 5'10" at best. If he were really 5'11" he would have called himself 6', like everyone else does.

My current flat boots have got holes in the sides where my bunions stick out, and are clearly in need of some proper cleaning, now they are five years old. There is no getting away from it. My standards have slipped and I have become a Dartmoor Hillbilly. Even my haircut is rubbish and somebody from the Unhealth club stole the only conditioner I have that works. I'm horribly badly dressed, wrinkly, overweight, and white; with two blobs of sparkly gold nail Shellac left on my big toes - the rest has fallen off.

My slatternly looks are all down to Faye's school merger, of course. In the olden days, the Mums had their hair done in London and any carrier bags were Pinks, Hacketts, or Harrods. The new class of Mum (who is probably more friendly, and certainly more down to earth and relaxed) cuts her hair herself, is make-up free, wears an anorak and heavy flat shoes, and her carrier bags are Lidl. So appearance-wise, I have mucked in and sunk to her level, and my make-over is going to take some time and money. I'm never going to have achieved it by Thursday! Help!

Tennis Elbow

08/03/2015

I've got Tennis Elbow even though I haven't played tennis since I was thirteen.

It's pain in that ligament on the inside of your elbow. I've had it for months now, and it won't go away, however much I sit around doing nothing. It might be called Housewife's Elbow, but I'm no longer a wife, and Sashka does nearly all my housework. It could be Riders Elbow - but she does nearly all my grooming and mucking out too.

And the other day, driving to see some old school friends for lunch, I discovered what's causing it. It's Golden Monster's Elbow. I've got the back of the seat adjusted so that my arms are quite high and straight reaching out for the steering wheel. The problem is exacerbated when turning the wheel to park, and if I'm tense. Which I was. I hadn't seen one of the guys for nearly forty years, and had never met his wife. I very much wanted him to think I was still glamorous, as he was drop-dead gorgeous at school, and slightly scarily cool, arty and clever.

Well it was the most wonderful day, with sublime rib of beef cooked by his lovely wife who I'm hoping to see lots more of on my way to and from Will's school. My old friends made me believe I was still beautiful, funny and special. Oh, I feel quite wobbly writing this..

And the next trip is to London to meet up with Him, and back via Bath. I am filled with apprehension, meanwhile my Elbow will be complaining like billy-oh!

More Retailer Wars

08/03/2015

Apparently, these days, the most common place for relationships to start, after the workplace, is in the gym. I heard it on Radio 2 last week, so it must be true.

So guess why I'm changing health clubs!

The Exeter David Lloyd Health Centre is full of beautiful, healthy-looking people who you feel you know already, or would like to get to know. I want to become a part of that scene. Apparently teenagers from around Exeter even do their homework there, between tennis and/or swimming, and in the summer they all hang out around the outdoor pool. What dreams are made of! I'm joining. I don't care how much it costs - a lot, as it happens. About double the monthly cost of Encounters. Let's hope the David Lloyd works better!

My new home must be somewhere near it. Which means near a 24hr garage and Sainsbury too, as well as the A38, A30, A303 and the M5. And most importantly, the Exeter Chiefs rugby ground.

Anyway, so the most recent meeting of the Jilted Wives Club took place at what might prove to be my future 'local' in Ide, and afterwards I quickly popped into the nearby Sainsbury Superstore to pick up some frozen croissants and quality orange juice for my B&Bers, because my normal supermarket doesn't appear to sell either on-line anymore.

Well. What an experience! It was lovely! Everywhere I looked I wanted to buy everything. It was all clean, and light, and bright, and beautifully packaged, and fresh, and looked really expensive, but wasn't.

Do you remember when you avoided being seen in the downmarket supermarkets because they were so grotty and cheap - a bit like Lidl five years ago?

Do you remember that brilliant series of Sainsbury ads back in the eighties, which featured famous people making the simplest, most delicious recipes, and the strapline was: "Everybody's Favourite Ingredient". I was doing PR for Bramley apples at the time and had a go at getting them included in a Sainsbury ad - in an apple pie or something. The marketing director said 'non', and, oddly, the store went downhill for the next thirty years, so beware of refusing Mary Nicholson!

Well last night my normal retailer didn't bring me my B&B delivery. This time it really was their fault and it's a total mystery as to what has happened. It meant that my guests didn't get strawberries in their fruit salad, nor any crème fraiche for breakfast.

I called the store immediately it was possible - this morning at 10am and not before. Anyway. Can you believe it. They said they couldn't get the order out today either. Well I went into a rant about how if I was the manager I would 'pick' the short order myself and bring it in my own car. Or get a friend or child to do it. I would do anything to prevent anyone ever saying anything horrid about my business. And now because of them, I would be getting a black mark in turn. Me! The top B&B on Dartmoor! "Bring back Terry Leahy!" I yelled. But I don't think the

Scottish lady manning Customer Services on a Sunday had ever heard of him.

So. No strawberries or crème fraiche for breakfast tomorrow morning either.

House Sale Progress (Lack of)

09/03/2015

Wydemeet has received 848 clicks on 'AdWords' costing me £353, with the most popular Google search being 'houses for sale in Dartmoor', clicked 173 times.

Shame this hasn't translated into 173 sales. Mind you, one would be enough.

But it has produced two enquiries.

The couple who keep their horses up the road have been back again. I couldn't quite cope with the idea of removing all the mole hills for a second time, nor with making every bedroom immaculate all over again, so I hope I haven't blown things through laziness. They still need to sell their house in Henley, but were unaware that you can exchange now, and not complete for a year or whenever. That would suit me very nicely, as it would mean that finding the next place would be miles less stressful because I could then do the same. So they are looking into the delayed completion option, I hope. They pointed out that a million quid appears to be rather more than equivalent house prices in the area, of which they say there are eighteen. So I'd better look into that.

And then there's a lovely sounding lady from Guernsey. She sounds already smitten, but is worried that her husband might think Wydemeet too remote. I emphasised that we are nearer Exeter and London than Tavistock or Horrabridge are, where they are also looking, and that the best prep school in the southwest is less than 25 minutes away, so her two young sons would no longer need to board, and the school is good enough to get them into Eton if they're brainy enough. Her husband is coming to see the house this Monday - she is not allowed to attend first viewings, because she is too emotional about it all, she tells me. I hope I can persuade him that it doesn't take terribly long to fetch a pint of milk from a shop, and the drive to school is very beautiful. We will see.

Meanwhile the agent who has put me onto Zoopla tells me that someone drove all the way from London to see Wydemeet, with no appointment, and wondered whether he had gone to the wrong place because "it's in the middle of a timber yard." Hopefully he had indeed gone to the wrong place and ended up in Neighbour's farmyard, because Neighbour has already removed half the wood - the piles are nothing like as bad as they were! If, to the objective observer, we still look as though we're in a timber yard, then I'm a bit stuffed.

So I expect I will still be launching properly using the tried and tested method of Estate Agents, as soon as everywhere has started to turn green and flowery.

My horses have escaped into the garden again, so the 'lawn' is full of deep hoof prints in amongst the molehills, and the wind has meant the whole place is covered in branches, dead leaves and twigs. Euurrggh. More hard work. I think I must pay someone to rake them up at some stage.

Thursday

09/03/2015

Ha ha! Are you in suspenders as to how Thursday went?

Well now I am going to put you out of your misery.

I put on my new black spray-on trousers, my 'best' old black jumper, and decided that I would prefer to have longer legs as a result of wearing heels and be taller than him, rather than being smaller than him, squat, in my ancient, holey old brown boots. I topped the look off with my fake suede, fake fur, -lined moss green Betty Barclay jacket, bought in a Peter Jones sale years ago - well before the bust-up. These days it smells of mildew.

I arrived suffering the normal Golden Monster Elbow and discovered I'd parked rather a long way from the restaurant. I put the one £1 coin I had in the meter, knowing it would only last ten minutes, and legged it to our eatery. He wasn't there, but as I turned round, I saw him outlined in the doorway.

He is an extremely youthful 63 - hardly any lines, not a hint of grey hair, very trim and relaxed in quality lambs wool (possibly cashmere?) sweater and jeans. The very definition of what I would expect a successful actor of his generation to look like. And reassuringly taller than what I had feared - probably 5'10 1/2".

We arranged for me to move the car - he charmingly extracted 12 x £1 coins from the newsagent's next door; while I raced off to get the Golden Monster, hoping he was admiring my long legs and sunglasses as I ran, meanwhile he stood saving an empty parking bay for me, right outside the restaurant window. While I was away his old mate Rory Bremner passed by for a quick chat; and then he was nearly run over by somebody who was determined to pinch the space. He was a bit shaken by the time I roared up in my huge truck.

Well. Four hours of non-stop chat and banter. He knows everybody and my goodness the tales. I cannot repeat them here. I would be arrested! And he kept touching my arm because he is a touchy-feelie actor darling. I nearly found myself reaching for his hand! Eeek!

I could have stayed there forever but I had to whizz off through the sunny London rush-hour to get to my mates for dinner at their new house in Bath. We hugged goodbye several times, and each said, "Can I see you again?"

But, on reflection, our lives have almost nothing in common. If he lived around here we might be together all the time at one another's houses. Similarly if I lived in West London. But he is frantically busy with the most enormous amount of extremely high profile productions on TV, Edinburgh, and in the West End. Meanwhile, despite my new life starting today, ie Faye boarding three nights a week, I still appear to be up to my neck in country pursuits and child-rearing. I never intended to be rural particularly. What is going on?

And could I be a luvvie? I'm not at all sure about that. I can't do the pink ones in Trivial Pursuit, and I never call anybody darling – not even my children.

I Hate Poldark

10/03/2015

Dark and brooding Poldark, beloved of Daily Mail readers, finally, after what seems like weeks, got shunted off page 3 back to page 5 today. Instead, on page 3, was a piece about how men don't like funny women.

Well I don't think Poldark's a bundle of laughs either, actually. Imagine having dinner with him. How gloomy would that be? He wouldn't even taste the food. He'd just be gazing into his half-empty glass, away with the fairies, being all sad and moralistic about his tin-mine, and you'd have to spend the evening trying to cheer him up. Exhausting. You would look over to that other jolly couple on the table next to yours, laughing, laughing, laughing, and wonder whether, however good-looking your date might be, you had really made the right choice.

But what annoys me most about Poldark is its stratospheric success. Because since it all went ballistic my Famous Film Star, who is involved with it, hasn't got time nor inclination to send me long hilarious emails anymore.

His world has gone potty and is much too frantic to include little old Dartmoor Hillbilly me in it. He is now made, because of the success of stupid Poldark. There are another ten books left to film for God's sake! Years and years of the stupid programme! Whereas if it had been a disaster there wouldn't be another series, the media wouldn't have gone mad about everyone in it, and he would have had time to think about coming to visit me here on Dartmoor.

So, Mr Aidan Turner. Don't be anticipating any fan mail from me.

It's A New Life - Or Is It?

12/03/2015

A whole new life started this morning.

Faye started full time boarding, so now I am free to play, all day, every day, anytime, anyplace, anywhere. Freedom! No deadlines! Relax and indulge!

But first I have to make breakfast for the B&Bers. Then I have to catch up on emails, do some blog, do some book etc.

It's 7pm by the time I've got space in my day to set off for the unhealth club, anticipating peace and calm, and hunky employed single men, rather than the losers and retired people who hang around the Jacuzzi during the daytime, once the ancient aquarobics ladies and Mr Lunchbox have disappeared.

Well, Miss Arrogance. Today I got my comeuppance .

Instead of the swimming lanes being blocked off as they are during Monday morning aquarobics, the club managers have added a third lane, and in each of the three lanes were three health-freaks pounding up and down - fast crawl - faster than you could run along the edge, even. Not a trace of fat on any of them. They made me look like a porky, wrinkly, old walrus as I completed my slow 40 lengths of side-stroke, coughing and choking my way through the waves they created.

So some athletes do belong to my unhealth club after all. I don't know what's worse. Them, or the fat people. The answer - I must join Exeter's David Lloyd asap!

Urban or Rural?

12/03/2015

Muddy Matches asks you to say in your profile what percentage urban vs rural you are.

When I was a subscriber I put that I was 90% rural because I thought I would get more 'fans' that way.

But actually I don't know what I am, and recent events have underlined this dilemma.

Famous Film Star has gone cold. Boo hoo. I reminded him that I am visiting London for a dinner organised termly by Ex for London based parents of children in Will's school year. And this time I'm included too, even though I live 180 miles away. The dinner is to be held a short Boris-bike ride from Famous Film Star's home. But he is too busy with Poldark and everything else to see me. I am not quite gutted, but it's a bit of a bummer.

A couple of days ago, when I was hacking home on Perfect Panda, a lone, young, male foot-follower wound down his car-window and, smiling warmly, asked me if I had far to go.

I have noticed him being around and about before. He is so rural that he wears walking gaiters. I did a bit of research and discovered his page on Facebook. He is 'passionate about hunting, shooting, and fishing'. He's the sort who has an on-going subscription to the Countryside Alliance and yomps for fun across the moors. Whereas I would rather relax in my hot tub with its flashing fluorescent lights.

So I'm off to London for this dinner with the school parents shortly. I've booked myself into a hotel in East Horsley which has a swimming pool and only costs £55. I've also got to pay for the dinner, the diesel, and for Sashka to do all my work on top of what she normally does while I'm away. And then I shall race back for Faye performing Dulce et Decorum Est in her school's Spoken English Final. The highlight of the week.

Buying and Selling Houses

17/03/2015

Which is more important: position? Or community?

I find myself in a dilemma.

I'm on various estate agents' lists to be told about new properties available, and one has just sent me details of a nice Georgian house on at £595,000, five miles nearer than Wydemeet is to the A38.

What is so attractive about it is that it is within walking distance of two of my 'Thunderbirds' group - the South Hams Mums I meet up with every month. And both have individually told me what a lovely community theirs is. If I moved there, I would be nearer my friends and it's good riding, but I'd be hardly any nearer to the David Lloyd Club, my children's schools, my Mum, London, England, The World, The Galaxy, or The Universe. So it wouldn't really help with building up a new social life, if that's what I really want to do. Do I?

Meanwhile my 'viewer' from Guernsey arrived 1 1/2hrs early yesterday. He caught me enjoying a light, rather smelly lunch of Weightwatchers Beef Hot Pot for one, accompanied with a sherry glass of Cava, at 4.45pm. At least I wasn't still in my pyjamas. Luckily Sashka had performed miracles in tidying up the house, but it was rather cold and I hadn't yet got round to lighting the fire, making the place smell of coffee, or creating some 'mood lighting'.

The man told me about some other places he had been looking at. I think Wydemeet is rather outclassed by them. Grimstone Manor has an indoor pool and is priced at £1.25 million. Rather out of our league. I emphasised how cosy and homely Wydemeet is, and how its rooms don't echo. I had a sudden thought that the man might like Her house, which I believe She is shortly to put on the market. Perhaps I should tell him about it? Maybe not.

And then I learned that my Georgian potential purchase has already been snapped up for just under the asking price. No decisions necessary after all that.

The Book's Done!

17/03/2015

I'm still in my pyjamas.

It's 5.45pm.

I wonder what the Tesco delivery man thought when he arrived here just now?

But it's done! Surviving Solo is complete!

I have ordered a couple of memory sticks and will pop it onto those and send it to some friends for checking, tomorrow.

Meanwhile I shall investigate self-publishing options and report back.

Perhaps all the publicity my marketing of it will generate might even help me sell Wydemeet and find a boyfriend!

Tiny Tims

17/03/2015

There are currently five intelligent, articulate Dates who are interested in me.

All five are under 5'9", two are called Tim, and two are called Richard. Or, to be more precise, one is called Dick.

"You're not really called 'Dick' are you?????????????" I wrote back. So now I'm calling him Richard in order to take him a bit seriously. And the fifth one is my old mate Little John.

It's a bit of a bugger, sometimes, being tall. I'm really not at all sure I could fancy anybody as little as these guys are. I expect that's why they've ended up on an Online Dating site.

A bit mean of God, this, don't you think? To be so Height-ist?

Direct to the Top

20/03/2015

Nobody ever wants to sit next to the company chairman at Christmas office parties.

Except me.

So, as the newest, most junior executive in the PR firm - I was the only one to volunteer for the position. And what was the result?

"Do you want to hear all about what really goes on in your company?" I whisper to him, over our flaccid roast turkey.

Of course he does. So I tell him, and the result is that I am well paid, quickly promoted, and remain great friends with him to this day.

So my policy is always to go directly to the top.

When our McVitie's Penguin Polar Relay team of 25 jubilant women returned triumphant from their expedition, back in 1997, I called Tony Blair's new office at No 10 and invited us all to tea.

And now I've done it again.

I've asked the new headmaster and his family for Sunday lunch. But not content with that, I've also invited the new vice headmaster and his family, and two other families, that I don't know all that well either, who I like a lot because they appear to be along the same lines as us.

I'm not quite sure anymore why I've done it. I've chosen a day when Ex is here to help. One of the families was extremely kind to me all day last Saturday, when Mad Vegas went potty at their hunt meet. And the other family has been very hospitable to Faye and me over the past few months.

But I think it's mostly because on the face of it, I just think they're all really nice, and I want to get to know them better over a jolly meal.

I'm wondering to myself whether I have a hidden agenda, but if I did - I've forgotten what it was!

∞

On the Telly!

∞

A Bit Of A Day

26/03/2015

Four In A Bed is (or is it are?) definitely happening! They're going to film Wydemeet on Wednesday May 6th. Yikes! They've just called to confirm. They're putting me as last visit on the programme itself - no surprises there - they always put the posh people on last, when everyone is really tired and hating each other.

So I've emailed my great mate at Prince Hall Hotel, and also Clydesdale Adventures (riding massive carthorses across the moor), inviting them to save that day if they want to be involved, and warned the school that Faye will need the day off.

The whole project will take up two weeks, from April 27th, staying at the B&Bs in the competition, interspersed with other accommodation between filming. I must think about how I'm going to handle running my own B&B side of things during that time.

So that happened this morning.

Also - I have just sent my book to all those most involved with it, including Ex. I am quaking in my Uggs about what their reactions are going to be. The pressure is on now, to have it ready for purchase by the time the Four In A Bed thing gets aired.

Aaaghh! I really am on the edge of making myself famous. How scary! I wonder how famous I will go?

Also of major import is what to do about Will's school that he loves so much. I have spent a long time discussing the issue with Ex this morning. Will is lucky enough to be blessed with the most extraordinary physique and athletic ability, yet is about to enter the sixth form totally turned off sport because of the attitude towards it at his school.

But he's arguably the happiest, kindest, most balanced and most emotionally intelligent young person that I have ever come across. You can't ask for much more really.

I suppose we must grit our teeth and let his GCSE results speak for themselves.

Decisions, decisions. At least Ex and I agree on almost everything regarding our children, so I am not screaming in the wilderness.

And then this morning Faye was playing in the School Music Competition, for her last ever time, and the new regime wouldn't let parents in! After all my weeks driving 70 miles each way to her flute lessons because the school's teacher makes her cry. And then my having to find her a sax to borrow - she's having a go at that this term - because the school couldn't provide one! I am furious!

All this when I'm off to Austria on the school ski trip in two days' time, and am about to rent the house out for a week. I've done nothing at all to prepare it. I must go and mow the grass for the first time this year. It looks like a field. Bloody moles.

What would I do without Sashka?

A Sad Ending to A Happy Holiday

06/04/2015

Lying on a picnic rug in the sunshine after a ritualistic lamb shoulder lunch at my mother's house is my definition of Heaven.

Except I feel a bit funny.

I can't really move properly.

Arriving at Mum's, on our way home to still-rented-out Wydemeet, after our wonderful school ski trip, Will, Faye and I found ourselves at Granny's house in a small kitchen full of three octogenarians, all fighting over how to cook the broccoli. I love them all, and Will found himself even flirting a little, with scary Auntie Rhonda.

I had offered to drive her to the station this morning, to save Mum the effort, and to achieve the event in half the time Mum would take, but I had to give up on my offer because I felt too strange.

The skiing holiday itself had felt almost character-changing.

During the last few days' freneticism prior to departure, I think I developed IBS. That's what the internet told me when I checked out the symptoms, which I'm not going to go into here, because I'm too embarrassed to.

I think it was caused by stress – something that is not supposed to be on my repertoire. Bum. So to speak.

Anyhow, over the first few days' of the skiing holiday – which I hadn't gone on for the skiing, by the way – it gradually disappeared as I became happier and happier and happier.

It seemed as though everybody loved my presence and wanted to be near me. I have never felt so popular. It was absolutely lovely and I was encouraged to behave as badly as possible. I felt surrounded by warmth, trust, support and love.

All the men who came along were extremely attentive and I felt free even to practise a little flirting! I haven't done that for a couple of decades!

The whole thing has worked to be the best possible confidence-builder in advance of the looming filming of Four In A Bed.

But I appear to have caught something on the last day of the trip. If I have, I do hope it will go away soon. With my stupid lifestyle, I absolutely cannot possibly afford to be ill.

Ill, ill, ill

22/04/2015

I am screaming.

But no voice is coming out. Just a hoarse, moaning, rasping sound. There is no air.

The wire for the toaster is too short so I can't plug it in. It's just one thing too many. The last straw. Too much to bear.

Tears trickle slowly down the side of my face.

I haven't unpacked everything from letting out the house two weeks ago.

But my next B&B guests are due at teatime, and I'm not confident that even a 'hello' will come out of my voice box!

I crawl up the stairs to my unmade Bellever bed, meanwhile the enticing bright sunshine through the window laughs at me: "Come and ride your horses! It couldn't be more beautiful on the moor! They need looking after, exercising and enjoying!"

My head flops onto the pillow and I am virtually oblivious to what Jeremy Vine's yacking on about on Radio 2.

This feeling just won't go away. It's been days now. I have so little energy I can't think straight, let alone plan stuff.

I have no back-up support. Sashka is as ill as I am, but with something different.

I call up Ex.

"You know you offered to help? Well I need you."

That was 2 1/2 weeks ago. Since my lovely holiday. And I still feel more-or-less the same.

Life is no fun with flu.

And on top of all this, it appears that my friends don't appear to be very impressed with my book. Bugger. After all that. What am I going to do about it? I can't just give up, after so much time spent on it. Eerrgghh.

And now, looking back through everything I have written, it is clear that I seem to be constantly ill these days. How many times have I felt that the option of dying might be preferable to mowing the lawn before my guests arrive?

I always used to be completely robust. Something's going to have to change. As things are, life is proving a bit terrifying. I am responsible for my guests having the really happy time that they've been looking forward to for months. I've got to be all jolly on TV next week. And then I need to rewrite my book, leaving out 40,000+ words of boring, repetitive and irrelevant introduction, according to my many amateur critics.

I need to be firing on all four, or is it eight, cylinders if I am going to pull this lot off.

But all I want to do is to lie in bed moaning.

Four In A Bed - the master interview

22/04/2015

Five hours!

Of that, I expect they will use one minute.

They are going to portray me as the mother from Hell.

The camera's whirling, and I'm excited to bits, shouting at Faye: "Cinderella - make sure there's not a single curly to be seen on that bed! Each one will cost us a fiver!" as I pretend to polish the mirror over and over again, and she keeps straightening the already straight duvet cover. How we luuurve that camera!

The producer from Four In A Bed who has come to interview me tells me that she has also worked on The Apprentice and X-Factor. Respect!

She's only done a couple of Four In A Beds so far, which were in fact Three In A Beds, but the episode she was involved with that I saw featured two posh girls, both of whom seemed delightful. God I hope she can pull off the same for me!

I haven't the faintest idea how I'm coming across, saying what seems to me to be the same thing over and over again.

I'm sure we'll come last, whatever happens. I think the B&Bers the programme sends won't be able to sleep because it's too quiet here. They'll hate the intimacy of the layout of the house, and all the personal stuff in their rooms, and they won't be into walking, which is really what Wydemeet is all about.

My B&B is priced to reflect its unique location and my utterly totally fantastic unbeatable immaculate 24hr service.

Would I wash my guests' feet with my hair? Probably – if only my hair were long enough, and provided I hadn't just returned from carefully blow-drying it at the health club.

I'll even make guests' kiddies fish fingers for nothing – or go out in the Golden Monster to collect fat people who can't quite make it back from their over-ambitious walks!

This sort of thing looks good and generates blobs on TripAdvisor, without causing me much trouble at all. But you can't really measure such acts of kindness on the telly programme – they don't count in the scoring system.

During the endless interview, I'm trying really hard to be utterly hilarious, but that would be easier if I wasn't on my own talking to myself, sitting on a sofa, feeling half dead.

I'm wearing a fake-silk light pink top, white straight-legs from Per Una, and pink high heels. Faye wouldn't let me wear cut-offs because she tells me that my legs have gone purple with age and need hiding.

I had originally slapped on a new No 7 'Beautifully Matte Mousse' foundation in 'cool beige', but luckily, just before going on film, caught sight of myself in a mirror. Aagghh! I looked like a ghost complete with a face covered in deep ravines. I've had to do something drastic to repair it, with no minutes to spare! I feel as though I've gone back in time, preparing for a teenage party, trying to hide my spots with Clearasil!

I wonder what I look like on camera? Guess I won't know until the programme's finally transmitted. "Next January" they said. January??!!! God – I'll be dead from flu well before then!

I am absolutely freezing by the end of my interview, rather wishing I'd stuck to my normal black merino/cashmere.

Too late to change now though. On to another 'housework' scene.

Complete with Faye's miniature frilly black apron, I pretend to wash around Dartmeet's loo. I casually lean on its rim, forgetting for the moment that proper cleaners would probably wear some Marri's if they're anywhere near one of the guests' lavatory bowls.

"Yah," I drawl. "I've turned full circle. I was a chamber-maid at 17. Went to probably the best school in the world. MD of a PR consultancy. Now back cleaning lavatories again." I grin manically at the camera.

"They call me Lady Muck around here.....Blue wellies or pink?" I hiss at Faye.

 "Pink!"

So now we're filming in the garden, and here I am, resplendent in fake Victoria Beckham sunglasses, pink silky top, spray-on white trousers and bright pink wellies, struggling along behind an ancient rusty red rotary mower, attempting to cut the grass between the ubiquitous mole-hills, dog-poo, fallen twigs and stones.

I can't wait til the filming proper starts. I'm longing to be told what to do by somebody else, from dawn til midnight. It will be a total holiday.

I've got to visit the Isle of Wight, Cambridge, and Shropshire. Driving for miles! I hope I make a massive great profit on travel expenses! I'm off to Super Sexy Dick tomorrow to collect some new tyres for the Golden Monster, as I think my truck is going to be the biggest star of this show.

Today's experience would all have been huge fun if I wasn't feeling so terrible.

After the five hour marathon I lie, drenched in sunshine, on a sunbed - trusty Cava and fag by my side, feeling as though I would rather be dead for the rest of the day, even though I now have to drive Faye back to school, together with huge suitcase and laundry bag for her first and last term of full boarding. Blimey – her little prep school costs not far short of Eton's fees!

Faye is on a total pedestal at the moment. Outside of filming, she has spent nearly the entire weekend sewing on fifty name-tapes. The one occasion some years ago when I had a go, it made my finger hurt, and I've never tried again since.

"My time's worth around £40 an hour, so I would rather buy a new sock than sew a name-tape onto an old one," I gasp at her. And collapse back into bed.

Boring? Moi?

29/04/2015

I hurl myself off my Wetbike, which is travelling at 40mph, and dive into the sea, just in front of a Red Funnel ferry. The assembled crowd on the promenade roars.

That was in 1980, and now here I am, back again at what used to be the Groves and Gutteridge Boat Yard on the Isle of Wight, thirty-five years later, even more excited!

I had spent the most extraordinary summer 'Demonstrating Wetbikes' during the university summer holidays when I was twenty. Wetbikes are very noisy 50hp motorbikes that travel across water on skis instead of wheels –much to the displeasure of the Cowes Royal Yacht Squadron.

I love the Isle of Wight. For me it is boiling over with happy memories. Earlier I had parked the Golden Monster in an 'immobile home' carpark, crossed a quiet lane, and made my way to what appeared to be a rather ordinary house, with a little fountain in the front garden, and exquisitely manicured borders.

"Ring the doorbell," ordered a cameraman filming from behind a bush.

There was a proper bell hanging next to the normal bell, so I ding-donged on that.

Lots and lots of times, while the cameras followed me from different angles. "Lucky there doesn't seem to be a guard-dog barking on the other side of the door," I thought to myself. "It would have been driven mental."

After an eternity, the door finally opened, and there in the frame stood a smart-casually dressed bloke of about 50, smiling "come in! come in!". He quickly shut the door behind me so the cameramen could no longer see us, and -

Oh my God! There's another bloke in there! They're a gay couple! Of course! How typically Four In A Bed!

"SSSSHHHHHHHH!!! SSSSSSHHHHHHHHHHHHHH!!!" they grinned and giggled, giving me a group squeeze and a kiss. "We're only in this for fun! It's going to be really good," they enthused, and I fell in love with both of them on the spot, my feelings and views never to change over the next, intense, fortnight.

They showed me upstairs to a bright, light, pristine room, all coordinated and sparkling clean, with a chandelier made of what appeared to be glass bubbles. The loo was clean enough to eat your dinner off, and I could do my make-up in the reflection off the bathroom floor. £75 for the night including breakfast is miles too cheap!

As we were about to be whisked off to our 'activity', the boys looked doubtfully at my high heeled black suede boots.

"Would low, brown leather boots be better?" I suggested, but still no enthusiasm.

No one was prepared to even hint at what 'the activity' might be, and I've got to look my best at all times on this show – that's the whole point! So, belt and braces, so to speak. I lugged my entire suitcase into the minibus, and off we set.

And now, here we are at the old boatyard. And how glad am I that I brought everything I've got!

I disappear into a café lavatory, and substitute my' black' for a navy blue top, white jeans and a pair of white trainers that I have never worn in ten years. I'm terribly pleased, and immensely relieved, about my sudden nautical look.

There's a rumour about, that we may be kayaking. Yuck.

But the activity turns out to be tying knots, on the boys' old yacht. Callum demonstrates 'the bowline'.

I hate knots. Always have since I failed my 'knot badge' in the Brownies.

And now I finally get to meet the other two sets of 'contributors'.

Introducing Tessa and Ivor. Tessa is Sharon Osborne, but made of flesh and blood rather than silicone. It turns out we're the owners of identical horses -Tessa even has a photo on her phone of herself hunting! Ivor is a great big northern bloke with tattoos, who, holding hands with Tessa, suddenly does a skip to the side, like Piglet.

The other pair are Joan and Thomas. They have been listening carefully to Callum's instructions and are now tying their bowline, very efficiently and expertly. Oh my God. They're 'In It To Win It'! Tessa and Ivor mess up theirs, and it's my turn.

"I'll do a horse knot instead," I say. I tie something known as a 'quick release', and give up.

"All aboard," we heave anchor, and off we potter along the lovely river that I know so intimately. Soon the producer asks me to take the helm. Hurray! I'm centre-stage and star attraction, perfectly turned out in my boaty kit - the sun's smiling, there aren't any inconvenient waves nor wind, and I'm lurving that camera!

Back on land, and we're each ushered off for our first, of many, many, many 'LittleChats'. These provide us with the opportunity to slag off all the other B&Bers behind their backs. After all – they'll never know what we said about them until the programme is shown months away!

"Isn't Joan feisty? Isn't she good fun? Isn't she centre of the party?" asks my interviewer.

Eh? Instead of saying that I think quite the opposite – that in my opinion she's predictable, unimaginative, irritating and boring - I say that it is too soon to comment. I am also bland about the knot-tying and sailing experiences, because nearly all my friends in Devon have a boat, so I can sail whenever I want to – ie, never.

So I mutter, "I can't quite be doing with all this clapping."

Everyone else is gathered up, but I am taken to one side by the producer. Oh good. Something else special for me to do!

"You do realise that I can't use anything you've said," I'm told in an urgent whisper. "You of all people understand what we need for television. If you don't say anything more interesting, we can't show you."

Oops. That wasn't quite the reaction I had expected.

Let's hope I can pull off something better over supper.

Loving the Camera

30/04/2015

They've put me nearest to the cameras, towards the front of the table, next to the boys.

I can tell, or am I imagining things, that the programme makers are aiming to use me as 'the character' in this show.

I rise to the occasion.

I am hilarious. I am interesting. I am to the point.

"Pilot!" I explode. "You - uniform - travelling and all that!" I shout, pointing at Don. "You're a pilot!"

"I wish," he replies. "Purser."

"Oh, you mean head air steward type thing?" I enquire. This fits. He looks the definition of one. "On Thomsons? My children love Thomsons - you have tellies!" I cry.

I am so noisy that I am worried that I am becoming overbearing.

"What does Tessa think?" I ask, and push my chair back out of the way, so that the camera can see the others.

It has been a brilliant evening, in a restaurant set on the banks of the river. Quite beautiful as the sun sets across the water. As I complete my last LittleChat of the day, various middle-aged, middle-class, rather drunk yachties wobble past. They are fascinated by the cameras, and clearly want to be included. I am worried that they are going to fall into the river.

"Much better," says a relieved producer, later on in the evening, as I turn out the light.

Sobbing Live On Telly

30/04/2015

AAAAAAGGGGGGGGGGGGGGGGGGGGGGGGGGGGGHHHHHHHHHHHHHHHHHHHHH HHHHHHHHHH!!!!!!!!!!!!!!!!!!!!!!!!!!!!!!!!!!!!!!

That's me gasping out really loud - not quite screaming - I've only genuinely screamed once, and that was giving birth to my beloved daughter, Faye.

But - I think with what's just happened, I am likely to go viral on YouTube!

I am absolutely so shocked! Shocked to pieces! I leap back in abject terror! I can't believe it! I can't look! Aagghh - I feel sick! Urrghh! I clutch my tummy!

I have been checking out my new mate Tessa's gaff. It is immaculate - totally, utterly pristine, just as I would have expected of her. She is the ultimate professional. Everything is white. And new. Even the mattress! And mattress protector. And real soft white leather sofa and chair (well we are on the Essex border). And a carpet which looks like the most enormous sheep that was ever bred, or a rather small polar bear. So I lie down on it and find, as anticipated, it's fake. Jolly sensible. Dartmoor real sheep carpets are too small to be any use, and smell.

Anyhow, so I walk confidently into the perfect bathroom, complete with plastic roll top bath just like mine, but much better quality. Tessa's bath still has its silver feet, whereas I have painted mine gold. I nonchalantly open the plastic white shiny lid of the white shiny loo - and - OH MY GOD!!!!!!!!!!

There's this thin red worm about six inches long wriggling around in the water!

OH MY GOD!!!!!!!!!!!!!

Well. It's all caught on camera.

"It's a fix!!" I shout.

Which it actually couldn't possibly be, and which is an incredibly dreadful thing for the tv crew to have recorded. It could get them into terrible trouble with some 'compliance' thing or something.

But what dawned on me immediately, being a marketing/PR-type person, is that this is disastrous business-wise for Tessa and Ivor. It is worse than never having appeared on the programme at all! They will have been investing so heavily into preparations for weeks, to get the place looking like it does. Tessa has even handmade a massive - I mean literally ten foot tall - 3-D wraparound headboard!

"We've got to tell them - I mean I've got to tell them - what I've found," I whisper to the crew.

Tessa and Ivor are summoned, and I start:

"I..I...I.. I... there's a THING in the loo," I manage to get out, and suddenly I am in tears. Streaming down. They are going to hate me now. I always felt I liked Tessa more than she liked me, and now she is going to hate me!

The pair peer into the loo and are entirely calm, professional and smiling.

"I can't believe it! It should be you crying, not me!" I wail hysterically.

Me. Tough old me. Who never cries. I didn't even cry about the divorce.

And now it's all on celluloid. Or digital or whatever they use these days.

To be repeated on global television over and over again, for years to come, to the vicarious amusement of literally millions of happy viewers.

Speed Freak

01/05/20150

Big, big, slow, wide yawn.

"Is that really the time?" I sigh, checking my watch, and rubbing my eyes sleepily.

Joan and Thomas are driving a beaten up old Discovery, achingly slowly around a chicane, manoeuvring the car so that it doesn't touch any of the tyres marking out their path. Joan, in the driving seat, is blindfold.

We've already watched Tessa and Ivor kangaroo jumping along the course, and Callum and Don making rather an expert job of it, Callum guiding blindfold Don as though he were on the Golden Shot - "Left a bit, right a bit..."

I'm bored. And also slightly shaken, jittery, sad and upset about 'Wormgate'. But it's not allowed to be discussed with anybody now, not until the denouement at the end of filming in eight days' time. I must concentrate - it's my turn to drive now.

I choose Callum as my navigator.

I have to stick on the blindfold and somehow climb into the car. I fumble around for the gear stick, clutch etc.

"Right - I'm used to driving these things - I used to have a Range Rover," I challenge Callum. "Let's go fast!"

I find a small lever at the bottom of the driving well, and Callum assures me that it says 'L' for low range gears at one end and 'H' for high range at the other. I shove it towards what I hope is 'H'. I've got butterflies. I've no idea whether the car will even move now!

"Hurry up!" I'm thinking. And finally we're off.

I've no idea how fast we're going, but it feels quick enough to me. If we knock down a tree or a portacabin it doesn't really matter in this old banger.

"You need to go much faster!" says Callum. I put my foot down. We're still in first gear, but it feels as though we're flying, and I know that the other three couples only used the lower register.

"Right, right, right, no left, left, right, left," cries Callum. I appear to have done two circles, and then I have to leap into reverse for a bit, and then another circle and suddenly it's all over.

I get out to find that the guiding tyres are lying scattered all around the arena, but we appear to have completed the whole circuit quite quickly, if in a rather maniacal sort of a way.

The others are laughing. Phew. I think it was a success.

Ugly Bug Ball

01/05/2015

Charlene is filming me going to bed.

I have bought three new pairs of pyjamas especially for this bit. Two are polyester, meant to look like silk, and the third is a rather pretty floral cotton print. Tonight I am in the shiny baby blue ones.

Wormgate has been sorted as far as is possible, and I go back into the bathroom to go to the loo and on to bed.

Oh, NO! NO! NO! "There's a spider in here!" I involuntarily cry, before I've given what I'm saying any further thought. The spider is about three inches long and very spindly, making itself a little web in the ceiling corner over the bath.

"No, you're not getting this one. I won't have it. They've suffered enough," I yell at poor Charlene, who's hovering with her camera just outside the bathroom door. And I do one of the bravest things I've ever done in my life. I don't like spiders. But I grab some bog roll, climb into the bath, and aim to grab the spider.

But aagghh! It falls to the floor! It's still alive! Eeek!

Quick as a flash, in one movement, I jump out of the bath, stamp on the spider, pick up the gunge which is what's left of him with the bogroll, lift up the top of the loo, and flush.

Charlene doesn't quite know what to do. She leaves to ask the boss, and the matter is closed.

Unbelievably, in the early hours of the next morning, when I am caught short as is my wont, I hobble into the bathroom - and this time there is a woodlouse crawling along the floor under the basin! I ignore it, do my business, and return to bed.

Unusually for me, I don't tell anyone about it.

In the morning there are more grim-faced words.

I'm in trouble over the feedback forms. "You have been nothing but gushing about the boys' B&B," I am admonished. "You need to say something more interesting." It hasn't gone down well that I have paid the boys £15 over the odds because I think their B&B is worth £90 including breakfast.

Next, it appears to be a real problem that I have decided to give Tessa and Ivor nine out of ten for cleanliness, despite Wormgate.

"Obviously I can't give them ten, but the room is absolutely spotless, and you can tell it's always like this," I insist. "Wormgate did not make it dirty, it's not the result of it being dirty, and it's a one-off. The room is pristine."

And then comes the biggie.

"How much are you going to pay them?"

"You can't do that."

"I can, and I am. Their place may be a little impersonal for my taste, but in my opinion the room is worth £115."

So there.

The Horsehair Worm

01/05/2015

"SHRIEK!! Live worm in the toilet bowl! I don't suppose there is any chance it didn't come from someone's bottom is there? About 2-3 inches long, fairly thin and it was WRIGGLING. Bleurgh. Stool samples all round I think"

I've googled 'Worm In Toilet' and this is what has come up on mumsnet. Looks like I'm not the only one who was so shaken by my wormy surprise...

> "Eewwwwww , it could just be a stray worm gone the wrong way on its mid-afternoon walk..."

> "2-3 inches long is far too long to be a pinworm/threadworm from what I know. Pinworms look like little tiny threads not "fairly thin" and 2-3 inches long. Does it look like an earthworm?"

> "Did it look like an earthworm or not??? (Running off to puke in a non wormy toilet)"

> "Looked thinner than an earthworm. Too big for a threadworm and no itchy bums in the house. Feeling a bit sick since I saw it......."

> "Erm hate to say this but where else would it have come from? Or have you got an 8 year old boy who might have dug up some earth worms and put them there for a joke?"

> "Didn't look like a tapeworm (have been researching worms frantically since seeing the ruddy thing) but am clutching at the "maybe it got there another way" straw"

> "Don't google human worms - one image is horrific!"

So I've done a couple of hours' research, and I think I now know what it is. I think it's a horsehair worm. They can come up from the sewer, but live on insects. Apparently they tend to turn up after particularly heavy rain when the sewer is high, and wriggle their way into downstairs or basement loos which haven't been flushed for a day or two.

This would all fit, even though it is the most unbelievably bad luck and coincidence. I dare say that a large proportion of the television viewing public will simply assume that the worm was put there. But I am satisfied that it wasn't. And it is actually so sad that it has happened. It's going to affect everything. It's not really funny at all.

The Wheels on the Bus

02/05/2015

I'm sitting in the minibus between Don and Callum, waving both my arms in a circular motion, and merrily singing along at the top of my voice to 'The Wheels on the Bus'.

It is only after several verses that I suddenly jerk back to my senses. "Could someone please turn that racket off!" I yell to the front, but it is too late.

My weak moment has been caught on film. Indelibly. For ever. What an idiot I have made of myself to the global television viewership.

Apart from that, I think I have survived the first week of 'Four In A Bed' without saying something I will regret for the rest of my life. But you never know. And they do very funny things with the editing.

So far, it has been a blast!

For me, it is like reading a fairy tale and then finding that you are living it for real. All the images you thought were just imaginary have come to life, and are all around you.

Shag Fest

02/05/2015

"There've been some issues, but they're all under control now," says Sashka's message on my answerphone, the first time I have heard from home for five days.

What????!!!!!!!!!!!!!!!!!!!!! The stupid electric gate? The Aga again? The boiler? A burst pipe? The bloody Mazzarator? Ponies on my lawn? What could it be? I lie awake all night in trepidation as to what has gone wrong with my wretched house this time.

"Hya, yes. A colt stallion escaped from a nearby farm, got into the field, and has been shagging Vegas and Panda senseless, over and over again, for the past 24 hours," Sashka informs me, when I finally get through to her.

"Lucky them!" I exclaim. "I am so glad - Panda's nearly eighteen and has been longing for it all her life. What fun they must both have had. So what happens about the morning after pill then?"

I gather from Sashka that this kind of incident is so rare that immediate post-coital contraception doesn't really exist for horses, but Veronica, our vet, is sourcing an injection which has to be carried out within the next fortnight.

"I hope the farmer's paying," I say, and of course Sashka has already sorted that.

I wonder whether both mares will be suffering from morning sickness by the time I get home?

Getting to Wales

03/05/2015

We're very modern here.

X and his girlfriend and her two daughters are staying for the weekend, in order to help get Faye to the horse show on Monday.

Meanwhile my great mate Alice's husband is also joining us for supper - he is staying at nearby Buckfast monastery.

And also a Dutch couple have just arrived to stay for three nights, Faye's lovely friend Vivian and her Mum are coming in the morning to do some riding, and then a bloke's due to arrive who wants to look around the house, to see whether his sister, who lives abroad, might be interested in buying it.

Just when Sashka needs to get everything ready for the descent of the Four In A Bed cameras in three days' time.

We are all suffering from mild hysteria, while I'm rushing around writing this before I forget what I think; trying to pack so that I look reasonably attractive doing whatever the next activity turns out to be - it might be basket weaving - prior to setting off for Knighton, just beyond Hay-on-Wye, which, according to the AA will take me 3 1/2 hours. The thing is that judging by previous experience the AA man drives faster than I do, so I think it will be more like four.

I've washed all my black gear (that's all I've been wearing so far, apart from for the knot-tying activity). Louise, from the crew, who is permanently dressed as Marilyn Monroe, calls my black look my 'signature'. I've also washed my white trousers so that hopefully they can rival Tessa's for brightness. But they're still wet.

Most of the horsey girls involved with these episodes of Four In A Bed (and it would appear that there are now an incredible five of us, including Marilyn and Charlene) possess exactly the same kit, which is tight white trousers tucked into long brown boots, and a blue top. I am worried if I put on this uniform that everyone might think I'm copying Tessa and Charlene, so I may just stick to black. They are all so going to love my 'activity', but I'm not allowed to reveal what it is yet.

I am now having to be chaperoned at all times, because we have discovered that I am a real chatterbox, instinctively interrogating everybody I meet without even realising that I'm doing it! Whilst I am finally aware that you're not allowed to talk to anyone off-camera on this programme, I don't seem to be able to help it. It's absolutely not deliberate. So I keep getting into trouble, as everything has to be a surprise so that the camera can capture the contributors' genuine reactions to anything that's said.

I keep trying to second-guess what is going to happen next, but have so far been completely wrong every time.

I am chuffed to bits that Joan appears to 'get' me, rather than assuming I'm a posh bitch. "You and your one-liners - you should be on the stage!"

she said to me over breakfast at Don and Callum's. Oh how I preened! Oh how I warmed to Joan!

I've trawled through TripAdvisor, and I'm fairly sure that Joan and Thomas's place is going to be a small cottage with a music/craft/writing studio, in beautiful surroundings, with not great bedrooms. I think the activity is going to be either making sort of folk music, or learning a Ceilidh. I don't hate Ceilidhs as much as Morris Dancing, so I won't mind too much if it's that, provided we don't have to dress up. I hope it's not boring basket weaving. I would love to learn to play Frere Jacque on Joan's accordion, which she calls 'Flora', and takes with her everywhere she goes.

All will be revealed soon enough. I can't wait. I am permanently so excited in my Four In A Bed bubble that soon I am going to get a tummy ache.

Sorry Seems to be the Easiest Word

09/05/2015

Plop! The £1000 mike falls, splash, into my wee wee. Quickly I grab it by its wire and pull it out dripping wet, and wrap it in some bog roll.

I am festooned with wires and furry bits stuck to the inside of my jumper, attempting to go to the loo without any of the clobber falling off - forgetting that I am wearing two mikes, not just one.

"Oh no, Sixties Steve is going to be really cross with me now!" I panic.

Something about the stress of all this filming has turned me into a deeply clumsy person. First I throw chocolate powder all over The Boys' white carpet, having mistakenly thought it was a delicious low calorie chocolate mint, and attempting to rip it open with my teeth. Next, I trip over the leg of the TV crew's light, and send coffee flying all over Ivor and Tessa's Farrow and Ball immaculate stone coloured wall. And now this! All in just a couple of days' filming!

I have never said 'sorry' so often in my life! About once an hour, on average, I think. If I'm not bumping into things, breaking things, or making things dirty, I'm saying the wrong thing.

There is a technique to this interviewing business. You can never say 'they' - you always have to say "Tessa and Ivor" or whoever, as being a 'talking head' no interviewer is ever shown, and otherwise the thread of the story doesn't make sense.

Likewise, you must never look into the camera lens. "Sorry, oh so sorry, oh sorry silly me," I am saying, over and over again; until it is my challenge to myself to ensure that I am the quickest and easiest of the contributors to interview, requiring the fewest 'takes'. I will never find out whether I manage this, but I so want to come across as professional.

Sixties Steve has long straight hair, long curly sideburns, and dresses from head to toe in black. He is the soundman and initially has appeared rather reserved. He carries a big box around his neck with hundreds of aerials sticking out of it, and hides behind doors, listening to us chatting away all at once. I am intrigued as to what he has heard that he shouldn't have.

Gradually over the days, as I drop more and more mikes on hard floors (I find it entirely impossible to go to the loo with my elasticated pencil-line mini-skirt riding up above my bum, whilst at the same time retaining the mike in its place on my waistband) his expression begins to soften.

Steve originates from Shrewsbury; but I refer to it as Shroseberry, and tell him that there is a jolly good school there.

"It depends which side of the tracks you come from, whether it's Shrewsbury or Shroseberry," replies Steve. "Michael Palin went to the school there. I know because I've worked alongside his daughter who's great!"

Bog Snorkling

09/05/2015

Suddenly I snort out loud to myself with laughter.

I recognise this place. It's near where I once came to compete against Ex in the famous 'Man vs Horse' race.

Ex had been asked to start the event.

"This is the first time I'm going to beat my wife in public," he announced to the large crowd of runners, and off they set - hundreds of them.

Half an hour later, the horses trotted off from the car-park just outside the centre of the little town of Llanwrtyd Wells in central Wales, where the event is held every year, quickly catching up with the slowest of the runners.

The race is 26 miles long, over four mountains, taking place that year in 80 degrees Fahrenheit. Neither Ex nor I had done any preparation for it, and towards the end my horse, Foggles, could hardly move. I kept getting on and off him to give him a bit of rest, but I had to lean against him as we went on, as I could hardly walk upright!

That year the race was won by a man, with the first horse coming in third. Foggles and I did quite well, not all that surprisingly completing the race an hour before Ex. But Foggles wasn't a great horse for Dartmoor, and I managed to sell him to some other race participants, returning home with an empty trailer, legs so stiff I could only walk up and down the stairs backwards, and a cheque for £4000.

Anyway, the organisers, a company called Green Events, also stage the annual 'Bog Snorkling' contest.

So now it has suddenly dawned on me what our next activity is going to be.

"Oh no," I think. "How very Four In A Bed. They are going to completely humiliate us. Oh yuck. How disgusting – they're going to make us swim through mud."

I am otherwise so happy and excited by my whole Four In A Bed experience so far, that I find I am singing "He's a walking miracle; oooh

oooh!" very loudly, as I merrily drive the 179 miles from Dartmoor to the third B&B in the competition.

'That would be a good sing-along to include in the programme,' I think, but remember they can't use any modern tunes at all, even in the background, because of licensing and copyright issues. Presumably accounting for why there is so much more classical music used by the media than is probably reflected in real life. I quickly change to 'Men of Harlech', but can't remember any words other than 'gaily prancing'.

By now I am just on the Shropshire/Welsh border, and suddenly all along both sides of the road are pictures of my old mate Peter Downe - the best looking boy when I was at school. He would now be 56 and appears to be standing for the Conservatives in the election in a couple of days' time.

I meet with the TV crew at an impersonal hotel for another LittleChat, and then follow two of them to the third B&B, doing a few 'drive by' shots as we go. As ever, curious passers-by gather - dying to know what's going on, half-hoping they might get included, and half-hoping that they won't. This one looks like a rather threatening indigenous Forest of Dean type of person, shaking his fist at us.

On we go through countryside that looks like the cover of my copy of 'The Sound of Music'.

"Aagghh!" We have just driven past a large blue sign saying "Therapy Centre for Humans and Animals, and B&B".

"I don't want to be therapised!" I mumble. "I like me the way I am!"

So we're here, driving up a steep rough track to a rather tumbledown looking collection of sheds and a farmhouse, past an elderly-looking horse grazing calmly in a field.

As ever, I have to reverse, and then drive up to the house again several times, so that they can take shots of me arriving from different angles, 'tight' and 'wide'.

And finally I am allowed to meet up again with Thomas and Joan - tonight's hosts.

It turns out that the pair met when Thomas was Joan's temporary bank manager. "Oh dear - I do my banking on-line" I wail. "No wonder I find it so impossible to meet anyone!"

They take me up a narrow stairway to a small, pretty bedroom. I am very agreeably surprised. It's called 'The Lilac Room' even though everything is blue, and there is a picture of a hyacinth on the wall.

The twin beds appear to have new mattresses, bedlinen and pillows. "Not bad," I think. And then I am told that we have 'shared facilities'. There's a loo along the passage, and a bathroom down the stairs, through Thomas and Joan's kitchen, past a couple of large, rather smelly dogs in big cages, and through another doorway or two.

I am filmed examining the bathroom's cleanliness, and discover lots of drip marks on the shower, an old bath mat with hairs underneath it, and some very healthy-looking plants hanging over the edge of the bath where your head would normally go.

"I probably won't use this, as I had a bath this morning, and it's a rather long way to come from the bedroom," I say to the camera.

If talking to yourself is the first sign of madness, any viewers of this programme will think I'm completely barking, as I do very little else. And I return to my room to prepare for the 'activity'.

We are led into Thomas and Joan's smallish sitting room where Joan kneels with a fluffy welsh collie on her lap.

"We are going to be learning shiatsu for dogs today," she starts.

She shows us where all the energy lines are along the dog's back, an inch or so away on each side of the spine, and then each B&B is presented with a dog of our own.

They're quite nice dogs, and I have a go, but really it's just easier to stroke it. I am partnered with Thomas, so when it's his turn to massage the dog I say, "Presumably you've massaged dogs millions of times. Why don't you massage me instead? " and I lie down on the rug which has been put down for the dogs.

Joan is not amused and inadvertently calls me the name for a female dog in front of everybody and on-camera. "Do you really want all the men to lie on you?!" she exclaims.

Ooops. I pretend I have hardly heard, but really - she does get it wrong sometimes!

Come morning I realise that I must wash my hair yet again, if I'm going to continue to be of universal appeal to all man once this programme gets aired, and I wander the 1/2 mile down to the bathroom in my fake silk polyester dressing gown. Cold water! Aggh! My pet hate! But I just have to wash my hair, so I do it quickly, leap out of the bath, and am so cold that I run back upstairs, forgetting to leave everything nice for the next person, or to pick the mat up off the floor, while the hairy grungy tepid water slowly runs out of the bath.

Trying to blow dry my hair is tricky with a mirror of a 2" diameter – that's all there is in the bedroom. I have to keep running from the hairdryer to the bigger mirror in the upstairs loo to sort out my fringe.

Thomas and Joan don't serve a full English breakfast, just their own eggs and continental everything else.

"Oooh that's a big one!" I hear myself saying, as I help myself to the largest croissant that I have ever seen. Meanwhile Ivor, who likes his bacon, launches into a discussion about which is least healthy: a grilled cooked breakfast, or a sugary fatty croissant, sugary cereals and sugary yogurt.

Joan, meanwhile, is in a state because she has prepared her cooked eggs for the agreed time of 9.30am, whereas everything is running late as ever, the eggs are all going hard, and her hens haven't laid any more.

The feedback form is tricky. I haven't slept for weeks, last night mostly because of the mild, invasive smell of dog which I simply can't stand. Mine looks as though it's a new carpet, but I can't help wondering how many different visiting dogs have slept on it. At 4am, or anyway some time well before dawn, an insistent cockerel starts up and won't stop. I'd always thought I would like to keep chickens, but this one I hope we'll have for breakfast.

I mark Thomas and Joan's 'facilities' with a 5, and circle the 'No' at the bottom of the form, to let them know that I don't want to come back.

Having said that, at £55 for two, this is the perfect place for impecunious dog-lovers. Cheaper than staying at home, utterly stunning location, and interesting hosts too. Joan is a very qualified horsewoman and animal shiatsu expert, while Thomas is president of some Carp Fishing Society and drives cars between destinations as his professional occupation.

If you don't like a fair amount of animal dirt, shared not immaculate facilities, and hundreds and thousands of animals everywhere you look, however, steer clear of this place by five miles!

Playing the Game

09/05/2015

The original verbal agreement with the programme's producers had been that I was taking part 'in order to find a new boyfriend'.

But it seems that the people involved in the programme change almost by the hour, and today's producer wasn't party to this discussion.

Which makes things difficult for both of us, because, in retrospect, I don't think that she would have supported the idea.

As filming progresses, things seem to be becoming increasingly tricky. After all – it is supposed to be a competition. I am a bit paranoid that I am constantly doing or saying the wrong thing.

We agreed from the start that I won't let on to anybody that my house is up for sale.

It's beginning to drive me nuts that I'm not allowed to ask anybody anything except 'have you seen the weather for tomorrow?' Perhaps I am affected particularly strongly because I haven't anybody with me to share my experiences.

But it's a shame, because I think it means 'Wormgate' is beginning to fester.

The camera crew members however, are absolutely delightful, cheerful, interested and enthusiastic, and so easy to talk to that I am beginning to wonder what I have found myself saying to their cameras. The more charming they are, the less discreet I become. I am playing for laughs and I love those cameras!

But one of my concerns now, is that by being so keen to please and 'play the game', dear Joan is unwittingly turning herself into the fall guy.

Charlene asks during one LittleChat: "Are you afraid of Joan?"

I explode with spontaneous mirth, gasping for air.

"What are you on? No, of course not! But I am afraid of hurting her."

I am beginning to think that Joan is a well-meaning, straightforward, rather vulnerable and fragile person, however loud, bossy and opinionated she might be.

I have always felt that it would be in my interests to be nice to, and about, everybody in this show – I even wrote to the original producers saying so - and I'm sticking with my decision, however hard it is sometimes. "Be nice, nice, nice, nice, always nice," is my daily mantra to myself.

It is confusing being in a competition which you've never had the slightest intention of trying to win. "Don't you think that's a bit defeatist?" I am asked, when yet again I state with conviction that I am going to come last, because the competition criteria simply don't fit my niche business.

But I just won't compromise my integrity by saying something that I don't mean.

"If it were called 'The happiest remotest luxury B&B in Southern England' then I might go all competitive on you," I explain to the producer.

The format just doesn't seem to work smoothly with me being more interested in selling myself, than in selling my B&B.

Eventually I am clearly advised that the programme cannot include the fact that I'm looking for a boyfriend in the final edit. And by now, as it happens, I have reached the same conclusion myself. There are just too many weirdos out there, and I am too vulnerable, living alone with my young daughter in the middle of nowhere.

The thing's not going to be transmitted until next January anyway, and who knows what will have happened by then? I should have sold the house, I may have new a boyfriend. I may even be dead!

Meanwhile, taking part is proving even more fun and interesting than I thought it would. My biggest worry now, is that if Tessa and The Boys get any funnier, I am going to wet myself in front of 10 million people all around the world!

And then Chazza, the most junior member of the crew, suddenly asks me whether I have considered appearing on 'Gogglebox' - an incredibly popular television programme that his company also makes, featuring normal people (if you can call them that) sitting on their sofas watching telly and commenting on what they see.

"Well of course I have," I reply, monumentally flattered. "Can you get me onto it?"

Like Gogglebox, one of the most endearing characteristics of Four In A Bed, I think, is its quirkiness. While the contract states that contributors should adhere to 'the spirit of the game' – it's not spelled out anywhere that I can find, what this actually is. We carefully complete all the feedback forms, yet the marks and comments we give have little or no bearing on the final outcome of the competition. We're not allowed to use half-marks on the form – but God knows why not. For instance, I wanted to mark Tessa and Ivor 9.9 recurring for 'cleanliness', but wasn't allowed to!

Meanwhile, in my experience, the low-budget generalist types of accommodation tend to do better, though not always, than the niche operators such as Joan and myself.

Each participant's interpretation of what a 'best value B&B' should comprise is just so wonderfully personal, individual - and unpredictable.

And it's all these imponderables and constant surprises that, for me at any rate, give Four In A Bed its uniquely addictive charm and appeal.

At Home to Four In A Bed

09/05/2015

"It's just beautiful!" I breathe down the phone to Sashka.

I am home from Shropshire and have examined, in microscopic detail, the three bedrooms that our guests are going to use. The only fault I have picked up is a forgotten coffee pot in one room. Sashka has achieved a miracle!

I can almost feel the determination and stress that she and Godfrey have undergone as they've been touching up this, and mending that - even repainting an entire wall in the dining room - because the congealed food stuck to it over the last decade, behind my grandmother's rusty old plate heater (I've replaced it with a new one off eBay), looked so unedifying.

I race out into the garden, through the howling gale and rain, in the dark, to do the mowing, while Faye is ordered to sweep up leaves off the steps, clean the weird stone sculpture, and put away the garden chairs' dripping cushions. As I chug my way up and down last week's stripes in the lawn, I pause to stuff torn up bits of old rag, drenched in petrol, down the mole hills - perhaps that will finally stop the blighters in their earthy tracks.

That night, I have to choose between sleeping in Will's room in the attic, or on the sofa in the sun (or more appropriately named rain) room. I opt for the latter, and at last Faye and I bed down, leaving the three immaculate bedrooms and en-suite bathrooms ready for the TV crew to invade at 8am the following morning.

I am not at all surprised that I don't sleep - as usual - and to make things worse, the light floods in through the skylight early the next morning.

The producer can't include me raving on about Sashka in the programme unless she is actually filmed, as it doesn't make logical sense for me to refer to someone that the viewers don't get to see. So, rather reluctantly, she arrives too, just as the film crew draws up.

We all stand in the kitchen and I am given another friendly warning about behaving myself — rather similar to what I'm in the habit of receiving from Sashka — but she has known me for ten years!

Sixties Steve wanders in, wondering, apologetically, whether he might exchange his instant coffee for real. He appears to be something of a coffee connoisseur, buying his own brew from Regent Street and preparing it in a Nespresso machine, he explains.

My first B&Bers are about to arrive and I am genuinely excited and looking forward to entertaining them! They are so nice! I am longing to show off my lovely home to them!

The first pair to arrive are Tessa and Ivor. "It's exactly what I thought it would be!" exclaims Tessa, hugging me and jumping up and down.

"Good - she's got me," I think to myself, relieved. We film their arrival, including Twiglet, a few times, and then I take them up to Hexworthy, and we have about three takes of that too. Ivor and Tessa appear to be OK about the room. Ivor's not quite sure what the genuine Corby trouser press thing is. Meanwhile I think to myself how glorious the large south-facing, pristine room looks, with sunshine (all of a sudden) flooding in.

I retire downstairs and twiddle my thumbs for a while, until The Boys arrive. How I love them! I show them up to Dartmeet a few times for the cameras, and then retire back to the kitchen to twiddle my thumbs some more.

Finally Thomas and Joan turn up in their old banger. (Ivor and Tessa drive an enormous, white, bling truck, very like mine.) I have been worrying about Joan. My sense is that she has been annihilated on her feedback forms, and that she will be very upset. But she seems perfectly sanguine and cheerful, and I give her a long, hard, meaningful hug - which has to be done again because we have squashed the microphone.

I take them up to Bellever and start twiddling my thumbs some more.

I am extremely troubled because Sashka disappeared without saying anything, while I was completing my first LittleChat of the day. I am anxious that she is twitchy and tired from working so hard on my behalf, and possibly upset that I asked her to make a different kind of coffee, and has gone off hurt after all that she's done for me, and now I can't credit her in the final programme, which will really matter when it's on air and all this is over.

I can't really think or concentrate on anything else actually. If I have inadvertently made Sashka unhappy, this is miles more serious than appearing on a TV reality show.

Suddenly the pressure is on, and I'm no longer enjoying things quite so much.

Adventure Clydesdale

10/05/2015

"You look like someone from a Jilly Cooper book," says Thomas.

Ooops. Maybe I have gone a bit far. I am wearing Christmas stocking present brand new bright white spray-on jodhpurs, long black riding boots, a well cut tight brown shooting jacket, hairnet and hat, and swishing around a very long, very whippy, dressage whip. Maybe I'd better drop the whip.

I've displayed a couple of fishing rods by the entrance of the house, to put the contributors off the scent of what we are really going to do, because - of course - we are going to be riding for our 'activity'!

But not just any old riding. We're off to see the magnificent Clydesdale horses who live up the road. These are huge heavy horses, originating from Scotland. They look quite regal, striding in a line out across the moor. A couple of weeks ago at the local point to point, I won £8 on 'Tom Parker' who came in first in the special Clydesdale race.

How incredibly fortunate we have been regarding 'activities' on this programme. Boating, off-road driving, 'dogging' and riding. No silly dressing up, no humiliation, all genuinely interesting, sensible on the whole, and enjoyable things to do. What a relief!

We climb into various cars, and enjoy all the normal guessing games as we approach the horses' yard about, "I wonder what the activity's going to be?" Finally we're led into four roomy stables, each housing a horse for us to groom and prepare for hacking.

Tessa gets on with the job in hand, while Ivor looks on, meanwhile Joan goes into mega horsey-woman mode. "I am a qualified whatever in this, and an advanced thingy in that," she informs Tarquin, the owner. She grooms her horse in two minutes flat and then looks at me.

"Not like that Mary! Is that all you've done?" she cries, and comes into my box. My horse is called Cyril.

"You'll be kicked if you brush the tail that way," she says. "Look, I'll show you!"

So she puts the not very clean thick tail across her thigh, facing the back of the box, brushing it vigorously. "That's how you do it!" she says triumphantly.

"But I'll get my new jodhpurs dirty if I do that," I wail, and go to rub Cyril's forehead, as I have seen Monty Roberts, the horse whisperer, do on telly.

"Actually, it's a good thing to work with animals slowly and quietly," comments Tarquin, as I softly murmur "who is this bossy lady?" into Cyril's ear.

Joan is now busy doing all my work for me, as I go to lean against the side of the box. I am knackered. "How is it that I so often, and so easily, get other people to do everything for me?" I wonder to myself for the millionth time.

And now we are ready to mount these enormous, gentle creatures. It is extraordinary how you can tell how good a rider is, almost right from the moment they first approach a horse. I am not disappointed. It is clear that both Joan and Tessa know what they are doing. I am in love with Tessa's lower leg position. Heels down, feet steady. I wish I could ride like that.

We proceed in a stately fashion to a nearby field, and walk around it, with Callum on a leading rein, astride the glorious Tom Parker. I am fairly scared. Panda and Mad Vegas are the only two equines I have ridden in six years! Riding a new horse is much more frightening than, say, driving an unfamiliar car.

To start with, everything is sort of OK, but then they want us to walk away from the TV crew, and canter back, towards them, which is also slightly downhill and towards home for the horses. Oo-er. If I were organising such a thing I would opt for an enclosed track leading up a hill and away from home.

Anyhow - so we three riders walk our horses away from the assembled group of spectators and cameramen, reach the end of the field, prepare to turn around, and suddenly - bingo! The horses turn on their haunches and fly into a fast and extremely bouncy canter, swooping up and down like dolphins, if that makes sense. I am taken totally unawares. I can't stop Cyril, and am conscious that his bounciness is infecting the others. It feels as though I am charging back towards home, but dammit, I've gone the wrong way round the camera. So we have to do it again.

This time Tessa's horse does the most enormous leap into the air. She sits it well, and it feels as though mine wants to copy her. Oh no! "One more time!" cry the cameramen. The horses are beginning to go a bit bonkers now. They're not machines. Off we go, attempting to walk away but they're jogging. We try to turn them right instead of left, which is the direction they're used to, but no - off they bomb again.

"I'm bottling out," I announce, and go to stand next to Callum. Tom Parker the wonder-horse, continues to stand quietly, while the two more proficient riders have one more go at the canter.

At last it's time to ride the horses back to their boxes, and I heave a sigh of relief. Phew! That was a bit exciting! They don't behave like that out on the moor!

The Last Supper

10/05/2015

Supper with all my new friends is to be at the lovely Rugglestone Inn, just outside Widecombe - the pub of choice with the locals because of its good food, genuine rural atmosphere and friendly service. This is going to be the most wonderful finale to our adventure! And even better, Sashka has replied to the two devasted phone messages I've left her, explaining that she simply had to leave in order to do some work for her other clients! Phew, phew, phew.

"So why have you taken part in this programme?" Joan turns to me, over her shepherd's pie.

"Move the camera!" shouts the producer, before I have a chance to make up a reply.

And then Ivor gets going. With his back to me, and looking at the wall, he challenges me on my dog policy, and asks me why I run a B&B in the first place.

All these questions would be fine if my inquisitors looked me in the eye and questioned me in a smiley friendly way, but suddenly everything seems to have gone cold and aggressive.

I'm flustered, I go all defensive, I start banging on about private schools in a stupid way as nobody has attacked me on that front as yet.

And then I make my biggest gaff of all time.

"If you're so broke, why don't you open your smallest room for one night at a time?" somebody asks me, perfectly nicely and innocently.

"Oh because I can't be arsed," I reply nonchalantly.

Oh dear. There's a sudden atmosphere.

"Oh, quick, can you change that to 'because it's not efficient for me'?" I yell to the cameras, but no, of course they can't. Deary me. I've really buggered it up now.

I have been found out. I am arrogant. I am flippant. I don't take this business seriously. I look down on people who rely on it. I clearly don't need the money. I don't do it as my livelihood. I'm all platinum spoon after all. Oh dear.

I am deeply distressed. I have lost my new mates in one throw-away remark.

I am incredibly uncomfortable, and so massively, massively disappointed after what I had thought was going to be a thoroughly enjoyable evening.

And then, before anything has a chance to be resolved, or any of us has been allowed to have pudding, the crew is clearing up the cameras, ready for our LittleChats, which take part in various nooks and crannies of the pub, and/or outside in the freezing cold.

I tell the camera that I think Ivor has asked some useful, pertinent and fair questions, but that I am terribly upset by his body language.

When we get home I 'prep' breakfast - putting out all the pots, pans, bowls, utensils etc that last week I wrote down that I would be needing. Breakfast tomorrow will be the biggest challenge of the whole adventure - breakfast for six people, each of them asking for something different.

Thank God I made that list well in advance. I am in such a state after that dinner that I can't really think straight.

Then I do what the TV crew do. I write up a Q&A crib sheet for myself.

"Why am I taking part in Four In A Bed?"

"Because I want to learn how to run my Bed and Breakfast better, from the most experienced and knowledgeable, and most critical judges I could possibly ever find," I lie merrily.

"What is your attitude to dogs?"

Well I have discovered that on the Home Page of my website, in the third paragraph I have written "sorry no dogs as they eat Twiglet and whine, and upset the other guests", and then further down in the fifth paragraph I've called Wydemeet a dog friendly B&B! Stupid me. So I immediately make up a new policy. I will take dogs in low season, but not at peak times. Hah! Sorted!

And finally ...

"I run the B&B because after the marital bust-up I lost my family - and I wasn't prepared to also lose the home that I know and love, that I bought for us all twenty years ago; or to take my children out of their schools, or sell my horses," I wrote down. "In the event, I did actually have to sell the car that I adored, replacing it with a Ford Focus I bought off eBay for eight hundred quid.

"My income was slashed, but I am hugely lucky enough to retain some, and the B&B is an attempt at enabling me to continue with my ridiculously grand lifestyle. Incidentally, I don't see any of you having to sleep on the sofa, or live without a bedroom."

".... But I am massively busy looking after the children all on my own, and time is my enemy. So everything I do has to be highly efficient. It doesn't make sense for me to use the smallest room for B&B for a night at a time. I can make far more money, miles more quickly, by simply using the two big rooms, for a minimum of two nights each."

Well. Ivor has inadvertently forced me to address the real issue. He has taught me what it is that my oldest friends have failed to get through to me over the past 55 years. That I have a habit of getting carried away, in order to be provocative, to show off, to get attention, exaggerating, saying things that I don't entirely mean, in order to cause a reaction.

And sometimes, most especially with strangers from very different backgrounds, my audience doesn't get it, takes what I am saying at face value, and without even realising what I am doing, I cause massive, massive offence.

A fifth reason that I got involved with Four In A Bed was to find out how I come across. Well I have just found out. And I am shocked and shaken. And now I understand so much.

So, with my answers all written down and sorted in my head, I am ready to face the contributors and the cameras over breakfast tomorrow, and at the denouement on Friday. Now that I know what I am going to say, I am finally so relaxed that I oversleep on my big white sofa.

A Circus Act

10/05/2015

Faye, until today, had never heard of AbFab. Well now she has. She's watched eight old episodes and laughed her head off.

All starts calmly. Cooking breakfast for six on a two plate Aga is a challenge for anybody, but I've remembered to turn it up the previous night, and I'm heating all the water separately in an electric kettle, so that it doesn't lose all its heat.

Initially I had said to the programme makers that I would just be offering a full English to the other contributors. But it turns out that this is against the rules - you have to offer them what you would normally offer to your guests.

Oh dear.

I habitually say - "You can have whatever you can think of for breakfast, except things that I don't like, such as kippers, haddock, black pudding and stuff. So here's a suggested menu, but you can try me with any other ideas, and I will have a go."

So that's what I am going to have to say. And I know Four In A Bed types - "A full English with no beans"; "A double full English with two sausages but only one egg," "Eggs Royale combined with Florentine", etc etc etc.

So I have had a wizard wheeze. I will cook eggs to order, but get Faye, aka Cinderella, to do silver service, or at least stainless steel service, with the rest.

I have decided that we will take the orders together, since this is Faye's first attempt at being a breakfast waitress, and under the cameras it appears to be so very difficult to get everything right, even though it looks a bit weird for us both to be standing there, pens and notepads poised.

"So, teas and coffees?" I query. Five English Breakfast Teas and one coffee are requested. Not too difficult, yet somehow even this simple order immediately flies out of my head.

Very soon all is ready, and I pour Joan a nice, big cafetiere full of coffee.

Oh no! There isn't enough hot water left in the poxy plastic electric kettle to fill three further teapots! I put enough in each one for a single cup of tea, and we take them through.

Dammit. Don lifts up his teapot, realizes it's very light, and looks inside.

"There's no water in here, Mary!" he laughs. There's not enough in Tessa's and Ivor's shared silver teapot for a cup of tea either. I can't believe it! How could I have been so stupid?! I pretend to shoot myself as I am filmed.

Once the hot beverages have been sorted, even lactose free warm milk for Joan's coffee, Faye and I go back again into the dining room, to take the dreaded cooked breakfast order, and I explain what's on offer.

Unlike the other contributors, I am cooking breakfast for six, not five, and then Joan goes and orders two breakfasts: a cheese omelette and a baked egg, so in the final analysis I am actually preparing seven breakfasts. Aaagghhh!

Meanwhile Faye reappears in the kitchen, interrupting my flow of intense concentration. "Joan says her bowl is dirty, and there aren't any more of the proper ones," she informs me. And calmly, in front of the cameras and everybody else, she gives Joan a little plastic baby bowl with a picture of Donald Duck's wife on it, with 'oops!' written on the bottom, left behind by the last people who rented Wydemeet.

Next, I reappear in the dining room with more pots of tea, porridge for Don, and we need a couple more mats to protect the rather nice polished mahogany table from all these hot utensils.

"Over there, Cinders!" I order Faye.

She opens a drawer.

"There's nothing but your old love letters in here," she says, and howls with laughter, tears streaming down her face.

I return to all my pans and quite quickly everything is ready in all its different dishes. I ask Faye to take through the sausages and (both back and streaky) dry cured bacon, all kept warm under silver foil, and put them on the new plate heater in the dining room. I stick the dish of tomatoes, sautéed potatoes and mushrooms on the side of the Aga while I complete the eggs.

Oh no! I've cooked fried instead of poached for Callum! Quickly I put more hot water on for the poached egg, and slide three fried eggs onto Ivor's plate - after all he did say, "As it comes."

I am about to send Ivor's eggs out with Faye to the table, when I notice a 'curly' stuck in one of them. I am shaking so much by now that I can't pick it off. I nearly have to ask Faye to do it.

Meanwhile - baked egg????!!!! I haven't done one of those since I was on the Cordon Bleu School of Cookery's Brides' Cookery Course which I did with a bloke when I was 17, and nearly got flung out for drinking the wine instead of putting it in the cooking.

I butter a little pot, break an egg into it and shove it into the top oven of the Aga for a few minutes.

Nigel the cameraman, who has been filming my activities in the kitchen, asks me to take it out and put it back in again. "NO!" I scream, aware that I am shaking so much by now that I will definitely drop it.

Faye takes the plates with their eggs on into the dining room, and together we provide our stainless steel service, moving to each contributor around the table, and then we leave them to it, to enjoy.

"How do you think it went?" queries Nigel, camera up close.

"God (by mistake I seem to prefix everything with 'God', which they can't use on a family TV show) - that was worse than a 2'9" cross country course," I exclaim. "But not as bad as a 3' one."

I go back in to clear the plates.

"That breakfast was absolutely divine!" exclaims Joan. I am touched to my core.

"My sausage was cold," says Ivor.

"I'm afraid my food was rather cold too," says lovely Callum.

Oh dear. Faye, not realising what it was for, had inadvertently taken the silver foil covering off the sausages and bacon.

Tessa has left both her specifically requested white toast (I actually gave her a 'Bit of Both' - slightly mouldy - all I had) and her rather runny scrambled egg. She will be hungry for the rest of the day because of me.

Aagghh!

"How did you all sleep?" I chirrup.

"We ran out of hot water in the shower," says Tessa.

"Ours went cold too," Callum says reluctantly.

Oh dear. My two absolute no-no's. Cold water and cold food. Oh well. I'm not 'In It To Win It' anyway - I have always said we would come last. These people are not my normal customer base. I do not normally cook for six or seven people all asking for different things at once. And I am targetting my real customers through the telly. It doesn't much matter what these six think - it is what the viewers think, and I am simply praying that the entire fiasco has looked like tremendous fun and very appealing.

Anyone with any intelligence will be able to see that cold food here is an anomaly (I hope!) Faye and I have been trying out a new system and it hasn't quite worked. But it will another time. And it did mean that anybody could change their mind about what they had at the last minute, if they wanted to.

The couples are taken away for their LittleChats and I go and sit outside in the sun, which has suddenly come out – hurray! A sheep and her lamb have appeared on the lawn, another favourite cameraman, Bob, is taking lovely pictures of the house, and all is looking gorgeous.

Faye and Twiglet bounce over. "That was SO FUN!!!" exclaims Faye, as Twiglet jumps six foot straight up in the air to retrieve a proffered dog treat. Faye is, without doubt, Television Gold.

But, I, on the other hand, am finding it very, very difficult to calm down. I have been so very outside my comfort zone.

"Sort yourself out, girl," I scold myself. "It went well! It was funny! And it was also perfectly clear that you can cook a really good breakfast under normal conditions too!"

The next stage is the goodbyes, each of which has to be shot from several different angles several times. Poor Ivor has to lug an enormous suitcase up and down my steps over and over again. Never mind. He's a strong, fit man. He was selected to play prop for the English rugby team, but then had a mining accident, and now has two metal plates in his back. A story that, if prompted, will make him break down and cry when repeated.

I am dying of curiosity to know whether Wydemeet is what my new friends expected. In a quick private moment, Tessa whispers to me off-air: "I thought it was going to be immaculate!" and Joan says so too. I am chuffed to bits. Clearly they are both of the opinion that I have been looking chic and smart, in my three new, identical, black woollen jumpers. So they didn't notice my shellac manicure beginning to chip after disposing of mole hills, the fact that my socks are different lengths, and that under normal circumstances, I have flat greasy hair and am covered in straw.

I wave them all off, and now it is reading the Feedback Forms time. The most emotionally demanding part of this entire experience. I am absolutely scared stiff of what is about to be revealed.

No, No, Yes!

10/05/2015

"It's as though it's alive; pulsating and evil!" I exclaim to the camera, as I eye the "Four In A Bed" blue book in front of me, not allowed to open the front page until I'm told 'go'.

"How good was your hostess?" is the first question, and I've scored a 9. There's a smiley face, but also a sad one. This form has clearly been completed by Tessa.

Shame. I've always thought my best thing is my hostessing. The sad face is about their confusion as to who I am, and what exactly I am trying to say and do.

The rest of the marks, considering Wydemeet is the sort of place that they would never, ever choose to stay in, I think are relatively generous. Clever Tessa has spotted that my curtains haven't been cleaned for years. They hate the feeling that they're in 'my' room, they had cold water, but they like the spaciousness and the 'accessories'.

It's a 'no' to coming back again. No surprises there.

The next form is from Joan and Thomas. They've given me a relatively poor eight for my hostessing skills. "Welcoming, but lacked the one-to-one service that we would normally expect from a B&B," they write.

"What's that about?" I wonder to myself.

I move down to facilities. They've given me a 4. No wardrobe, marks on the wall, room too small for two, unfinished light fitting, knobs loose on bedhead - on and on it goes.

Damn. They've lifted up the dead sheep on the floor, and discovered the hole in the carpet where the old basin used to be. Bellever was a wash room complete with showers and loos when we bought the house, as Wydemeet used to be an adventure centre, accommodating 36 children at a time!

It's another 'no' as far as coming back is concerned. Again not a surprise. Joan has been clear that she doesn't like the look of Dartmoor. "Bleak, featureless and thin ponies" is how she describes it, compared with her beloved Shropshire.

This is all becoming a farce. I am beginning to laugh about the whole thing. Then I turn to the last page.

Hostessing skills: "TEN!!!!!!!!!!!!! FANTASTIC!!!!!!!!!!!!! A giggle a minute!!!!!!" have written The Boys. Cleanliness: 10, Spotless! Sleep quality: 10.

Facilities: "very upset that the hat didn't fit" they comment - as they have been trying on the skiing clothes stored in the bottom two drawers of the large chest.

Would you come back? The biggest roundest YES ever - circled again and again until the pen has gone through the paper. "Can't wait for the next performance!" they add.

"That was absolutely great!" enthuses the camera crew. The producer is all smiley and helpful. "I can't believe we didn't have to go back over anything. Really, really good!"

I preen. Perhaps I will be able to get some regular part on the telly after all?

We move through to where Bob has moved things around in my sitting room, making it look much nicer than it normally does, for the final LittleChat of the day.

I explain to the camera that according to the competition criteria I can't possibly win this competition as it stands. I charge more than I think the room would otherwise be worth because of its unique location, and because I offer a 24/7 service with no rules, opening up my home to my guests as I would to family and friends, and waiting on them accordingly.

And my guests are really paying for 'probably the most remote B&B in southern England, with footpaths and bridleways stretching in every direction from the garden gate.'

"You can't say that - you'll just make the others cross," I am advised. "Their B&Bs are all unique in their different ways too, and anyway - yours is worth what you charge as a stand alone B&B, as it is."

I am chuffed by this. Of all people, the producers of Four In A Bed must know!

The Denouement

10/05/2015

I oversleep again. This has been my first really good night's sleep of a fortnight!

It's all over now. I can hardly even be bothered to wash my hair for the nth time, and I put on an old pair of tights with snags in them.

I make myself realise that we are still being featured on global TV, with an audience of ten million, and begin to panic as it's clear that I'm about to be late for the 8am sharp start time requested, at the same rather bland hotel in Tavistock where last September I celebrated my birthday so happily with the school Mums.

I drive at 70mph across the moor - at a sharp bend, overtaking what looks to be the camera crew. As I might have predicted, when I finally get to the hotel, all is not ready and I am not needed for over an hour. It feels very, very odd being in this familiar lobby, surrounded by television cameras and these unlikely new friends of mine.

A school Mum I've known slightly for the past ten years suddenly appears - we first met at Faye's toddlers' tap dance class - and we settle down to discuss stollen dough, until the crew is finally ready.

The contributors are rounded up, and we all troop in to the meeting room and sit in our allotted places, round an enormous table. As ever they have put me nearest the cameras, making me feel as though the whole thing is revolving around me and my general hilarity. How I love that feeling. How much will I live to regret it?

We go through the feedback forms starting with Callum and Don. There is an endless argument between Joan and Callum about whose fault it was that the boys' new coffee percolator fell to pieces in Thomas's hands. In fact, the list of things that seem to have broken in Joan and Thomas's room at the boys' place is so long that the whole thing begins to sound farcical. Thomas went through a wicker chair in the courtyard. Their shower flooded. On and on it goes. I feel like banging my head on the table with boredom.

Then it's Tessa's and Ivor's turn. Wormgate. I have butterflies and am nearly shaking. Due to all the cloak and daggers, the subject has not been raised now for eight days! Festering! The others aren't even aware that it happened! I don't want to talk about it any further, as I don't want the disastrous story to be given even more airtime.

Oh F***. It turns out that what has happened is that my hysteria, wailing "Oh Tessa, this is a PR disaster for you, I am so, so sorry!" has, of course, proved self-fulfilling. My extreme reaction has inadvertently served to inflame the situation, making things much worse for Tessa and Ivor than they need have been. What a total and entire F*** Up. Agghh! And, of course, because they don't know me properly, they assume that my histrionics are all part of some sort of sophisticated rich-bitch game, and I have played the situation up on purpose. They don't trust me, because they think I'm one of the posh, shallow, horse-racing-types that typically frequent their B&B.

They are totally confused because they can also see that I appear to have no interest in winning this competition. They absolutely cannot, cannot, cannot get their heads around why I have given them a 9 for cleanliness, and paid them the full asking price for their room.

"Because the worm thing has never happened before, will never happen again, and the room was pristine," I explain slowly and clearly, over and over again.

"I paid you the full amount because that is what I feel the room is worth."

Time for another LittleChat in the chilly hotel garden, and a spot of lunch, and we're back in 'the room' again.

It's Joan and Thomas's turn for a roasting.

Callum and Don have been quite nice about Joan's B&B until it comes to cleanliness. The boys found a huge matted ball of fluff on their bedroom floor. And then the bath, after I had used it, was full of my hair, and I'd left leaving a a dirty tide mark around it. I immediately hold my hand up as the culprit on this one.

Things are getting a bit twitchy.

"I paid Joan and Thomas full whack, despite the unremitting smell of dog, because at £27.50 each, if there were two of me, it's cheaper to move into their place than to live at home," I explain. "So for the right person, it's priced appropriately. But for me, well I would prefer to pay more for a bit of additional luxury, and not be surrounded by everybody's dogs all the time."

Again, the other contributors just don't seem to 'get' my approach, although it seems so straightforward to me.

By now, we are all, including the crew, extremely tired, hot, and on edge.

Finally it's my turn. I am under Ivor's spotlight, and I repeat the lines in answer to his questions that I taught myself the night before last. My drivel seems to go on endlessly. I am asked to start again, this time using short, sharp answers. I have no idea how much I have managed to explain on camera, but at least I have, at last, had an opportunity to discuss where I am coming from with Ivor and Tessa, whether they understand me yet, or not.

Going through Callum and Don's comments sheet is easy. "You can't possibly give me a ten for cleanliness!" I exclaim. "Didn't you look under the bed? It's disgusting!"

Everybody is most surprised by this outburst. But I know that under the bed there are bits of felt and canvas hanging down, from the 100 year old box sprung mattress which I have deliberately chosen to retain because it's so comfortable. Tessa would have had a fit if she'd seen it!

In the end, Callum and Don have docked me a fiver because of their cold hot water. Ivor and Tessa have given me £100 for my £130 room because of the water issue, the cold breakfast, undercooked scrambled egg, no wardrobe, dirty curtains, dirty drawers under the lining paper, feeling of invading someone's home, being in the middle of nowhere with nothing to do except walk/ride/fish/cycle/explore/rock climb/relax etc.

And then we come to Joan and Thomas. I query my apparent lack of hostessing skills, and discover that I've been docked two marks because they have been made to feel like 'the poor relations' - being put in the smallest room, and because I didn't come up to check how they were getting on.

"I put everybody in rooms according to what they charge, so that the most expensive B&B got my most expensive room, and so on," I explain. "It seemed to me to be the fairest way of allocating them."

I find Joan so utterly predictable, and I can't help being rather fond of her as a result. In some ways she reminds me of Faye when she was six. I open the envelope and discover just what I was expecting, as I had predicted to the camera in the last LittleChat. Joan has paid me what she charges. £55. How hilarious! I can't even work out quickly how much the underpayment is, but it's a lot. And I don't care in the least, because, to the appropriate audience watching on TV, I think Wydemeet has come out looking utterly beautiful and compelling. Meanwhile Thomas mumbles that actually he would have liked to have come back, and Joan admits that she now thinks the part of Dartmoor she has travelled through this morning on the way to the hotel is nicer than the rough part around Wydemeet.

I think that Joan has probably inadvertently made herself look rather mean and a bit idiotic, whereas I hope and pray that, however mad, I have come out looking like a nice, decent person who is being given an unnecessarily hard time and is responding with good humour and grace.

Later, upon further reflection, though, I think that for the pair of them to pay me basically half of my asking price, equating my offering with theirs, and knowing how this will affect the final outcome of 'the game' is actually quite rude, unjustified, and not very funny really. I have only once, out of hundreds of Four In A Bed episodes, seen anybody underpay by such an enormous margin. And in that case I think it was probably justified.

Time for a coffee break and at last we are allowed to talk openly to each other.

"I haven't been able to tell you until now, but Wydemeet's been on the market since November!" I whisper loudly to all the other contributors. "That's why my behaviour has been so odd! I wasn't allowed to tell anyone - I'm so sorry! But by the time this all gets aired the house will hopefully have been sold. So unlike you guys, I never got involved with this in order to market my B&B - it was, from the start, in order to find a boyfriend!" I reveal to them all. At last!

"If your hysteria wasn't put on in order to win, I will feel quite bad," comments Tessa. I am so very disappointed that she and Ivor didn't trust me, just because I am posh. Wormgate has actually turned out to have rather ruined this whole experience for me, as I had anticipated it might.

"Why haven't you pushed the fact that Wydemeet is for walkers?" enquires Tessa.

"Because I was advised not to - I was told it would make you cross," I reply.

"Why on earth should it? Of course you should emphasise that!" she says firmly.

Bloody hell. I've got one last LittleChat to go - five minutes left of two weeks filming, in which to properly and clearly push my B&B, in the right way, to the right people, in words of one syllable. In fact, simply to repeat the first two sentences of my website, which have taken me a couple of years to perfect.

"My market is affluent walkers and fishermen (thank you Bob for reminding me about the fishermen). I believe Wydemeet is possibly the most remote B&B in southern England," I manage to squeeze into my final interview, this time with my favourite cameraman, Nigel.

But afterwards I am still kicking myself, because I think that I have forgotten to add: "We have footpaths and bridleways stretching in every direction, north, south, east and west, from right outside our garden gate; yet we are only 20 minutes from the A38 highway between Exeter and Plymouth."

Never mind.

And I've got one last little job that I think I must perform. I am sharing a beautifully presented, three-tiered, afternoon tea of titchy little sandwiches and cakes, with Joan and Thomas.

"Joan," I start (there are no cameras now). "Might you do a little something for me? Do you think that when your guests arrive, instead of shutting Thomas in the kitchen, you could push him forward and announce proudly,

'This is my husband Thomas. He is my rock, and without him, I couldn't do any of this.' "

There. I've said it. I do hope she thinks about that. So at least I've learned something from my divorce.

And I've thought of something else too. Here I have been, all on my own, Billy No-Mates, surrounded by these lovey-dovey couples for two whole weeks. Tessa and Ivor, and Callum and Don, have been together for over 25 years! But who is actually the luckiest of us all? It turns out that Tessa and Ivor, and Joan and Thomas all wanted children, but never managed to have any.

I am the only contributor here who is lucky enough to have a brace.

And now it's time for the winners' announcement.

I am not surprised that they choose me to do the job. Apparently the final B&B to be visited generally has a useful sitting room that the crew can use, and the person selected to read out the results is the owner of that B&B, so perhaps this is pure coincidence. Whatever - I am absolutely delighted to be doing it! I am so enjoying all this showing off.

The top envelope says 'Fourth'.

"Last!" I cry. I open the envelope up. It is quite clear whose name is going to be on the card.

"ME!!" I shout grinning. "Well what a surprise!!!!!"

I slowly open the 'Third' envelope, keeping everybody waiting for the announcement, like they do on X-Factor. No surprises again. Dog Heaven for poor people.

So then I turn to the envelope saying 'First' and wave it around a lot, keeping everybody in suspenders. I have been told that the percentage difference in payment between the top two B&Bs is very close.

Slowly I open up the envelope, and even more slowly, I reveal the contents.

"The Boys!" I cry jubilantly, and rush over and hug them both.

Would I Do It Again?

10/05/2015

It's 9pm, and filming is finally over. I am free to collect Faye from her school on my way home from the hotel, where we have now been under the spotlight for thirteen hours. The others have still got nearly 200 miles to drive tonight.

While my head is bursting with all that has gone on over the past couple of weeks, Faye blithely fills me in on her school day as we drive home, and, as if I haven't had enough of it all by now, she insists on watching an episode of Four In A Bed for a laugh before going to bed.

I'm surprised that I feel rather down.

Is it because I am exhausted?

This morning I still feel down. I have been going over and over everything that has happened without stopping, trying to work out what the problem is.

It was all such fun to begin with. I was singing excitedly as I drove along. I had new friends. I was on holiday. I was getting masses of attention and believing that I was being really funny. It was great!

And then, when everybody descended on my house, the stress and negativity kicked in.

I hope and believe that I have succeeded in remaining genial throughout the entire experience, and I am very proud of myself for that. I have found the last few days both slightly depressing, and very tiring, yet I have continued to smile.

I have been anticipating coming last of the four B&Bs in the competition, but I think perhaps it is beginning to grate that beautiful, successful, much-loved Wydemeet B&B, after all our care, excitement and hard work, has been publicly voted 'least good value' B&B. Especially by such a very enormous margin, however ridiculous the reasons behind the outcome, and however stunningly my home eventually comes across on the programme itself.

During the last two weeks I have achieved almost all of what I set out to do. For one thing, I now have a much better idea of how I come across to other people.

I have learned what it is that I do that makes people so very cross, that I never understood before.

And I have had it objectively reaffirmed that there is 'something about me' that could possibly be turned into 'Television Gold'.

How the programme makers choose to edit me, after all that, is anybody's guess.

But however they choose to portray me, there will always be at least 54 genuinely objective five-blob reviews on TripAdvisor, united in their agreement about the wonderful Wydemeet experience.

So, in the meantime, I might just write to the programme-makers, Studio Lambert, asking for a job.

Would I do it again? Yes. But it will take a day or two for this sense of 'down-ness' to dissipate. By the time the programme is actually aired, I don't suppose I will care what's in it all that much. But I hope that I can launch this book at the same time, and that it will lead to even more extraordinary adventures!

She Loved It!

20/05/2015

"We both had so much fun and just LOVED the experience and wish we could do it all again!"

This is what the other Dartmoor B&B, who also used the Rugglestone Inn at Widecombe for their Four, well actually Three, In A Bed dinner, thought of being on the programme.

"All in all it really was one of - if not THE - best experience of our lives," continued delightful Margaret.

I had emailed her to find out how she had felt about the whole thing, and to discover what had happened once it was transmitted. No hate mail and, interestingly, no booking requests, she commented, and that's despite her coming across as extraordinarily charming, and her B&B, although simple, appeared to be utterly beautiful.

And then came the best bit of all. Apparently one chap had contacted her to say that he thought that her step-daughter was 'a cracking bit of stuff' and could he marry her?!

Dreams Come True?

21/05/2015

This morning I found the house of my dreams. It is priced at £300,000 less than Wydemeet's on for. I could be rich!

Then I spoke to an Encounters Date who sounds even more interesting and funny than I am - and he is taller than me.

And most exciting of all - I bumped into one of my best friends who recently nearly died after a skiing accident; and, although very thin, and having to wear a little helmet, she is completely 'with it', and we were able to hug and I felt like crying.

This afternoon I dyed myself as brown as an abo, in anticipation of a second meeting with the guy that I snogged last January.

I joined my mate Sarah for supper just now, checked myself in the loo mirror, and I'm so brown that I look rather odd.

Love Nest

24/05/2015

"WOW!" breathed Faye. Four times. Trying not to, because she knew that was what I wanted her to say.

This was the fifth house today that she had been forced to look at.

Being 13, what impressed her most about it were some modern light fittings, and a sunken trampoline.

There aren't very many houses in my special triangle of choice, so even fewer available for purchase at any one time, and we were doing well to find so many to look at, I thought - any one of which I would have been happy to live in.

But this little love nest - a Scandinavian wooden single storey chalet - has the 'wow' factor, as it looks across the entire Exe valley towards Ottery St Mary. It would be like buying a two-seater open-top sports car. A mid-life crisis, mad, impractical thing to do. I think all three of us - Faye, Will, and myself - would be intensely proud to bring friends back to it.

I have urgently invited the estate agent to ask the owner, a rock star who used to play for Tangerine Dream, whether he might accept an early exchange on a low percentage, and delayed completion, until I sell wonderful Wydemeet.

But it's Bank Holiday Monday.

So all is in the lap of the Gods.

I am trembling with excitement and apprehension.

Oo-er

30/05/2015

"I loved the house and can see why you love it. It's very different and the views are awesome," wrote Charming Charles, my estate agent.

"It's a unique property, but one that I think will always fetch more than expected for the right buyer."

The green light.

I email Mr Rockstar saying I want to buy his home for the asking price, exchanging straight away (I can cash in a pension I'd forgotten about, thanks to the government and to my being so old) with a delayed completion; and head off to the health club, heart pounding.

"Twist and Shout!!" Faye and I sing along to my iPhone plugged into the Golden Monster's stereo system on the way home.

"Could you just check my emails?" I ask her.

3G leaps into action. "Time is not an issue," reads Faye.

"WHAT???????????!!!!!!!!!!!!!!!!!" I scream at her. "Read that again!"

"Time is not an issue," she repeats.

Mr Rockstar is prepared to wait for a delayed completion!

WOW! WOW! WOW!

So I'm buying it!

WOW!

This is scary. Nearly as life-changing as finding a new partner. The one difference being that once you've found the house you want, it doesn't have to like you back.

So we're off. I'm buying the first house I've looked at, before mine is even properly on the market, let alone sold. This could prove quite a roller coaster! And it feels perfect!

What Do Other People Think?

13/06/2015

"Crazy house! Hope it hasn't got woodworm," emailed back my sister, when I sent her details of my exciting new home. She likes to be funnier than me. And succeeds occasionally.

So I'm sort of laughing now, and sort of worrying a bit too - what if it has? Well - I guess I could just burn it down and buy another flat pack, and ask Faye to knock up a new wooden chalet out of it for me. She's good at that sort of thing.

"Hi Mum - would you like to lend me £50,000 to exchange on a little wooden house I like - I'll complete once I sell Wydemeet," I enquire casually over the phone of my mother, hoping to avoid cashing in my pension and incurring income tax on three-quarters of it.

"I think I'm a bit too old for that kind of thing," she replies. Damn. She thinks I'm mad, taking the risk of not selling my house in time to complete on the new one.

Time to garner some more opinions.

An old school friend who plays in a very successful band and is a multi-millionaire as a result of the advertising agency he set up thirty years ago, just happens to live 2 1/2 miles down the road from my potential new lodgings. He is 6'4" tall, retains loads of thick red hair and a beard, and has a very loud, low, posh voice. Over the years, he has become a bigger character than I am. Anyhow - I ask him whether, as a new neighbour, he would like to visit my new home and see what he thinks.

"Why don't you go out with the owner?" is the first comment of his gorgeous wife, post-viewing.

I then send my sister-in-law over to take a look.

"It will be the most brilliant hang-out place for Ben (her son, my nephew) when he starts at Exeter University," I say. "The bus comes from central Exeter right past the drive!"

"I love it! Why don't you go out with the owner?" is her verdict, when I meet up with her later, at the David Lloyd Health Club, which I've finally joined, but where I still haven't yet succeeded in bumping into any potential new totty.

We're On

12/06/2015

We've gone live!

Wydemeet is now officially for sale.

Two hundred full colour brochures have been printed, and we are listed on 'RightMove'.

And we have already had two viewings through the estate agent - someone who recognised me from my London days (circa 1985); and a couple who drove a Mitsubishi Shogun. No further news from either of them.

I won't be able to comment on further potential buyers coming to see round my house, as I am banned from being present.

"First time viewers feel much more comfortable if the vendor isn't there," I was told by charming Charles the estate agent. I am still unsure whether to take this personally or not.

Meanwhile, the little family who came to stay a few weeks ago, on a B&B basis, with a view to buying Wydemeet, have offered me a £10,000 deposit while they wait for their Reading house to sell.

I said "I'd be nuts to go along with that in my current position - Wydemeet's only been officially on the market for a week!"

Everywhere I look I appear to be selling something. Myself on Encounters, my B&B on TripAdvisor, my holiday rental on Owners Direct, and Wydemeet itself via Knight Frank. Sell, sell, sell. It's really hard work. I am exhausted. That's a lot of 'no's to experience every day. Oh well. Chin up.

And what's worse, I can't keep the stupid moles which are wrecking my 'lawn' at bay, so soon no one will want to buy, or even stay at Wydemeet anyway. I have stuffed all my odd socks soaked in petrol down the many, many mole holes, but this doesn't seem to have helped at all. Every time it rains - up pops another small mound of top-soil! Usually directly beneath the solar-powered mole scarers as the beasts' special little joke. And now there is an entire line of mounds winding its way right across the whole of my grassed area.

Perhaps I had better get a cat.

13555083R00208

Printed in Great Britain
by Amazon.co.uk, Ltd.,
Marston Gate.